The Ottoman Empire, 1700–1922

The Ottoman Empire was one of the most important non-Western states to survive from medieval to modern times, and played a vital role in European and global history. It continues to affect the peoples of the Middle East, the Balkans, and Central and Western Europe to the present day. This new survey examines the major trends during the latter years of the empire; it pays attention to gender issues and to hotly debated topics such as the treatment of minorities. In this second edition, Donald Quataert has updated his lively and authoritative text, revised the bibliographies, and included brief bibliographies of major works on the Byzantine Empire and the post–Ottoman Middle East. This accessible narrative is supported by maps, illustrations, and genealogical and chronological tables, which will be of help to students and non-specialists alike. It will appeal to anyone interested in the history of the Middle East.

DONALD QUATAERT is Professor of History at Binghamton University, State University of New York. He has published many books on Middle East and Ottoman history, including *An Economic and Social History of the Ottoman Empire, 1300–1914* (1994).

NEW APPROACHES TO EUROPEAN HISTORY

Series editors
WILLIAM BEIK *Emory University*
T. C. W. BLANNING *Sidney Sussex College, Cambridge*

New Approaches to European History is an important textbook series, which provides concise but authoritative surveys of major themes and problems in European history since the Renaissance. Written at a level and length accessible to advanced school students and undergraduates, each book in the series addresses topics or themes that students of European history encounter daily: the series will embrace both some of the more "traditional" subjects of study, and those cultural and social issues to which increasing numbers of school and college courses are devoted. A particular effort is made to consider the wider international implications of the subject under scrutiny.

To aid the student reader scholarly apparatus and annotation is light, but each work has full supplementary bibliographies and notes for further reading: where appropriate chronologies, maps, diagrams, and other illustrative material are also provided.

For a list of titles published in the series, please see end of book.

The Ottoman Empire, 1700–1922

Second Edition

DONALD QUATAERT

Binghamton University,
State University of New York

CAMBRIDGE UNIVERSITY PRESS
Cambridge, New York, Melbourne, Madrid, Cape Town, Singapore, São Paulo

Cambridge University Press
The Edinburgh Building, Cambridge CB2 2RU, UK

Published in the United States of America by Cambridge University Press,
New York

www.cambridge.org
information on this title: www.cambridge.org/9780521547826

First published 2000 and reprinted five times
Second edition 2005

Printed in the United Kingdom at the University Press, Cambridge

A catalogue record for this book is available from the British Library

ISBN-13 978-0-521-83910-5 hardback
ISBN-10 0-521-83910-6 hardback

ISBN-13 978-0-521-54782-6 paperback
ISBN-10 0-521-54782-2 paperback

To my brothers and sisters
Patricia, Phyllis, Pamela, Michael, Peter,
Robert, and Helen
in the hopes this book will help them to
understand my whereabouts over the years

Contents

Plates

Maps

Preface

The writing of the history of the Ottoman Empire, 1300–1922, has changed dramatically during the past several decades. In the early 1970s, when I began my graduate studies, a handful of scholars, at a very few elite schools, studied and wrote on this extraordinary empire, with roots in the Byzantine, Turkish, Islamic, and Renaissance political and cultural traditions. Nowadays, by contrast, Ottoman history appropriately is becoming an integral part of the curriculum at scores of colleges and universities, public and private.

And yet, semester after semester I have been faced with the same dilemma when making textbook assignments for my undergraduate courses in Middle East and Ottoman history. Either use textbooks that were too detailed for most students or adopt briefer studies that were deeply flawed, mainly by their a-historical approach that described a non-changing empire, hopelessly corrupt and backward, awaiting rescue or a merciful death.

This textbook is an effort to make Ottoman history intelligible, and exciting, to the university undergraduate student and the general reader. I make liberal use of my own previous research. Moreover, I rely quite heavily on the research of others and seek to bring to the general reader the wonderful specialized research that until now largely has remained inaccessible. At the end of each chapter are lists of suggested readings, not always those used in preparing the section. Given the intended audience, only English-language works are cited (with just a few exceptions). These works, however, each contain substantial bibliographies in many languages that can provide a springboard for further reading. To gain an overview of Ottoman history writing today, examine an annual bibliography, named *Turcology Annual*,[1] that lists hundreds of books and articles – in languages as diverse as English, Japanese, Arabic, French, Russian,

---

[1] *Turcology Annual/Turkologischer Anzeiger*, published at the Institut für Orientalistik der Universität Wien, Vienna, Austria

Turkish, Spanish, German, Chinese, and Armenian. The bibliography is an indispensable source.

I have tried to give what I believe is a more widely comprehensive presentation – including not only political history, but social, economic, and labor history as well. Too often the state has been overemphasized in Ottoman history writing. In part this is because the sources from which the history is written are those produced by the state itself. This text seeks to give agency to groups in the "civil society," outside the government. Despite my effort to more equally weight the various aspects of the Ottoman experience, there are numerous gaps, a function of both space limitations and my own shortcomings. In preparing this second edition, I continue to underrepresent the field of cultural studies, mainly for fear of not doing it justice. Also, my original treatment of the religious classes, both the Muslim ulema and the Jewish and Christian clergy, also remains basically unrevised. In the end, I concluded that a fuller treatment of these groups would require comparably specialized treatments of various other important elements in Ottoman society such as merchants, soldiers, and artisans and that such analyses belong to a specialized monograph and not a general text. Slavery remains largely excluded. There is, however, some mounting evidence that the issue of economic slavery may need revisiting. Such slavery was not widespread and domestic slavery did dominate; but some slaves were working in manufacture and agriculture and their activities may require further discussion at a later point. In this regard, I also mention the possibly connected presence of Africans in the northern Ottoman Empire during, for example, the nineteenth century.

Some of the revisions seek to correct errors that generously were called to my attention by reviewers or in private correspondence – to both sets of individuals I am very grateful. Most of the changes result from my readings of the literature published since the first section or rethinking points of interpretation.

A caution: the Ottoman experiences were rich, diverse, and sometimes unusual. But they were not sui generis, one of a kind. We can understand them by using the same categories of analysis that historians employ to examine states and societies in Ming China, Tokugawa Japan, the Habsburg Empire, and Victorian England. I believe that Ottoman institutions and peoples were particularly fashioned by a special set of historical contingencies. But so too, political and social organizations across the globe each were uniquely fashioned by their own sets of contingencies. When appropriate, I have underscored the unique qualities of the Ottoman experience. But throughout, I also have sought to present the process of change in the Ottoman world as sharing much with those of states, societies, and economies elsewhere. That is, common patterns are to be expected and, within those, we find the Ottoman particularities formed by specific contingencies.

The first chapter situates Ottoman history in a larger context and its role in the evolution of western Europe. The following three chapters, 2–4, are chronological surveys of the period before 1683, the eighteenth century, and the 1800–1922 era. Chapters 5–10 are thematic in nature, exploring various major issues: international and domestic politics; the economy; society, and popular culture; identity; and the question of inter-subject relations. The final chapter explores the resonance of the Ottoman past in the experiences of people living in the more than thirty states that exist on the lands once Ottoman.

In preparing the first edition of this book, numerous friends and colleagues have offered invaluable guidance that I usually welcomed but sometimes rejected. Thus, errors and misjudgments are my responsibility. Colleagues at Binghamton University and especially the world history group – including Rifaat Abou-El-Haj, John Chaffee, Brendan McConville, Tiffany Patterson, and Jean Quataert – have changed the way I think about history. I also wish to thank Elif Akşıt, Lynda Carroll, Eric Crahan, Kasım Kopuz, Thomas Page, and Margarita Poutouridou for reading earlier versions of this manuscript. Faruk Tabak was exceptionally helpful and read two, quite different, drafts of the text; his comments were very useful. The biennial conferences on Ottoman history at Binghamton University have served as a powerful learning device for me. For various specific points, I thank Virginia Aksan, Selçuk Esenbel, Carter Findley, Heath Lowry, Nancy Micklewright, Zafer Toprak, as well as Andreas Tietze. For their criticisms and comments on the published first edition, I especially thank Carter Findley, Fred Lawson, Viorel Panaite, Christine Philliou, Michael Quataert, and Yunus Uğur. More generally, I have found the discussions on H-Turk to be very useful.

Guide to pronunciation of Turkish words[1] and a note on place names

Pronunciation

C, c = "j" as in juice
Ç, ç = "ch" as in cheek
Ğ, ğ = soft "g", hardly pronounced
I, ı = without a dot, pronounced like the first syllable of "earnest"
İ, i = with a dot, somewhere between "in" and "eel"
Ö, ö = as in the umlaut ö in German or as French eu in peu
Ş, ş = as in "sheet"
Ü, ü = as in the umlat ü in German or as French u in tu
∧ = used to denote a lenghtened vowel (a, i, and u) or to palatize a preceding g, k, or l

Place names

The issue of place names is a thorny one. To call places as they were in the past can cause confusion for modern readers. The old names often but not always have completely disappeared from the present memory of all but a few devotees of the area or subject. In many areas of the former empire – including the Balkans, Anatolia, and Palestine – a large proportion of the contemporary place names are radically different from their Ottoman labels. To use these past names would be historically accurate but overly confusing for a textbook. Similarly, it does not seem useful to use place names in a form that is known only within the country of origin or to specialists. Throughout this text, therefore, I have preferred to call places according to the general international usage. Hence, for example, I use Belgrade not Beograd and Aleppo not Halep. For the Ottoman capital, I use the current designation of Istanbul even though the Ottomans called it Konstantiniyye or Dersaadet. However, I use Constantinople to denote the Byzantine city before the Ottoman conquest in 1453.

[1] After Cornell H. Fleischer, *Bureaucrat and intellectual in the Ottoman Empire: the historian Mustafa Ali (1541–1600)* (Princeton, 1986), xiv.

The convention for place names used in this textbook has the advantage of clarity and is not intended necessarily to endorse the policies of those who changed the name. It should enable students to refer to standard international atlases and readily find the places mentioned in this work.

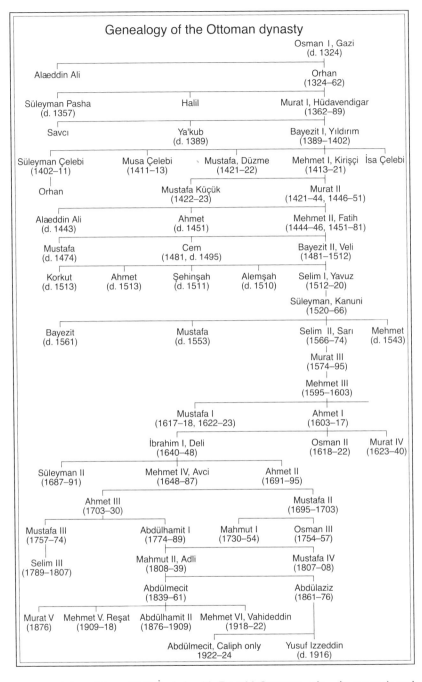

Genealogy of the Ottoman dynasty

Osman I, Gazi
(d. 1324)

Alaeddin Ali

Orhan
(1324–62)

Süleyman Pasha
(d. 1357)

Halil

Murat I, Hüdavendigar
(1362–89)

Savcı

Ya'kub
(d. 1389)

Bayezit I, Yıldırım
(1389–1402)

Süleyman Çelebi
(1402–11)

Musa Çelebi
(1411–13)

Mustafa, Düzme
(1421–22)

Mehmet I, Kirişçi
(1413–21)

İsa Çelebi

Orhan

Mustafa Küçük
(1422–23)

Murat II
(1421–44, 1446–51)

Alaeddin Ali
(d. 1443)

Ahmet
(d. 1451)

Mehmet II, Fatih
(1444–46, 1451–81)

Mustafa
(d. 1474)

Cem
(1481, d. 1495)

Bayezit II, Veli
(1481–1512)

Korkut
(d. 1513)

Ahmet
(d. 1513)

Şehinşah
(d. 1511)

Alemşah
(d. 1510)

Selim I, Yavuz
(1512–20)

Süleyman, Kanuni
(1520–66)

Bayezit
(d. 1561)

Mustafa
(d. 1553)

Selim II, Sarı
(1566–74)

Mehmet
(d. 1543)

Murat III
(1574–95)

Mehmet III
(1595–1603)

Mustafa I
(1617–18, 1622–23)

Ahmet I
(1603–17)

İbrahim I, Deli
(1640–48)

Osman II
(1618–22)

Murat IV
(1623–40)

Süleyman II
(1687–91)

Mehmet IV, Avci
(1648–87)

Ahmet II
(1691–95)

Ahmet III
(1703–30)

Mustafa II
(1695–1703)

Mustafa III
(1757–74)

Abdülhamit I
(1774–89)

Mahmut I
(1730–54)

Osman III
(1754–57)

Selim III
(1789–1807)

Mahmut II, Adli
(1808–39)

Mustafa IV
(1807–08)

Abdülmecit
(1839–61)

Abdülaziz
(1861–76)

Murat V
(1876)

Mehmet V. Reşat
(1909–18)

Abdülhamit II
(1876–1909)

Mehmet VI, Vahideddin
(1918–22)

Abdülmecit, Caliph only
1922–24

Yusuf Izzeddin
(d. 1916)

Adapted from Halil İnalcık with Donald Quataert, eds., *An economic and social history of the Ottoman Empire, 1300–1914* (Cambridge, 1994), xvii

Chronology of Ottoman history, 1260–1923

1261–1300	foundation of the principalities of Menteşe, Aydın, Saruhan, Karesi, and Osmanlı (Ottoman) in western Anatolia
c. 1290–1324	**Osman I**
1324–62	**Orhan**
1326	Ottoman conquest of Bursa
1331	Ottoman conquest of Nicaea (İznik)
1335	fall of the Mongol empire in Iran
1354	Ottoman occupation of Ankara and Gallipoli
1361	Ottoman conquest of Adrianople
1362–89	**Murat I**
1363–65	Ottoman expansion in southern Bulgaria and Thrace
1371–73	Ottoman victory at Chermanon; Byzantium, the Balkan rulers recognize Ottoman suzerainty
1385	Ottoman conquest of Sofia
1389	Ottoman victory at Kossovo-Polje over a coalition of the Balkan states
1389–1402	**Bayezit I, Yıldırım**
1396	battle of Nicopolis
1402	battle of Ankara, collapse of Bayezit I's empire
1403–13	civil war among Bayezit's sons for sultanate
1413–21	**Mehmet I**
1421–44	**Murat II**
1446–51	
1423–30	Ottoman–Venetian war for Salonica
1425	Ottoman annexation of Izmir and the reconquest of western Anatolia
1439	Ottoman annexation of Serbia
1443	John Hunyadi invades the Balkans

Adapted from Halil İnalcık with Donald Quataert, eds., *An economic and social history of the Ottoman Empire, 1300–1914* (Cambridge, 1994), xviii–xxiv.

1444	revival of Serbian despotate, battle of Varna
1444–46,	**Mehmet II, Fatih**
1451–81	
1448	second battle of Kossovo-Polje
1453	conquest of Constantinople; fall of Pera
1459	conquest of Serbia and the Morea
1461	conquest of the empire of Trabzon
1463–79	war with Venice
1468	conquest of Karaman
1473	battle of Başkent
1475	conquest of the Genoese colonies in the Crimea
1481–1512	**Bayezit II**
1485–91	war with the Mamluks of Egypt
1499–1503	war with Venice; conquest of Lepanto, Coron, and Modon
1512–20	**Selim I**
1514	Selim defeats Shah Ismail at Çaldıran
1516	conquest of Diyarbakir; annexation of eastern Anatolia; defeat of the Mamluks at Marj Dabık
1517	battle of Ridaniyya, conquest of Egypt; submission of the sharif of Mecca
1520–66	**Süleyman I, Kanuni**
1521	conquest of Belgrade
1522	conquest of Rhodes
1526	battle of Mohács; Hungary becomes a vassal
1529	siege of Vienna
1534	conquest of Tabriz and Baghdad
1537–40	war with Venice
1538	siege of Diu in India
1541	annexation of Hungary
1553–55	war with Iran
1565	siege of Malta
1566–74	**Selim II**
1569	French capitulations; first Ottoman expedition against Russia; siege of Astrakhan
1570	Uluç Ali captures Tunis; expedition to Cyprus; fall of Nicosia
1571	battle of Lepanto
1573	peace with Venice and the emperor
1574–95	**Murat III**
1578–90	war with Iran, annexation of Azerbaijan
1580	English capitulations
1589	Janissary revolt in Istanbul

1591–92	further Janissary uprisings
1593–1606	war with the Habsburgs
1595–1603	**Mehmet III**
1596	Celali rebellions in Anatolia
1603–39	Iranian wars
1603–17	**Ahmet I**
1606	Peace of Sitva-Torok with the Habsburgs
1609	suppression of the Celalis in Anatolia
1612	extension of capitulations to the Dutch
1613–35	rebellion of Ma'noğlu Fahreddin
1618	peace with Iran, Ottoman withdrawal from Azerbaijan
1618–22	**Osman II**
1621	invasion of Poland
1622	assassination of Osman II
1617–18,	**Mustafa I**
1622–23	
1623–40	**Murat IV**
1624–28	rebellion in Asia Minor; anarchy in Istanbul
1632	Murat takes full control of the government
1635	siege of Erivan
1624–37	Cossack attacks on the Black Sea coast
1624–39	war with Iran, fall of Baghdad
1637	fall of Azov (Azak) to Cossacks
1638	Ottoman recovery of Baghdad
1640–48	**Ibrahim I**
1640	recovery of Azov
1645–69	war with Venice; invasion of Crete; siege of Candia
1648–56	Venetian blockade of the Dardanelles
1648	deposition and assassination of the sultan
1648–87	**Mehmet IV**
1648–51	the child sultan's mother Kösem in control
1649–51	Janissary dominance in Istanbul and Celali pashas in the Asiatic provinces
1651–55	anarchy in Istanbul, Venetian blockade continues
1656	Köprülü Mehmet appointed grand vizier with dictatorial powers
1656–59	re-establishment of the central government's control over the Janissaries and in the provinces
1657	lifting of Venetian blockade
1658–59	re-establishment of Ottoman control over Transylvania and Wallachia
1661–76	Köprülü Fazıl Ahmet's grand vizierate

1663	war with the Habsburgs
1664	battle of St. Gotthard, peace of Vasvar
1669	fall of Candia, peace with Venice
1672–76	war with Poland, annexation of Kaminiec with Podolia, Treaty of Zuravno
1676–83	Kara Mustafa's grand vizierate
1677–81	rivalry over Ukraine with Russia
1681	French attack against Chios
1683	siege of Vienna
1684	Holy League against the Ottomans between the emperor, Polish king and Venice
1686	fall of Buda, Russia joins the coalition; Venetians in the Morea
1687	second battle of Mohács; army's rebellion; deposition of Mehmet IV
1687–91	**Süleyman II**
1688	fall of Belgrade
1689	Austrians at Kosovo; Russians attack the Crimea
1689–91	Köprülü Fazıl Mustafa's grand vizierate; tax reforms
1690	recovery of Belgrade from Austrians
1691–95	**Ahmet II**
1691	battle of Slankamen; death of Fazıl Mustafa
1695–1703	**Mustafa II**
1695	fall of Azov
1696	Ottoman counter-attack in Hungary
1697	Ottoman defeat at Zenta
1698–1702	Köprülü Hüseyin's grand vizierate
1699	Treaty of Karlowitz
1700	peace with Russia
1703	army's rebellion; deposition of Mustafa II
1703–30	**Ahmet III**
1709	Charles XII, king of Sweden, takes refuge in Ottoman territory
1711	battle of Pruth, Ottoman victory over Peter I of Russia, insurrection at Cairo, realignment of Mamluks; Shihabi supremacy over Mount Lebanon
1713	peace treaty with Russia: Azov recovered, Charles XII returns to Sweden; introduction of Phanariote rule in principalities
1714–18	war with Venice, recovery of the Morea
1716	war with Austria
1717	fall of Belgrade

1718–30	Ibrahim Pasha's grand vizierate
1718	peace treaty of Passarowitz with Austria and Venice: Morea recovered, large parts of Serbia and Wallachia ceded to Austria
1723–27	war with Iran, Ottoman occupation of Azerbaijan and Hamadan
1730	Patrona Halil rebellion; deposition of Ahmet III; end of Tulip period
1730–36	Iran's counter-attack; loss of Azerbaijan and western Iran
1730–54	**Mahmut I**
1736–39	war with Russia and Austria
1739	peace treaty with Austria and Russia; recovery of Belgrade
1740	extension of French capitulations; Ottoman–Swedish alliance against Russia
1743–46	war with Iran under Nadir Shah
1754–57	**Osman III**
1757–74	**Mustafa III**
1768–74	war with the Russian empire
1770	Russian fleet in the Aegean; Ottoman defeat on the Danube
1771	Russian invasion of the Crimea
1773	Ali Bey's rebellion in Egypt
1774–89	**Abdülhamit I**
1774	treaty of Küçük Kaynarca, independence of the Crimea and northern coasts of the Black Sea from the Ottoman Empire
1783	Russian annexation of the Crimean khanate
1787	war with Russia
1788	Sweden declares war against the Russian Empire
1789–1807	**Selim III**
1792	Treaty of Jassy
1798	Napoleon invades Egypt
1804	Serb revolt
1805–48	Muhammad Ali as ruler of Egypt
1807	Selim's reform program crushed by revolt
1807–08	**Mustafa IV**
1808–39	**Mahmut II**
1808	Document of Alliance
1811	Muhammad Ali massacres Mamluk remnant in Egypt
1812	Treaty of Bucharest
1826	destruction of the Janissaries
1832	battle of Konya

1833	Treaty of Hünkiar-İskelesi with Russia
1838	Anglo-Turkish Convention
1839	battle of Nezib
1839–61	**Abdülmecit I**
1839	Tanzimat begins with Imperial Rescript of Gülhane
1853–56	Crimean war
1856	Imperial Rescript
1856	Treaty of Paris
1861–76	**Abdülaziz**
1875	*de facto* Ottoman bankruptcy
1876	first Ottoman Constitution
1876–1909	**Abdülhamit II**
1878	Treaty of Berlin
1881	formation of Public Debt Administration
1885	occupation by Bulgaria of eastern Rumelia
1896–97	insurrection in Crete; war with Greece
1908	Young Turk Revolution and the restoration of the Constitution of 1876
1909–18	**Mehmet V**
1911	war with Italy
1912	Balkan war
1914	World War I begins
1918–22	**Mehmet VI**
1920	establishment of French mandate over Syria and Lebanon and British mandates over Iraq and Palestine
1923	proclamation of the Republic of Turkey

1 Why study Ottoman history?

Introduction

This book owes its origins to an event that occurred in Vienna in the summer of 1983, when lines of schoolchildren wound their way through the sidewalks of the Austrian capital. The attraction they were lining up for was not a Disney movie or a theme park, but instead a museum exhibition, one of many celebrations held that year to commemorate the 300th anniversary of the second Ottoman siege of Vienna. In the minds of these children, their teachers, and the Austrian (and, for that matter, the general European) public, 1683 was a year in which they all were saved – from conquest by the alien Ottoman state, the "unspeakable Turk."

The Ottoman state had emerged, c. 1300, in western Asia Minor, not far from the modern city of Istanbul. In a steady process of territorial accretion, this state had expanded both west and east, defeating Byzantine, Serb, and Bulgarian kingdoms as well as Turkish nomadic principalities in Anatolia (Asia Minor) and the Mamluk sultanate based in Egypt. By the seventeenth century it held vast lands in west Asia, North Africa, and southeast Europe. In 1529 and again in 1683, Ottoman armies pressed to conquer Habsburg Vienna.

The artifacts in the Vienna museum exhibit told much about the nature of the 1683 events. For example, the display of the captured tent and personal effects of the Ottoman grand vizier illustrated the panicky flight of the Ottoman forces from their camps that, just days before, had encircled Vienna. The timely arrival of the central and east European allies, notably King John (Jan) Sobieski of Poland, had put the encircling Ottoman armies to flight and turned the second Ottoman effort to seize the city into a full-blown disaster. For hundreds of years the Ottoman forces had been pressing northward, ever deeper into the Balkan peninsula and closer to Vienna and the German-speaking lands. These Ottomans literally were the terror of their enemies, seemingly invincible. Viennese mothers put their children to bed warning them to behave lest the "Turks" come and gobble them up. This world changed in 1683. Somewhat to the surprise of both sets of protagonists, the Ottoman forces besieging Vienna were catastrophically defeated, an event that marked the permanent reversal of power relations between the Ottoman and the Habsburg empires.

By "Turks," these frightened mothers meant a more complex reality – the fighting forces, who may or may not have been ethnically Turkish, of the multi-ethnic, multi-religious Ottoman empire. Thus, a word here about the terms "Turks" and "Ottomans" seems in order. West, central, and east Europeans referred to the "Turkish empire" and to the "Turks" when discussing the state led by the Ottoman dynasty. This was as true in the fourteenth as in the twentieth century. The appellation "Turk" has some basis since the Ottoman family was ethnically Turkish in its origins, as were some of its supporters and subjects. But, as we shall see, the dynasty immediately lost this "Turkish" quality through intermarriage with many different ethnicities. As for a "Turkish empire," state power relied on a similarly heterogeneous mix of peoples. The Ottoman empire succeeded because it incorporated the energies of the vastly varied peoples it encountered, quickly transcending its roots in the Turkish nomadic migrations from central Asia into the Middle East (see chapter 2). Whatever ethnic meaning the word "Turk" may have held soon was lost and the term came to mean "Muslim." To turn Turk meant converting to Islam. Throughout this work, the term Ottoman is preferred since it conjures up more accurate images of a multi-ethnic, multi-religious enterprise that relied on inclusion for its success.

In hindsight, we can see that after 1683 the Ottomans never again threatened central Europe. They did, however, stay in occupation of southeast Europe for 200 more years, dominating the modern-day states of Bulgaria, Serbia, Greece, Rumania, and others. Finally, in the hardly unbiased words of the British politician, Gladstone, they were driven "bag and baggage" from their possessions. In its Asian and African provinces, the Ottoman Empire persisted even longer. Most parts of modern-day Turkey, Syria, Lebanon, Iraq, Israel, Palestine, Jordan, and Saudi Arabia remained part of the empire until World War I. During the last decades before it disappeared in 1922 the Ottoman Empire existed without the European provinces that for centuries had been its heart and soul. In its last days, but only then, it fairly could be called an Asiatic, Middle Eastern power. Until the 1878 Treaty of Berlin stripped away all but fragments of its Balkan holdings, the Ottoman Empire was a European power and was seen as such by its contemporaries, being deeply involved in European military and political affairs. Throughout nearly all of its 600-year history, the Ottoman state was as much a part of the European political order as were its French or Habsburg rivals.

Ottoman history in world history

The Ottoman Empire was one of the greatest, most extensive, and longest-lasting empires in the history of the world. It included most of the territories of the eastern Roman Empire and held portions of the northern Balkans and north Black Sea coast, areas that Byzantium had never ruled. Nor were these holdings ephemeral – the Ottoman Empire was born before 1300 and endured until after World War I. Thus, it began in the same century the powerful Sung state in China ended, in the era when Genghis Khan swept across the Euro-Asiatic world and built an empire from China to Poland while, in Europe, France and England were about to embark on their Hundred Years War. In west Africa the great Benin state was emerging while, in the Americas, the Aztec state in the valley of Mexico began its expansion, both events being nearly contemporaneous with the Ottomans' emergence in Asia Minor. Born in medieval times, this empire of the Ottomans disappeared only very recently, within the memory of many people still living today. My own father was nine years old and my mother five years old when the Ottoman Empire finally disappeared from the face of the earth. Large numbers of present-day citizens of the Ottoman successor states – such as Turkey, Syria, Lebanon, and Iraq – bear Ottoman personal names given to them by their parents and were educated and grew up in an Ottoman world. Thus, for many, this empire is a living legacy (see chapter 10).

In the sixteenth century the Ottoman Empire shared the world stage with a cluster of other powerful and wealthy states. To their far west lay distant Elizabethan England, Habsburg Spain, and the Holy Roman Empire as well as Valois France and the Dutch Republic. More closely at hand and of greater significance to the Ottomans in the short run, the city states of Venice and Genoa exerted enormous political and economic power, thanks to their far-flung fleets and commercial networks linking India, the Middle East, the Mediterranean, and west European worlds. To the east were two great empires, then at their peak of power and wealth: the Safevid state based in Iran and the Moghul Empire in the Indian subcontinent. The Ottoman, Safevid, and Moghul empires reached from Vienna in the west to the borders of China in the east and, in the sixteenth century, all prospered under careful administrators, enriched by the trade between Asia and Europe. The three together likely held the balance of economic and political global power, at the very moment when Spain and Portugal were conquering the New World and its treasure. But China, in the midst of Ming rule, certainly was the most powerful and wealthy single state in the world at the time.

The Ottomans, in 1453, had destroyed the second Rome, Byzantium, that had endured for one thousand years, from the fourth through the fifteenth centuries. Through this act, the Ottoman state changed in status from regional power to world empire. As destroyer, the Ottoman Empire in some ways also was the inheritor of the Roman heritage in its eastern Byzantine form. Indeed, Sultan Mehmet II, the conqueror of Constantinople, explicitly laid down the claim that he was a caesar, a latter-day emperor, and his sixteenth-century successor, Süleyman the Magnificent, sought Rome as the capstone of his career. Moreover, the Ottoman rulers, having conquered the second Rome, for the next four hundred-plus years honored its Roman founder in the name of the capital city. Until the end of the empire, the city's name – the city of Constantine – Konstantiniyye/Constantinople – remained in the Ottomans' official correspondence, their coins, and on their postage stamps, after these came into use in the nineteenth century. In some respects, the Ottomans followed certain Byzantine administrative models. Like the Byzantines, the Ottomans practiced a kind of caesaro-papism, the system in which the state controlled the clergy. In the Ottoman judiciary the courts were run by judges, members of the religious class, the ulema. The Ottoman sultans appointed these judges and thus, like their Byzantine imperial predecessors, exercised a direct control over members of the religious establishment. In addition, to give another example of Byzantine–Ottoman continuities, Byzantine forms of land tenure carried over into the Ottoman era. While the Ottomans forged their own unique synthesis and were no mere imitators of their predecessors, their debt to the Byzantines was real.

Other powerful influences shaped the Ottoman polity besides the Byzantine. As we shall see, the Ottoman Empire emerged out of the anarchy surrounding the Turkish nomadic movements into the Middle East after 1000 CE, population movements triggered by uncertain causes in their central Asiatic homelands. It was the last great Turco-Islamic state, following those of the Seljuks and of Tamerlane, born of the migration of the Turkish peoples out of central Asia westward into the Middle East and the Balkans (see chapter 2). The shamanist beliefs of those nomads remained deeply embedded in the spiritual practices and world view of the Ottoman dynasty. Similarly, pre-Islamic Turkish usages remained important in Ottoman administrative circles, despite the later influx of administrative and legal practices from the Islamic world of Iran and the eastern Mediterranean. Ultimately, the Ottoman system should be seen as a highly effective blend of influences deriving from Byzantium, the Turkish nomads, and the Balkan states, as well as the Islamic world.

Shaped by others, the Ottomans in their turn affected the evolution and formation of many central, east, and west European states and the shaping of their popular imagination. If there is such a thing as the paranoid style in twentieth-century Soviet Russian politics, we have the Ottomans to thank, in large measure. For the Czarist Russian state based in Moscow the presence of a powerful Ottoman state long blocked the way to Black Sea and Mediterranean warm water ports. For centuries, the Ottomans were the single most important foreign enemies of the Russian state; czars and sultans fought against each other in a seemingly endless series of wars between the seventeenth and twentieth centuries, until both disappeared. These wars had a powerful impact on the evolution and shaping of the emerging Russian power: the Muscovite state's deep fears of powerful enemies on its southern (and western) flanks permanently marked its polity with a need to seek safety in expansion and domination. The Habsburg state on the Danube, for its part, came into existence amid profound regional confusion in order to check further Ottoman expansion northwards. The Vienna-based state became a center of resistance and, over time, acquired the role and identity as the first line of defense for central Europe because the various kingdoms further south in the Balkan peninsula all had failed to check the Ottomans. Without question, the Ottomans played a decisive role in the formation and subsequent evolution of the Habsburg state, defining its very nature.

Its geopolitical position, at the crossroads of the Asian, European, and African continents, thus gave the Ottoman state an important role to play in world history. This importance did not vanish after the military catastrophe of 1683 and the failing ability of the Ottomans to defend their territorial integrity. Indeed, Ottoman weakness prompted international instability among expanding neighbors jealous to lop off Ottoman lands or, at the least, prevent them from falling into the hands of rivals. This "Eastern Question" – who would inherit which territories once the Ottoman state vanished – provoked strife among the Great Powers of the age and became a leading issue of international diplomacy in the nineteenth century. In 1914, the failure to resolve the Eastern Question helped bring on the first great catastrophe of the contemporary age, World War I.

A far more positive reason to study the Ottoman empire and assign it an important place in world history concerns the tolerant model of administration that it offered during most of its existence. For a contemporary world in which transportation and communication technologies and the migrations of peoples have brought about an unparalleled confrontation with difference, the Ottoman case warrants careful study. For centuries the Ottoman hand rested lightly on its subject populations. The Ottoman political system required its administrators and military officers to protect subjects in the exercise of their religion, whether Islam, Judaism, or Christianity in whatever variation – e.g. Sunni, Shii, Greek or Armenian or Syriac Orthodox or Catholic. This requirement was based on the Islamic principle of toleration of the "People of the Book," meaning Jews and Christians. These "people" had received God's revelation, even if incompletely and imperfectly; therefore, the Ottoman Islamic state had the responsibility to protect them in the exercise of their religions. Without question, these legal protections did fail. Christian and Jewish subjects sometimes were persecuted or killed because they did not share the Islamic faith of the state apparatus. But such actions were violations of the bedrock principle of toleration – a high standard to which the state expected and required adherence. Such principles of toleration governed inter-communal relations in the Ottoman empire for centuries. But, in the final years, there was mounting disharmony and inter-communal strife (see chapter 9). For most of its history, however, the Ottoman Empire offered an effective model of a multi-religious political system to the rest of the world.

The Ottoman Empire in European culture

Let us begin with a word of caution about the significance of the following pages, that outline the place of the Ottoman Empire in the history, imagination, and culture of western Europe. This discussion is not intended to imply that the Ottomans are important only to the extent they contributed to west European development. Instead, the discussion has this focus because the intended primary audience is those from the west European cultural tradition. The goal is to demonstrate for those readers the manner in which the Ottoman Empire affected the course of their own history and culture.

Because the Ottomans, by chance, were physically the most proximate to the west European states that came to dominate the globe in the modern era, they long bore the brunt of Europe's military, political, and ideological expansion. This proximity had a profound impact on the formation of identity, both of the Ottomans and of the Europeans. On each side proximity structured a complex identity formation process of repulsion and attraction. After all, a people comes to perceive of itself as distinct and separate, with particular and unique characteristics, often through using the "other" as a means of defining what it is and, equally, what it is not. Confronting the Byzantine, Balkan, east, and west European states, the Ottomans sometimes emphasized (perhaps like the Moghuls facing a Hindu enemy in the Indian subcontinent) their identity as Muslim warriors for the faith. This did not prevent the Ottoman rulers from simultaneously admiring and employing Byzantine, Bulgarian, Serb, west European, and other Christians as soldiers, artists, and technicians. For Europeans, including their descendants in the United States and elsewhere, the Ottomans were a vital means by which European culture defined itself as such. Sometimes the Ottoman served as a model for qualities the Europeans wished to possess. Thus Machiavelli and later European political thinkers such as Bodin and Montesquieu praised the Ottoman military and administrators' incorruptibility, discipline, and obedience in order to chastise Europeans. All of them, different political thinkers in different eras, wrote about the need for effective administrators and an effective state. In an age when direct criticism of a king might be dangerous, they used the example of the Ottomans to inspire European monarchs and their soldiers and statesmen to better behavior. These are the qualities, such writers were saying, which we in the West should possess. Further, as Europeans sought to define themselves, they did so in part by describing what they were not. Many European writers made the Ottomans the repository of evil; they identified the characteristics which they wished to have by attributing the opposite to their enemy. Thus, cruelty vs humaneness, barbarism vs civilization, infidels vs true believers. You could know who you were by defining who and what you were not. (In the places that we now know as England, France, and Germany, authors had assigned this role of "other" to the Muslims of Arab lands during the earliest days of Islam, back in the seventh century CE). In the imagination of these writers and their readers whose identity as Europeans was still in the making, the Ottomans (them) were described as possessing qualities which civilized persons (we) did/could not possess. In the world of the European mind, the Ottomans alternately were terrible, savage, and "unspeakable" and at the same time sex-crazed, harem-driven, and debauched. Even in the nineteenth century, European imaginings marked the Ottoman East as the degenerate site of pleasures supposedly absent or forbidden in the civilized and vigorous West, where Europeans by contrast allegedly were restrained, sober, just, sexually controlled, moderate, and rational.

In a truly intimate way the Ottomans became part and parcel of everyday European life, usually in ways that today are overlooked or forgotten. For example, most west Europeans or Americans surely would fail to acknowledge their debt to the Ottomans for the coffee and tulips they enjoy or the smallpox inoculations that protect their lives. But indeed, these are Ottoman contributions, arriving in western Europe between the sixteenth and the eighteenth centuries. From early times the Ottoman Empire has been intertwined in the daily lives, religion, and politics of what became Europe. Usually, as a rule of thumb, the extent of the intertwining is in inverse correlation to the distance. Hence, probably, the Ottoman legacy is greater in present day Austria than in Denmark. And yet, everywhere, including the United States where so many western European values have been maintained, the Ottoman presence is felt.

The Ottoman Empire played an important role in the European wars of religion, serving a didactic function. During the Reformation era, the Ottomans were the veritable scourge of God on earth for many of the contesting parties. Some radical reformers, called Anabaptists, held that the Ottomans were God's sign, about to conquer the world. The Anti-Christ then would come; the Elect would destroy the godless and bring about the Second Coming of Christ. Martin Luther, for his part, wrote that the Ottomans were God's punishment for a corrupt papacy, an instrument of God's anger. Catholics, from their side, considered these "Turks" divine punishment for allowing Luther and his followers to flourish.

The Ottomans similarly are embedded in European popular culture. In the seventeenth century, French imaginative literature frequently focused on the sultans, for example in the story of Sultan Bayezit I (1389–1402) in his cage and his captor, Timur (Tamerlane), which was published in 1648. Most stories, however, related the cruelty of these "Turks," such as that of Sultan Süleyman the Magnificent towards his favorite, the Grand Vizier Ibrahim. Sultan Mehmet the Conqueror, who actually was a cosmopolitan, sophisticated, multilingual Renaissance prince, instead was portrayed as a cruel and brutal tyrant in a 1612 French play that depicted his mother drinking the blood of a victim. Other, equally bizarre and inaccurate tales related stories of Ottoman soldiers making sacrifices to the Roman god of war, Mars. The receding of the Ottoman threat after the 1683 failure before Vienna, however, modified the image of the Ottomans.

And so, in the eighteenth century, west, central, and east Europeans felt safe enough to begin borrowing overtly, actively, from their Ottoman neighbor. During this period the Ottomans made important contributions in the realm of European classical music, adding to it the percussion sections of the modern orchestra. From the 1720s until the 1850s, so called "Turkish music" – a term once used for the percussion instruments in the orchestra – became the rage in Europe. European courts vied with one another to produce the Ottoman percussion sounds – cymbals, the single kettle drum, the side drum, and the bass drum, plus triangles, tambourines, and the "Jingling Johnny," a pavilion-shaped instrument of bells. This music had originated with the Janissary band that marched with the Ottoman armies to inspire the troops and strike terror into enemies' hearts. King Augustus II of Poland (1697–1733) so admired Janissary music that a sultan gifted him with a band of twelve to fifteen players. The king's neighbor, Empress Anne of Russia, enviously determined she needed one as well, and in 1725 sent to Istanbul for a similar group. By 1741, the Vienna Habsburgs had their own and, somewhat later, so did the Prussian king in Berlin. In each of these, the band members were Ottomans, whose careers abroad in these strange lands certainly deserve telling. In 1782, London received its own band but, in this instance, Africans were employed on the drums, cymbals, and tambourines, probably to further promote the sense of the exotic. One survival of this Janissary band craze is the mace throwing by drum majors. Over time, the mace became ceremonial, carried by the head of the Janissary band to keep time. This finally evolved into the baton of the drum majorettes, thrown into the air in parades and at football games everywhere in the United States.

The popularity of the Janissary sound spilled over from the orchestra and entered the mainstream of what we now call Western classical music. There is a wonderful passage in the final movement of Beethoven's Ninth Symphony, first published in 1824, that conjures up images of marching Janissaries. "Turkish music" can also be heard in the Fourth Symphony of Brahms and in Haydn's Military Symphony as well as in Rossini's *William Tell* overture and in the march of Wagner's *Tannhäuser*. Mozart's A major piano sonata K. 331 contains a marvellous *rondo alla turca*, a theme that carried over into American jazz and the repertories of musicians such as Dave Brubeck and Ahmad Jamal. In opera, not only Ottoman music but Ottoman settings became popular, the first being a three-act opera in 1686 produced in Hamburg, on the fate of Grand Vizier Kara Mustafa Pasha after the siege of Vienna (he was executed). Handel's opera *Tamerlane* (1724) portrayed the defeat, capture, and imprisonment of Sultan Bayezit I (1389–1402) by the central Asian world conqueror. The *Escape from the Seraglio* by Mozart in 1782 was preceded by several operas with similar plot lines and characters. Rossini's *The Turk in Italy* and to some extent *The Italian Girl in Algiers* carried on this tradition of Ottoman operatic themes.

As European music borrowed Ottoman musical themes and settings, "Turkish" fashions became the rage of late eighteenth-century Europe. Pseudo-Ottoman sultans and sultanas appeared everywhere, a fad started by Madame de Pompadour in the court of King Louis XV. During the Sarmation movement in Poland, for example, nobles wore Ottoman costumes and rode "Arab" horses. Ottoman-style coffee houses across Europe became populated with Europeans wearing bright silks, billowing trousers, and upturned "Turkish slippers," smoking "Turkish" pipes and eating "Turkish" sweets.

In the nineteenth century this "Turkomania" faded, to be replaced by yet other expressions of the Ottoman presence in European popular culture. The common motifs of cruelty, intrigue, jealousy and savagery continued, hence the ready reception accorded to the powerful British politician Gladstone's rantings against the "Bulgarian horrors." Alongside this old, ruthless image emerged that of the amorous or the buffoon Turk. The silly Turk already had become a stock figure, as we see in Molière's *The Bourgeois Gentleman* (1670), where a major character babbled gibberish which the audience was meant to understand as Ottoman Turkish. Now, in the nineteenth century, lustful Turks with enormous sex organs became an important feature of Victorian pornographic literature. Further, many Europeans, from Lord Byron to the novelist Pierre Loti to Lawrence of Arabia, came to consider the Ottoman Empire as the land of dreams where sexual or other fantasies could be realized. These three individuals and thousands of others sought escape from the tedium and monotony of modern industrial life in the imagined East – whether or not they traveled to the Ottoman realms. The paintings of Delacroix, Gérôme, and others abound in images of the exotic and erotic, the primitive, the savage, and the noble.

Thanks to the Ottoman artifacts displayed at the various world's fairs of the nineteenth century, including the 1876 American Centennial Exposition, a "Turkish corner" became commonplace in European and American homes. In the parlors of the wealthier classes, overstuffed armchairs with deep fringes and tassels appeared, often set off with a copper tray and always "Oriental" carpets. In 1900 Paris, for example, the designer Poiret was famed for his "Oriental" fantasies. In the homes of the less-well-off, a single piece of overstuffed furniture – a sofa, ottoman, or divan – often conjured up the exotic East. The great German novelist Thomas Mann's *The Magic Mountain* (1924) depicts a "Turkish corner," and also a figure who used a "Turkish" coffee mill and "Turkish" coffee for socializing. The grandfather of one of the main characters had "a funny little Turk in flowing silk robes, under which was a hard body with a mechanism inside. Once, when you wound him up, he had been able to leap about all over the table, but he was long since out of repair." In the United States, for example, in New York City, Portland, Oregon, and Chicago, architects built scores of motion picture theaters that borrowed very heavily from Islamic and Ottoman architectural details (as well as from other cultures, including the ancient Near East).

In sum, as is clear from the above examples, the Ottomans supplied much grist for the imaginative mill of the Europeans. The Anti-Christ and enemy of the Reformation and of the French imaginative literature of the seventeenth century had given way to more innocent images in the age of Ottoman military contraction. Hence we find the Janissary music and Turkomania fads of the eighteenth century, and then the exoticism and eroticism of the nineteenth century accompanied by the omnipresent Oriental rug and the movie theater. Even today, in the cultural world of Europe and its extensions, the Ottoman Empire is gone, but its legacies remain (see chapter 10).

In its last days, the Ottoman Empire persevered in the heyday of west European imperialism, when the empires of Britain and France physically dominated and occupied much of the globe. Everywhere peoples had fallen under the control of these and other west European states. In the late nineteenth-century world there were only a handful of independent states outside the European continent. The Ottomans, together with imperial China and Japan, were the most important of such states which survived with any strength. As independent states, they became models and sources of hope to the colonized peoples of the world in their struggles against European imperialism. Thus, peoples as diverse as Indian Muslims, the Turkic speakers of central Asia and the North Africans of the Maghreb all looked to the Ottoman Empire in their struggles against British, Russian, and French colonialism.

Suggested bibliography

Entries marked with a * designate recommended readings for new students of the subject.

*Asad, Talal. *Anthropology and the colonial encounter* (New York, 1973).

Bohnstedt, John Wolfgang. *The Infidel scourge of God: The Turkish menace as seen by German pamphleteers of the Reformation* (Philadelphia, 1968).

*Brown, L. Carl, ed. *Imperial legacy: The Ottoman imprint on the Balkans and the Middle East* (New York, 1996).

*Çelik, Zeynep. *Displaying the Orient: The architecture of Islam and nineteenth-century world fairs* (Berkeley, 1992).

Daniel, Norman. *Islam, Europe, and empire* (Edinburgh, 1966).

  Islam and the West: The making of an image (Edinburgh, 1962).

*Deringil, Selim. "The Ottoman twilight zone of the Middle East," in Henri J. Barkey, ed., *Reluctant neighbor: Turkey's role in the Middle East* (Washington, DC, 1996), 13–22.

Faroqhi, Suraiya. *Approaching Ottoman history: An introduction to the sources* (Cambridge, 1999).

Fischer-Galati, Stephen A. *Ottoman imperialism and German Protestantism, 1521–1555* (Cambridge, MA, 1959).

*Karpat, Kemal. *The Ottoman empire and its place in world history* (Leiden, 1974).

*Mansel, Philip. *Constantinople: City of the world's desire, 1453–1924* (London, 1995).

*Rodinson, Maxime. *Europe and the mystique of Islam* (Seattle, translation of original French 1980 edition, 1987).

Rouillard, Clarence. *The Turk in French history, thought and literature (1520–1660)* (Paris, 1938).

*Said, Edward. *Orientalism* (New York, 1978).

*Schacht, Joseph and C. E. Bosworth, eds. *The legacy of Islam* (Oxford, 2nd edn, 1979).

Schwoebel, Robert. *The shadow of the crescent: The Renaissance image of the Turk, 1453–1517* (Nieuwkoop, 1967).

Southern, R. W. *Western views of Islam in the Middle Ages* (Cambridge, 1968).

*Stevens, MaryAnne. *The Orientalists: Delacroix to Matisse* (London, 1984).

Thompson, James. *The East: Imagined, experienced, remembered* (Dublin, 1988).

*Valensi, Lucette. *The birth of the despot: Venice and the Sublime Porte* (Ithaca, 1993).

Suggestions on the history of the Byzantine Empire

Laiou-Thomadakis, A. E. *Peasant society in the late Byzantine Empire* (Princeton, 1977).

*Treadgold, Warren T. *A concise history of Byzantium* (New York, 2001).

*Vryonis, Speros, Jr. *The decline of medieval Hellenism in Asia Minor and the process of Islamization from the eleventh through the fifteenth century* (Berkeley, 1971).

2 The Ottoman Empire from its origins until 1683

Introduction

The era from 1300 until the later seventeenth century saw the remarkable expansion of the Ottoman state from a tiny, scarcely visible, chiefdom to an empire with vast territories. These dominions stretched from the Arabian peninsula and the cataracts of the Nile in the south, to Basra near the Persian Gulf and the Iranian plateau in the east, along the North African coast nearly to Gibraltar in the west, and to the Ukranian steppe and the walls of Vienna in the north. The period begins with an Ottoman dot on the map and ends with a world empire and its dominions along the Black, Aegean, Mediterranean, Caspian, and Red Seas.

Origins of the Ottoman state

Great events demand explanations: how are we to understand the rise of great empires such as those of Rome, the Inca, the Ming, Alexander, the British, or the Ottomans? How can these world shaking events be explained?

In brief, the Ottomans arose in the context of: Turkish nomadic invasions that shattered central Byzantine state domination in Asia Minor; a Mongol invasion of the Middle East that brought chaos and increased population pressure on the frontiers; Ottoman policies of pragmatism and flexibility that attracted a host of supporters regardless of religion and social rank; and luck, that placed the Ottomans in the geographic spot that controlled nomadic access to the Balkans, thus rallying additional supporters. In this section follows the more detailed story of the origins of the Ottoman state.

The Ottoman Empire was born around the turn of the thirteenth and fourteenth centuries, in the northwestern corner of the Anatolian peninsula, also called Asia Minor (map 1). Extreme confusion – political, cultural, religious, economic, and social – marked the era and the region. For more than a millennium, this area had been part of the Roman Empire

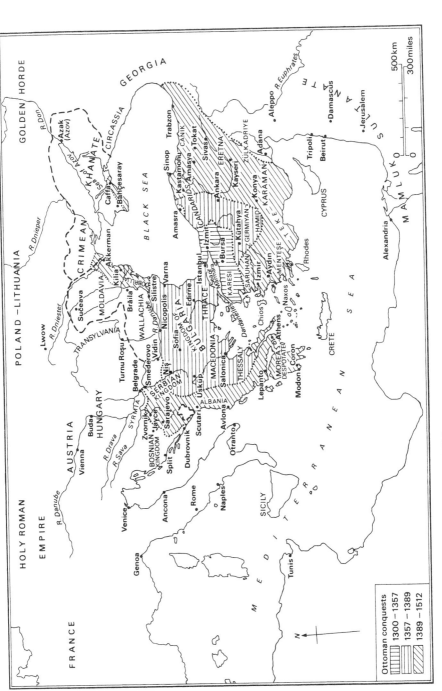

Map 1 The Ottoman Empire, 1300–1512
Adapted from Halil İnalcık with Donald Quataert, eds., *An economic and social history of the Ottoman Empire, 1300–1914* (Cambridge, 1994), xxxii.

and its successor state in the Eastern Mediterranean world, the Byzantine Empire, ruled from Constantinople. Byzantium had once ruled over virtually all of today's Middle East (except Iran) – the region of modern-day Egypt, Israel, Palestine, Lebanon, Syria, Jordan, Turkey, and parts of Iraq, as well as parts of southeast Europe, north Africa, and Italy. In the seventh century CE, however, it had lost many of those areas, mostly to the expanding new states based in Mecca, Damascus, and Baghdad. With some difficulty, the Byzantine state then reinvented itself and managed to retain its Anatolian provinces. In its reduced form, the Byzantine Empire faced three sets of enemies. From the Mediterranean, the Venetian and Genoese merchant states fought between themselves and (usually separately) against the Byzantines to gain strongholds and economic concessions on the rich Aegean, Black Sea, and eastern Mediterranean trade routes. To their north and west, the Byzantines faced expansive and powerful land-based states, especially the Bulgarian and Serbian kingdoms. And, beginning at the turn of the first millennium, the Turkish nomads (called Turcoman) appeared on their eastern frontiers. Turkish peoples with their origins in central Asia, in the area around Lake Baikal, began migrating out of these ancestral homes and, c. 1000 CE, started pouring into the Middle East. In their Central Asiatic homes, the Turcoman way of life was marked by shamanist beliefs in religion and economic dependence on animal raising and social values that celebrated personal bravery and considerable freedom and mobility for noble women. The Homeric-style epic, named *The Book of Dede Korkut*, recounts the stories of heroic men and women, and was written just before the Turcoman expansion into the Middle East. This epic also shows that the Turcoman polity was highly fragmented, with leadership by consensus rather than command. This set of migrations – a major event in world history – created a Turkic speaking belt of men, women, and children from the western borders of China to Asia Minor and led to the formation of the Ottoman state. The nomadic, politically fragmented Turcoman way of life began causing major disturbances in the lives of the settled populations of the Iranian plateau, who bore the brunt of the initial migrations/invasions. As the nomads moved towards and then into the sedentarized Middle East, they converted to Islam but retained many of their shamanist rituals and practices. Hence, Turkish Islam as it became practiced later on varied considerably in form from Iranian or Arab Islam. As they migrated, the Turcomans and their animals disrupted the economy of the settled regions and the flow of tax revenues which agriculturalists paid to their rulers. Among the Turkish nomadic invaders was the Seljuk family. One of many leaders in charge of smaller or larger nomadic groups drifting westward, the Seljuk family seized control of Iran and its agricultural populations, quickly assimilated into its prevailing Perso-Islamic civilization, and then confronted the problem of what to do with their nomadic followers who were disrupting the settled agricultural life of their new kingdom. A solution to the Seljuks' problem was to be found in Byzantine Anatolia.

The provinces of Byzantine Anatolia had two sets of features that seem important here. First, they were productive, heavily populated agrarian settlements and thus for the nomads appeared as very attractive targets of plunder. In a word, the Anatolian provinces were rich. They also were Christian. Therefore they offered doubly justified targets of warfare for these Turkish nomads recently converted to Islam and under the influence of popular preachers who had fused shamanist beliefs with Islam. Was Anatolia attractive to the nomads mainly because it was rich or because it was Christian? Like their crusading Christian contemporaries, the nomads' motives were a mixture of economic, political, and religious factors. The lands of Anatolia were rich and they were inhabited by (mainly) farmers of another, Christian, faith. For the vast numbers of nomads already in the Middle East, pressured by waves of nomads behind them in central Asia, these were powerful incentives. And so, not long after their entry into Iran, the Turcoman nomads began plundering and raiding the eastern provinces of Byzantium, pulled there by economics, politics, and faith, and pushed there by the centralizing Seljuk rulers of Iran. After enduring the raids for several decades, the central Byzantine state moved to crush the new threat. In 1071, however, the imperial army under the Emperor Romanus Diogenus decisively was crushed at the epochal battle of Manzikert, not far from Lake Van, by the combined military forces of the Turkish nomads temporarily allied with the army of the Seljuk Sultan Alp Arslan. This spelled the ruin of the imperial border defense system in the east, and Turkish nomads, now nearly unchecked, flooded into Byzantium.

For the next several centuries, until the mid-fifteenth century, the history of Anatolia, east and west, can be understood through the metaphor of islands of sedentarized life under Byzantine imperial and feudal lords struggling to exist in a flood tide of Turkish nomads whose leaders, in turn, came to form their own small states. In the short run, Turcoman principalities rose and fell and Byzantine control ebbed and flowed. Anatolia became a patchwork quilt of tiny Turcoman and Byzantine principalities and statelets, expanding and contracting. At times, Byzantine leaders, imperial and feudal, resisted more or less successfully. But inexorably, in the long run, Byzantine Christian, predominantly Greek-speaking, Anatolia underwent a profound transformation and over time became Turkish speaking and Muslim. This general atmosphere of confusion, indeed chaos, played a crucial role in the emergence of the Ottoman state. In the midst of the Turcoman invasions, the beleaguered Byzantines also were fighting against the Italian merchant states, losing to them chunks of land and other economic assets such as trade monopolies. Between 1204 and 1261, moreover, Constantinople became the capital of the erstwhile Crusaders, who instead of marching to Palestine, seized and sacked the riches of the imperial city and established their short-lived Latin Christian empire. Historians agree that the 1204 sack of the city struck a blow from which Constantinople never recovered.

The specific context in which the Ottoman state emerged also is linked to the rise of the Mongol Empire under Genghis Khan, its rapid expansion east and west, and its push into the Middle East during the thirteenth century. As the Mongol state expanded, it often accelerated the movement of Turkish nomads, who fled before it into areas that could support their numbers and their livestock. In the middle of the thirteenth century a Mongol general warred on a Seljuk state which had been established at Konya in central Anatolia. This Mongol victory wrecked the relatively large Seljuk sultanate there, which, before the Ottomans, had been the most successful state founded in post-Byzantine Anatolia, and triggered the rise of a number of small Turcoman principalities in its stead. The Mongol presence also prompted the flight of Turcoman nomads who sought pasture lands in the west. These were the border regions of the collapsing Seljuk state on the one hand and the crumbling Byzantine world on the other. This was a changing world, full of Serb and Bulgarian, Genoese and Venetian invaders and of Turkish Muslim nomads and Byzantine Greek Christian peasants. In these Anatolian highlands to the south and east of Byzantine Constantinople, the Ottoman Empire was born.

Historians who are Ottoman specialists like to argue about which was the most important single variable explaining the rise of this extraordinary empire. The question is a fair one since the founder of the dynasty after whom it was named, Osman, was just one of many leaders and not the most powerful, among the various and sundry Turcoman groups on the frontier. Looking down on this world in the year 1300, it would have been impossible to predict that his would be among the most successful states in history. At the time, Osman was in charge of some 40,000 tents of Turcoman nomads. Some of his Turkish-speaking rivals in other parts of the frontier were vastly more successful and commanded 70,000 and 100,000 tents (with two to five persons per tent). There were scores of other Turcoman principalities. All were part of a larger process in which Turcoman nomads of the Anatolian highlands pressed upon and finally occupied the valleys and the coastal plains. Alone among these, the dynasty of Osman triumphed while the others soon disappeared.

Osman and his followers, along with the other Turcoman leaders and groups, surely benefited from the confusion throughout Anatolia, especially in the borderland (as later Ottoman rulers would profit from political disintegration in the Balkans). Turkish nomadic incursions, commonly spontaneous and undirected, toppled local administrations and threw the prevailing political and economic order of Anatolia into confusion. The Mongol thrusts accelerated these movements which, altogether, seem to have built up considerable population pressures in the frontier zones. Warrior bands like Osman's flourished both because they could prey on settled populations and because their strength offered adherents a safety that governments seemed unable to provide. Such warrior encampments became an important form of political organization in thirteenth-century Anatolia.

Ottoman success in forming a state certainly was due to an exceptional flexibility, a readiness and ability to pragmatically adapt to changing conditions. The emerging Ottoman dynasty, that traced descent through the male line, was Turkish in origins, emerging in a highly heterogeneous zone populated by Christians and Muslims, Turkish and Greek speakers. Muslims and Christians alike from Anatolia and beyond flocked to the Ottoman standard for the economic benefits to be won. The Ottoman rulers also attracted some followers because of their self-appointed role as *gazi*s, warriors for the faith fighting against the Christians. But the power of this appeal to religion must be questioned since, at the very same moment, the Ottomans were recruiting large numbers of Greek Christian military commanders and rank-and-file soldiery into their growing military force. Thus, many Christians as well as Muslims followed the Ottomans not for God but for gold and glory – for the riches to be gained, the positions and power to be won.

Another argument against identifying the Ottoman state primarily as a religious one rests in the reality that Ottoman energies focused not only on fighting neighboring Byzantine feudal lords but also, from earliest times, other Turcoman leaders. Indeed, the Ottomans regularly warred against Turcoman principalities in Anatolia during the fourteenth through the sixteenth centuries. Despite their severity and frequency, the Ottoman wars with Turcomans often have been overlooked because historians' attention has been on the Ottoman attacks on Europe and on inappropriately casting the Ottomans' role primarily as warriors for the faith (*gazi*) rather than as state builders. Rival Turcoman dynasties – such as the Karaman and the Germiyan in Anatolia or the Timurids in central Asia – were formidable enemies and grave threats to the Ottoman state. From the beginning, Ottoman expansion was multi-directional – aimed not only west and northwest against Christian Byzantine and Balkan lands and rulers but always east and south as well, against rival Muslim Turcoman political systems. Thus, what seems crucial about the Ottomans was not their *gazi* or religious nature, although they sometimes had this appeal. Rather, what seems most striking about the Ottoman enterprise was its character as a state in the process of formation, of becoming, and of doing what was necessary to attract and retain followers. To put it more explicitly, this Ottoman enterprise was not a religious state in the making but rather a pragmatic, dynastic one. In this respect, it was no different from other contemporary states, such as those in England, Hungary, France, or China.

Geography played an important role in the rise of the Ottomans. Other leaders on the frontiers perhaps were similar to the Ottomans in their adaptiveness to conditions, in their willingness to utilize talent, to accept allegiance from many sources, and to make multi-sided appeals for support. At this distance in time it is difficult to judge how exceptional the Ottomans may have been in this regard. But when considering the reasons for Ottoman success we can point with more certainty to an event that occurred in 1354 – the Ottoman occupation of a town (Tzympe), on the European side of the Dardanelles, one of the three waterways that divide Europe and Asia (the others being the Bosphorus and the Sea of Marmara). Possession of the town gave the Ottomans a secure bridgehead in the Balkans, a territorial launching pad that instantly propelled the Ottomans ahead of their frontier rivals in Anatolia. With this possession, the Ottomans offered potential supporters vast new fields of enrichment – the Balkan lands – that simply were unavailable to the followers of other dynasts or chieftains on the other, Asiatic, side of the narrow waters. These lands were rich and at that time were empty of Turcomans. Appeals to action also could be made in the name of ideology – of war for the faith.

Thus, the earlier riches and political turmoil of Byzantine Anatolia were paralleled by the riches and turmoil of the fourteenth-century Balkans. Forces similar to those that earlier had brought the Turcomans into Byzantine Anatolia now brought the Ottomans and the nomads into the Balkans. The Balkans offered a relief valve for the population pressures building in western Asia Minor, and the Ottomans alone offered access to it. Ironically, the Ottoman crossover into Europe happened because of the ambitions of a Byzantine pretender to the Constantinople throne. Caught in a civil war, he granted the Ottomans this foothold in a new continent as a means of cementing their support. Irony compounded irony since the Ottomans then used their alliance with Genoa, a sometime enemy of the Byzantines, to expand their newly gained but precarious European holdings.

Like Anatolia in c. 1000 CE, the Balkans in the fourteenth century offered rich and vulnerable prizes ready for the taking. State building efforts in both the Bulgarian and Serbian areas had collapsed; the Byzantines were in a civil war as rival claimants fought one another for the imperial crown; and Venice and Genoa each moved to take advantage of the confusion. And so, a combination of flexibility, skilled policies, good luck, and good geography contributed to the Ottomans' ability to break out onto the path of world empire and gain supremacy over their rivals. Already successful, their crossing into the Balkans vaulted them into a new position with unparalleled advantages.

Expansion and consolidation of the Ottoman state, 1300–1683

From their beginnings in western Anatolia, the Ottoman state in the following centuries expanded steadily in a nearly unceasing series of successful wars that brought it vast territories at the junction of the European, Asian, and African continents. Before turning to the factors which explain the Ottomans' expansion from their initial west Anatolian–Balkan base, we need to briefly enumerate these victories (map 2).

Usually, historians like to point to the reigns of two sultans – Mehmet II (1451–1481) and Süleyman the Magnificent (1520–1566) – as particularly impressive. Each built on the extraordinary achievements of his predecessors. In the 100 plus years before Sultan Mehmet II assumed the throne, the Ottomans expanded deep into the Balkan and Anatolian lands. By the time of their crossover from west Anatolia into the Balkans, the Ottomans already had seized the important Byzantine city of Bursa and made it the capital of their expanding state. In 1361 they captured Adrianople (Edirne) in Europe, a major Byzantine city that became the new Ottoman capital, and used it as a major staging area for offensives into the Balkans. Less than half a lifetime later, in 1389, Ottoman forces annihilated their Serbian foes at Kossovo, in the western Balkans. After 1989, the reinvented memory of Kossovo became a powerful catalyst to the formation of modern Serbian identity. This great victory was followed by others, for example, the capture of Salonica from the Venetians in 1430. At Nicopolis in 1396 and Varna in 1444, the Ottomans defeated wide-ranging coalitions of west and central European states that were becoming painfully aware of the expanding Ottoman state and the increasing danger it posed to them. The international aspect of these battles was marked by the presence of forces from not only Serbia, Wallachia, Bosnia, Hungary, and Poland, but also, for example, France, the German states, Scotland, Burgundy, Flanders, Lombardy, and

Savoy. Scholars have considered Nicopolis and Varna as latter day Crusades, the continuation of eleventh-century European efforts to destroy local states in Palestine. And yet, at both battles (see below), Balkan princes were present who fought on the Ottoman side while Venice, at Nicopolis, negotiated with each side to gain commercial and political advantage.

So, when Mehmet the Conqueror took power, he had a strong foundation on which to build. Just two years later, in 1453, he fulfilled the long-standing Ottoman and Muslim dream of seizing thousand-year-old Constantinople, city of the Caesars. Mehmet immediately began restoring the city to its former glories; by 1478, the population had doubled from 30,000 living in villages scattered inside of the massive fortifications to 70,000 inhabitants. A century later, this great capital would boast over 400,000 residents. Mehmet's conquests continued and, between 1459 and 1461, he brought under Ottoman domination the last fragments of Byzantium in the Morea (southern Greece) and at Trabzon on the Black Sea; he also annexed the southern Crimea and established a long-standing set of ties with the Crimean khans, successors of the Mongols who earlier had conquered the region. For a time, perhaps as part of a plan to conquer Rome, his armies occupied Otranto on the heel of the Italian peninsula. But the effort failed, as did his siege of Rhodes, an island bastion of a crusading order of knights.

Sultan Süleyman the Magnificent had the good fortune of succeeding Selim I (1512–1520). In his short reign, Selim had thoroughly beaten a newly emergent foe, the Safevid state on the battlefield of Çaldıran in 1514. (The Safevids, a Turkish-speaking dynasty who had acquired an Islamic and Persian identity, became the major opponent on the Ottoman eastern frontiers during the fifteenth through the seventeenth centuries.) Selim then (1516–1517) conquered the Arab lands of the Mamluk sultanate based in Cairo, filling the treasury and bringing the Muslim Holy Cities of Mecca and Medina under the Ottoman rulers' dominion. During the long reign of Süleyman the Magnificent (1520–1566) the Ottomans enjoyed considerable power and wealth. Under Süleyman's leadership, the Ottomans fought a sixteenth-century world war. Sultan Süleyman supported Dutch rebels against their Spanish overlords while his navy battled in the western Mediterranean against the Spanish Habsburgs. At one point, Ottoman troops wintered on the modern-day Riviera at Toulon, by courtesy of King Francis I of France who also was fighting against the Habsburgs (see chapter 5). On the other side of their world, Ottoman navies warred in the Red Sea and the Indian Ocean, as far east as modern-day Indonesia. There they fought because the global balance of power and wealth had been overturned by the Portuguese voyages of

Boundary of the Ottoman Empire
Boundary of vassal states
Vassal states

Map 2 The Ottoman Empire, c. 1550
Adapted from Halil İnalcık with Donald Quataert, eds., *An economic and social history of the Ottoman Empire, 1300–1914* (Cambridge, 1994), xxxiv.

discovery around Africa, that opened all-water routes between India and south and southeast Asia. These new passages threatened to destroy a transit trade that Middle Eastern regimes for many centuries had dominated and profited from. To loosen the mounting Portuguese (and later Dutch and English) chokehold on this trade and break its growing dominance of the all-water routes, the Ottomans launched a series of offensives in the eastern seas. For example, they aided local rulers on the India coast who were fighting the Portuguese and sent fleets to aid the Moluccans (near modern Singapore) who were struggling to break mounting European maritime domination. On the Balkan fronts, Sultan Süleyman's forces similarly moved to impose Ottoman domination over trade routes, rich mines and other economic resources. In an important series of victories, the Ottomans seized Belgrade in 1521, crushed the Hungarian state at the battle of Mohács in 1526 and later (in 1544) annexed part of it. In 1529, Ottoman troops stood outside the walls of Habsburg Vienna, which neither they nor their successors in 1683 were able effectively to breach. By this date the Istanbul-based state stood astride the rich trade routes linking the Aegean and Mediterranean seas to east and central Europe. Thus both Venice and Genoa suffered grievous blows, losing the wealth and power that the trade routes and colonies of these regions had brought them.

If the phrase "expansion" aptly depicts the overall Ottoman military and political experiences until the later sixteenth century, then "consolidation" likely best summarizes the situation during the subsequent century or so. Following Süleyman's death, Ottoman victories continued but less frequently than before. The great island of Cyprus with its fertile lands became an Ottoman possession in 1571, bolstering Istanbul's dominance over the sea routes of the eastern Mediterranean. The Europeans' naval victory at Lepanto in 1571 and utter destruction of the Ottoman navy, one of the greatest in the Mediterranean at the time, proved ephemeral. The next year a new fleet re-established Ottoman dominion in the eastern Mediterranean, the locale of their recent defeat. On land, Ottoman armies captured Azerbaijan between 1578 and 1590 and regained Baghdad in 1638. Crete, the largest of the eastern Mediterranean islands after Cyprus, was incorporated into the state in 1669, followed by Podolia in 1676.

Not every battle was a victory but the overall record until the later seventeenth century was a successful one, bringing more extensive frontiers containing new treasures, taxes and populations. By the later seventeenth century, Ottoman garrisons overlooked the Russian steppe, the Hungarian plain, the Saharan and Syrian deserts, and the mountain fastness of the Caucasus. Ottoman military forces had achieved virtually full dominion over the entire Black Sea, Aegean, and eastern Mediterranean basins, including most or all of the drainages of the Danube, Dniester, Dnieper, and Bug rivers, as well as the Tigris–Euphrates and the Nile. Thus, the trade routes and resources that had supported Rome and Byzantium, but then had been divided among the warring states of Venice, Genoa, Serbia, Bulgaria, and others, now belonged to a single imperial system.

How to explain this remarkable record of Ottoman success?

Describing victories is much easier than explaining why they happened. The Ottomans certainly profited from the weaknesses and confusion of their enemies. For example, their ability to expand against the Byzantines in part must be credited to the enduring harm done to Byzantium by the terrible events in 1204. At that time, Venetians and other Crusaders occupied Constantinople and plundered it so ruthlessly that Byzantium never regained its former strength. Also, consider the bitter rivalries among and warring between the most powerful states in the eastern Mediterranean – Venice, Byzantium, and Genoa. In addition, the decline of the feudal order, c. 1350–1450, left many states in shambles both militarily and politically. Thus, the collapse of the once-powerful Serbian and Bulgarian kingdoms at the very moment of Ottoman expansion into the Balkans left the road open to the invaders. Then there is the matter of the eruption of the Black Death in 1348. Here, historians like to argue that the plague most heavily affected urban populations, relatively sparing the Ottomans and softening their mainly urban enemies. To counter this point, it must be said that we have no evidence on how horribly the plague struck the populous Ottoman encampments or the towns and cities (such as Bursa, Iznik, and Izmit) already under their control. Moreover, such arguments ignore the repeated and terrible plague outbreaks that later wracked Ottoman cities and, notably, undermined Mehmet the Conqueror's efforts to repopulate Ottoman Constantinople. Such emphases on the divisions and weaknesses of enemies and the impact of the plague underscore good fortune and downplay Ottoman achievements by attributing success to factors outside of their control.

It seems more useful to examine Ottoman policies and achievements – emphasizing what they achieved by their own efforts – rather than the mere luck they enjoyed because of their enemies' problems. In this analysis, stress is upon the character of the Ottoman enterprise as a dynastic state, not dissimilar from European or Asian contemporaries such as the

Ming in China or England and France during the time of the Wars of the Roses. Like most other dynasties in recorded history, the Ottomans relied exclusively on male heirs to perpetuate their rule (see chapter 6). In the formal political structure of the emerging state, women nonetheless sometimes are visible. For example, Nilufer, wife of the second Ottoman ruler, Sultan Orhan (1324–1362), served as governor of a newly conquered city. Such formal roles for women, however, seem uncommon. More usually, later Ottoman history makes it clear that the wives, mothers, and daughters of the dynasty and other leading families wielded power, influencing and making policy through informal channels. For the early period, c. 1300–1683, we do know that, in common with many other dynasties, the Ottomans frequently used marriage to consolidate or extend power. For example, Sultan Orhan married the daughter of a pretender to the Byzantine throne, John Cantacuzene, and received the strategically vital Gallipoli peninsula to boot. Sultan Murat I married the daughter of the Bulgarian king Sisman in 1376, while Bayezit I married the daughter of Lazar (son of the Serbian monarch Stephen Dușan) after the battle of Kossovo. Such marriages hardly were confined to the Christian neighbors of the Ottomans but often were with other Muslim dynasties as well. For example, Prince Bayezit, on the arrangement of his father Murat I, married the daughter of the Turcoman ruler of Germiyan in Anatolia and obtained one-half of his lands as dowry. Bayezit II (1481–1512) married into the family of Dulkadirid rulers of east Anatolia, in the last known case of marriage between the Ottomans and another dynasty.

Another important key to understanding Ottoman success is to look at the methods of conquest. Here, as in the realm of marriage politics, we encounter a flexible, pragmatic group of state makers. The Ottoman rulers at first often allied with neighbors on the basis of equality, sometimes cementing a relationship with marriage. Then, frequently, as the Ottomans became more powerful, they established a loose overlordship, often involving a type of vassalage over the former ally. Thus, local rulers – whether Byzantine princes, Bulgarian and Serbian kings, or tribal chieftains – accepted the status of vassals to the Ottoman sultan, acknowledging him as a superior to whom loyalty was due. In such cases, the newly subordinated vassals often continued with their previous titles and positions but nevertheless owed allegiance to another monarch. These patterns of changing relations with neighbors are evident from the earliest days and continued for centuries. Thus, for example, the founder Osman first allied with neighboring rulers, then made them his vassals, bound to him by ties of loyalty and obedience. During the latter part of the fourteenth century the Byzantine emperor himself was an Ottoman vassal, as were Bulgarian and Serbian princes, as well as the Karaman ruler from Anatolia. At Kossovo in 1389, Ottoman supporters on the battlefield included a Bulgarian prince, lesser Serb princes, and some Turcoman rulers from Anatolia. In many cases, patterns of equality between rulers gave way to vassalage and finally direct annexation. A sharp example of this final phase is 1453, when the relationship between the Ottoman and Byzantine empires completed its evolution from equality to vassalage to subordination and destruction. As Sultan Mehmet the Conqueror defeated the Byzantine emperor he not only destroyed the Byzantine Empire but also the vassal relationship which had existed, now bringing the dead emperor's state under direct Ottoman administration. Similarly, Sultan Mehmet ended the alliance and vassal relationships with the Turcoman rulers of Anatolia and brought them under direct Ottoman control. In the early sixteenth century, to give another example, the Ottomans first ruled Hungary as a vassal state but then annexed it to more effectively govern the frontier.

There was not, however, always a linear progression from alliance to vassalage to incorporation. Sultan Bayezit II (1481–1512), for example, reversed his father's policies and restored Turcoman autonomy (but it is true that his turnabout in turn was reversed). After c. 1550, local dynasties (elected or approved in some fashion by their nobles) retained their power in several areas north of the Danube, notably, Moldavia, Wallachia as well as Transylvania. In all three regions, these rulers professed allegiance to the sultan and paid tribute while, in the first two areas but not the third, Ottoman garrisons were present. Otherwise, there were few other traces of Ottoman rule; significantly, for example, no mosques were built. But these tribute payers served at the pleasure of the sultan and were obliged to provide troops on his demand. In a different form, native rule also held at Dubrovnik (Ragusa) on the Adriatic. The tradition of local rule in Moldavia and Wallachia, endured until just after the 1710–11 Ottoman campaign against Russia, ending because of the alleged "treachery" of the princes. The Ottomans' relationship with the Crimean khans is still more fascinating. These descendants of the Golden Horde (the Mongols of the Russian regions) became vassals of the Ottoman sultans in 1475 and remained so until 1774, when that tie was severed as a prelude to their annexation by the Czarist state in 1783 (see chapter 3). Throughout, they also were considered as heirs to the Istanbul throne in the event the Ottoman dynasty became extinct.

These examples from Transylvania, Moldavia, Wallachia, Dubrovnik and the Crimea thus show alliance or vassalage relationships rather than annexation continuing for centuries after the main thrust of the Ottoman conquests was over. The main trend between 1300 and 1550 nonetheless is of growing direct Ottoman control over neighboring lands. Thereafter, until the end of the empire, Ottoman methods of rule continued to evolve, into new and fascinating forms (see chapter 6).

As the Ottoman state imposed its direct control over an area – whether Anatolia, the Arab provinces or the southern or the northern Balkans – its rule usually worked to the economic advantage of the newly conquered or subordinated populations. The weakening or end of Byzantine central control in Anatolia and the Balkans often had meant the rise of Byzantine feudal or feudal-like lords who imposed brutally heavy tax burdens. Under the Ottomans, these trends were reversed; Ottoman officials took back under central state control many of the lands and revenues which had slipped into the hands of local lords and monasteries. Overall, the new Ottoman subjects found themselves rendering fewer taxes than they had to the officials of rulers preceding the Ottomans.

From not later than the end of the fourteenth century and into the fifteenth and sixteenth centuries, officials carried out careful surveys that enumerated all of the taxable resources of an area, immediately after the imposition of direct Ottoman control (but not in tributary areas such as Moldavia and Wallachia). An appointed official (a Christian one did the counting in an early fifteenth-century Albanian case) went from village to village: he enumerated the households and livestock, measured the land, its fertility, productivity and use – the kinds of crops, vineyards, and orchards – and recorded the information in account books (*tahrir defterleri*). He also counted the population – not every man, woman, and child but the people that mattered to the state, thus the tax-paying head of the household and males old enough to serve in the military.

Having inventoried its landed resources, the state apportioned their tax revenues out to Ottoman military and administrators in the form of timars – fiscal administrative units producing a certain level of tax revenue (originally, the timar was 20,000 *guruş* in value). Recipients of timar revenue sources were allowed to collect the tax revenues of the timar. The more crucial the service rendered by the timar holder, the greater the amount of the tax revenues he received the right to collect. The basic timar tax revenue was the amount of money considered necessary to maintain a cavalryman and his horse for a year. These cavalrymen fought during the war season (spring and summer), and then returned from campaigning to administer the holdings. Sections of the empire in the Balkans and Anatolia thus were divided into basic timar units. The physical size of the land set aside as a timar varied – in a more fertile area, the timar would be smaller in size since it was more productive; but in less fertile areas a larger amount of land was needed to provide the necessary amount of money. More valuable revenue units (in effect multiple timars each with a different Ottoman name) supported military commanders and higher-ranking government officials.

Such fiscal practices were common among so-called "pre-modern" states, which granted the use of revenue sources in exchange for services rendered (unlike contemporary states today which pay their officials in cash). Only the tax revenues from the land or resource were granted, not the land or resource itself. The whole timar concept was based on the practices of ancient Near Eastern priest kings who administered the lands in the name of the gods. All the land thus belonged to the (priest) king, who allowed others to use its revenues in exchange for services to the king. In Ottoman times the timar method granted tax revenues to the (*sipahi*) cavalry who were the backbone of the early Ottoman military forces, a large proportion of the warriors fighting on the battlefield. (There were Christian timar holders in Sultan Bayezit II's time (1481–1512) and they sometimes formed more than one-half of all "timariots"; but over time Christian timar holders gradually disappeared.) *Sipahi* soldiers had reason to favor conquests since the revenues of the new lands would become timars which they would gain. Similarly, such soldiers profited as the Ottoman dynasty's relations with neighbors moved from alliance to vassalage to direct administration. For example, the revenues of the lands of the Bulgarian king ultimately were taken over, carved up, and turned over to the Ottoman military. Originally, moreover, the state sought to keep better control by promoting the frequent turnover of timar holders, thus reducing the chance these individuals would develop local roots.

Efforts to block the emergence of such local power nodes notwithstanding, timars in the Balkan lands sometimes nevertheless went to the lords and monasteries which once had owned them. In Anatolia, similarly, many tribal leaders obtained the taxes of their tribes as timars. These examples reveal a state unable to fully impose control, one compelled to negotiate and not simply command the loyalty of the local elites.

Until the early sixteenth century most newly won revenue sources, especially lands in the Balkans and Anatolia, became timar holdings. But, when the Arab regions fell to the Ottomans in 1516–1517, the central state organized their revenues as tax farms (*iltizam*), a fiscal device which already existed on a small scale elsewhere in the empire. Chronically short of cash because of the difficulty of collecting cash taxes directly, pre-modern states across the globe routinely used tax farms. In tax farming, the state held auctions at specific times and places for the right to collect the taxes of a district, the annual value of which officials already had determined. The highest bidder paid the state in cash at the auction or soon thereafter. Armed with state authorization, the tax farmer went to the assigned area and, accompanied by state military personnel, collected the taxes. After deducting expenses, the tax farmer retained the difference between the tax farm bid and the sums actually collected.

From the sixteenth century, timars over time gave way increasingly to tax farms because the cash needs of the state were mounting. The state bureaucracy was becoming steadily larger, in part because the empire itself was bigger and also because of changes in the nature of the state (chapter 6). Increasingly complex warfare for its part demanded more cash. Until the sixteenth century, the *sipahi* cavalry armed with bows and lances had formed the core of the military, being tactically and numerically its most vital component, and supported by timars. In a development with fourteenth- and fifteenth-century roots, a standing fire-armed infantry replaced cavalry as the crucial battlefield element. Vastly more expensive to maintain, this infantry required large cash infusions that tax farms but not timars provided.

The rising importance of firearms – the product of a remarkable openness to technological innovation – also helps to explain Ottoman successes in the centuries after 1300. For several hundred years Ottoman armies used firearms on a vaster scale, more effectively, and earlier than competing dynasties. In the great Ottoman victories of the fourteenth, fifteenth, and early sixteenth centuries, technological superiority often played a key role. Cannon and fire-armed infantry were developed at very early dates and used to massive technological advantage in the Balkan as well as the Safevid wars. These firearms required a long training and discipline that often were incompatible with nomadic life. In many cultures, including the Ottoman, cavalry prevented or retarded the use of guns that took a long time to reload and grated on the warrior ethic of bravery and courage demonstrated through hand-to-hand combat. Further, sultans used newly created fire-armed troops in domestic power struggles against timar forces that were insufficiently docile. As firearms became more important, the cavalry and its timar financial base became decreasingly relevant.

The rising importance of firearms is linked to another factor in the Ottoman success story, the *devşirme*, or the so-called child levy system. This system had its origins in the era of Sultans Bayezit I, Murat I, and Mehmet II. Until the early seventeenth century, recruiting officials went to Christian villages in Anatolia and the Balkans as well as to Muslim communities in Bosnia on a regular basis. They assembled all the male children and selected the best and the brightest. These recruits then were taken from their village homes to the Ottoman capital or other administrative centers. There, in the so-called palace school system, they received the best years-long mental and physical education that the state could provide, including religious training and, as a matter of course, conversion to Islam. The *crème de la crème* of this group entered the state elites, becoming officers and administrators. Many rose to become commanders and grand viziers and played a distinguished role in Ottoman history. The others became members of the famed Janissary corps, an extraordinarily well-trained, fire-armed, infantry center of armies that won many victories in the early Ottoman centuries. The Janissaries for centuries technologically were the best-trained, best-armed fighting force in the Mediterranean world.

The *devşirme* system offered extreme social mobility for males, allowing peasant boys to rise to the highest military and administrative positions in the empire, except for the dynasty itself. Significantly, it served as a means for the empire to tap into the manpower resources of its numerous Christian subject populations. As the Ottoman state had matured during the fourteenth and fifteenth centuries and placed greater emphasis on its Islamic character, the military and bureaucratic service of unconverted Christians became more problematic. And so the earlier use of Christians to make the land usage surveys faded away as did the appointment of Christian timar holders. However, while such formal appointments of Ottoman Christians faded, imperial conquests in the Balkans mounted and Christians came to form a more important proportion of the total Ottoman subject populations than before. According to Islamic law, which the Ottoman administration claimed to uphold, the state could not compel the conversion of its own Christian subjects to Islam. The state's primary concerns, however, were not religious but rather political: to maintain and extend its power by whatever means necessary. Such considerations, so-called "reasons of state" (see chapter 6), therefore prevailed and, through an interpretive nicety, the *devşirme* system was retained as a legitimate state institution.

Although striking in our eyes, the *devşirme* system of reaching across religious boundaries had precedents in the Judaic and Christian experiences. In western Europe, as Christianity had solidified its hold on the later Roman period, it had become unacceptable for Christians to enslave other Christians. Hence, when the Slavs became Christian, west Europe turned to Africa and the Black Sea regions for slaves. Jewish merchants, because of the principle of not charging interest to coreligionists, preferred to lend money to non-Jews. Similarly, the Ottomans found trained soldiers and administrators in the same manner as had the Christian slavers and Jewish merchants, by reaching outside their own religious constituencies.

Evolution of the state until the late seventeenth century

Between c. 1300 and the end of the seventeenth century, the state underwent a quite radical evolution both in its form and in the concentration of power within the administrative apparatus. In the earlier part of the period, 1300–1453, the elites were frontier lords (*beys*), Turcoman leaders, and princes; and these leaders considered the Ottoman monarch as first among equals (*primus inter pares*). Entering Ottoman service with retinues, troops, and adherents independent of the sultans', these elites followed the Ottomans because such allegiance brought them still more power and wealth. The sultan, for his part, negotiated with these nearly equal elites rather than commanding them. At the same time, however, a powerful countervailing trend was developing, one that placed the sultan far above all others in rank and prestige. Some individuals who promoted sultanic superiority were creatures of the monarchs on whom they depended for position and power. But others were religious and legal scholars who invoked Islamic precedents. Already in the early fourteenth century, legal scholars were advocating that bureaucratic leaders and military commanders, despite their vast power, were in fact mere slaves of the sultan. They were not slaves in the American sense since they possessed and bequeathed property, married at will, and moved about freely. In a particularly Ottoman sense, however, being a servant/slave of the sultan meant enjoying privilege and power but without the protection of the law that all Ottoman subjects in principle possessed. From the early fourteenth century, the theory already was evolving – hotly contested by the old elites – that the sultan was no mere Turcoman ruler surrounded by near equals but rather a theoretically absolute monarch. The struggle went back and forth but Sultan Mehmet II, armed with vast prestige after his conquest of Constantinople in 1453, stripped away wealth and power from many of the great Turcoman leaders who often had been independent of him. Now enacting the theory of absolute power, Sultan Mehmet installed his own men, often recruited from the *devşirme*, persons who in theory were totally indebted to him and over whom he exercised full control. Thus 1453 marked a visible power shift to the person of the ruler. Thereafter, until the nineteenth century, the sultan possessed theoretically absolute power, with life and death control over his military and bureaucratic elites.

In reality, however, the sultan's power varied greatly over time. For a century following the capture of Constantinople, the sultan exercised a fairly full measure of personal rule. Thus, during the 1453–1550 era, the notion of the exalted, secluded, monarch superior to all took hold while the sultan exercised a very personal kind of control over the military and bureaucratic system. Sultan Süleyman the Magnificent (like Philip II of Spain) spent his reign assiduously poring over the record books of his empire and personally leading armies to war.

During the century spanning the reigns of Sultans Mehmet and Süleyman, some sense of an "Ottoman Empire" perhaps began to emerge among administrators and subjects. Although the frontiers were still expanding, a general sense was developing of living in the sultan's world, of being in the sultan's lands as opposed to those, for example, of the Habsburg king or the Safevid shah. At its most fundamental, those within received the sultan's protection from enemies and those outside were attacked by him. But more was involved. The sense of being inside of an Ottoman commonwealth in part also derived from the innumerable actions of the sultan to cement subjects' loyalties (chapter 6). On another level, the regularization of taxes and the repeated appearances of Ottoman officials on the local scene similarly reinforced subjects' sense of belonging to the same universe. Moreover, both Mehmet and Süleyman promulgated codes of law which set the sultanic standards, the norms, for behavior. Thus, the presence of a common system of justice, taxes, and a shared ruler who offered protection to every subject served to foster the wider sense of participating in a common "Ottoman" project. This was no small achievement and helps to explain the longevity of the Ottoman Empire.

Let us return now to the narrative of evolving political power within the state. The evolution that exalted the power of the sultan, described above, continued. Thus, later in the reign of Sultan Süleyman, power began passing from the person of the monarch to others in his household. Generally, this sultan's reign ended a nearly unbroken line of warrior kings going back to the founder of the Ottoman Empire. In this maturing empire, statecraft was changing as the wars of conquest slowed and then halted. As expansion faltered, administrative skills of both men and women became more important than those of the warrior: not fighting sultans but legitimizing sultans were needed. Hence, between the later sixteenth and mid-seventeenth centuries, the mothers and wives of sultans came more visibly to the fore in decision-making, wielding considerable if still informal political power. In the seventeenth century actual control rested only rarely in the hands of the monarch who, overall, reigned but did not rule. Sultan Murat IV, unusually for a seventeenth-century ruler, personally commanded during the latter part of his 1623–1640 reign. But during the earlier years his mother, Kösem, ably restored the state's finances after a period of severe inflation. Overall, sultans who actually ran the military and the state faded from Ottoman history until the nineteenth century and the reigns of Sultan Mahmut II and Abdülhamit II.

Sultan Mehmet IV (1648–1687) could be sultan although a child because he was not needed to actually rule. Instead, he served as a symbol of a system that functioned in his name. Power rested with his mother (the same Kösem) and other members of his household and, by that date, with members of important Istanbul households outside of the palace. Thus, between c. 1550 and 1650, policy-making and implementation shifted away from the sultanic person; but the central state in its Istanbul capital still directed affairs.

The state apparatus continued its intensive transformation during the seventeenth century. First of all, as seen, sultans became reigning not ruling monarchs who legitimized bureaucratic commands but themselves usually did not initiate policy. For example, during the second half of the seventeenth century (1656–1691), the remarkable Köprülü family truly directed state affairs, often serving as chief ministers (grand viziers). Second, by 1650, new elite groups in Istanbul outside the military (*sipahi* and *askeri*) classes, called vizier and pasha households, began making sultans and running affairs. A new collective leadership – a civilian oligarchy – had emerged and the sultans provided the facade of continuity as new practices in fact were replacing old ones. The central state, it is true, still commanded but others besides the ruler were in charge. This was the opposite of events in western and central Europe where monarchs were consolidating power.

These vizier and pasha households had new fiscal underpinnings, sources of wealth autonomous of the state that included, after 1695, lifetime tax farms as well as illegal seizures of state lands. Also important were the revenues based on the so-called pious foundations. These foundations (*vakif* or *waqf*) played a vital role in the economic life of Ottoman and other Islamic societies. These were sources of revenues set aside by male and female donors for pious purposes, such as the maintenance of a mosque, school (*medrese*), students, soup kitchen, library or orphanage. The revenue source might be cultivable lands or, perhaps, shops and stores. The donor prepared a document that turned over the land or shop to the foundation. Properly speaking, immediately upon formation of the foundation or on the death of the donor, the revenues would begin flowing to the intended purpose. But another form of foundation emerged, in which the revenues nominally were set aside for the pious purpose but in reality continued to go to the donors and their heirs under various and dubiously legal pretexts. Pious foundations (even such shady ones) could not be confiscated because of the provisions of Islamic law, jealously guarded by the religious scholars, the ulema. Thus, they offered a revenue source that was secure in a way that wealth from timars or tax farms could never be. Tax farms and timars derived directly from state action and therefore could be taken back from the holder in a moment.

Pious foundation revenues, however, did not and were safe from confis-
cation. Setting up such a pious foundation meant that the possessions of
a person – who as a member of the bureaucratic or military elite theoretically was the slave of the sultan – could not be seized, a remarkable turn
of events in Ottoman history. During the sixteenth century, pious foundations had been the preserve of the state and the prerogative of those
under sultanic control. But, by the eighteenth century, this monopoly
of access had faded and the formation of pious foundations had spread
to newly emergent groups. This was part of the process that weakened
the power of the sultans. The financial security which these foundations
offered likely stabilized the respective positions of the vizier and pasha
households and of the ulema as the new economic and political power
forces of the late seventeenth century.

Suggested bibliography

Entries marked with a * designate recommended readings for new students of
the subject.
*Abou-El-Haj, Rifaat. *The 1703 rebellion and the structure of Ottoman politics*
(Istanbul, 1984).
The formation of the modern state (Albany, 1991).
Barnes, John Robert. *An introduction to religious foundations in the Ottoman Empire*
(Leiden, 1986).
Blair, Sheila S. and Jonathan M. Bloom. *The art and architecture of Islam, 1250–
1800* (New Haven, corrected edn, 1995).
Brummet, Palmira. *Ottoman seapower and Levantine diplomacy in the age of discov-
ery* (Albany, 1994).
*Busbecq, O. G. de. *The Turkish letters of Ogier Ghiselin de Busbecq: Imperial Am-
bassador at Constantinople* (Oxford, 1968).
*Darling, Linda. "Another look at periodization in Ottoman history," *Turkish
Studies Association Journal* 26, 2 (Fall, 2002), 19–28.
Faroqhi, Suraiya. *Towns and townsmen in Ottoman Anatolia: Trade, crafts and food
production in an urban setting* (Cambridge, 1984).
*Men of modest substance. House owners and house property in seventeenth-century
Ankara and Kayseri* (Cambridge, 1987).
*"Crisis and change, 1590–1699," in Halil İnalcık with Donald Quataert, eds.,
An economic and social history of the Ottoman Empire, 1300–1914 (Cambridge,
1994), 411–636.
Fleischer, Cornell. *Bureaucrat and intellectual in the Ottoman Empire: The historian
Mustafa Ali* (Princeton, 1986).
*Goffman, Daniel. *The Ottoman Empire and early modern Europe* (Cambridge,
2002).
Goodwin, Godfrey. *A history of Ottoman architecture* (London, 1971).
Hess, Andrew. *The forgotten frontier: A history of the sixteenth century Ibero-African
frontier* (Chicago, 1978).
Hourani, Albert. *A history of the Arab peoples* (Cambridge, MA, 1991).

Howard, Douglas. "Ottoman historiography and the literature of 'decline' of the sixteenth and seventeenth centuries," *Journal of Asian History*, 22, 1 (1988), 52–77.

*Imber, Colin. *The Ottoman Empire, 1300–1650* (London, 2002).

İnalcık, Halil. "The Ottoman state: economy and society, 1300–1600," in Halil İnalcık with Donald Quataert, eds., *An economic and social history of the Ottoman Empire, 1300–1914* (Cambridge, 1994), 9–409.

İnalcık, Halil and Rhoads Murphey, eds. *The history of Mehmet the Conqueror* (Chicago and Minneapolis, 1978).

*Kafadar, Cemal. *Between two worlds: The construction of the Ottoman state* (Berkeley, 1995).

Karamustafa, Ahmet. *God's unruly friends: dervish groups in the Islamic later middle period, 1200–1550* (Salt Lake City, 1994).

*Keddie, Nikki, ed. *Women and gender in Middle Eastern history* (New Haven, 1991).

Köprülü, M. Fuad. *The origins of the Ottoman Empire*, trans. and ed. by Gary Leiser (Albany, 1992).

Lindner, Rudi Paul. *Nomads and Ottomans in medieval Anatolia* (Bloomington, 1983).

*Lowry, Heath W. *The nature of the early Ottoman state* (Albany, 2003).

"Pushing the stone uphill: the impact of bubonic plague on Ottoman urban society in the fifteenth and sixteenth centuries, *Ottoman studies*, 23 (2003), 93–132.

*Mansel, Philip. *Constantinople: City of the world's desire, 1453–1924* (New York, 1995).

*McNeill, William. *Europe's steppe frontier 1500–1800* (Chicago and London, 1964).

*Mihailovic, Konstantin. *Memoirs of a Janissary* (Ann Arbor, 1975).

*Necipoğlu, Gülru. *Architecture, ceremonial and power: The Topkapı palace in the fifteenth and sixteenth centuries* (Cambridge, MA, 1991).

Panaite, Viorel. "Power relationships in the Ottoman Empire. The sultans and the tribute-paying princes of Wallachia and Moldavia from the sixteenth to the eighteenth century," *International Journal of Turkish Studies*, 7, 1 & 2 (2001), 26–53.

"The status of the Kharâj-güzarlar. A case study: Wallachians, Moldavians and Transylvanians in the 15th to 17th centuries." *The Great Ottoman-Turkish Civilisation*, I, (Ankara, 2000), 227–238.

*Peirce, Leslie. *The imperial harem. Women and sovereignty in the Ottoman Empire* (Oxford, 1993).

Tietze, Andreas. *Mustafa Ali's counsel for sultans of 1581*, 2 vols. (Vienna, 1979–1982).

*Tucker, Judith. *Gender and Islamic history* (Washington, DC, reprint of 1993 edition).

Wittek, Paul. *The rise of the Ottoman Empire* (London, 1938).

*Zilfi, Madeline. *Women in the Ottoman Empire. Middle Eastern women in the early modern era* (Leiden, 1997).

3   The Ottoman Empire, 1683–1798

Introduction

In marked contrast to the military and political successes of the 1300–1683 era, defeats and territorial withdrawals characterized this long eighteenth century, 1683–1798. The political structure continued to evolve steadily, taking new forms in a process that should be seen as transformation but not decline. Central rule continued in a new and more disguised fashion as negotiation more frequently than command came to assure obedience. Important changes occurred in the Ottoman economy as well: the circulation of goods began to increase; levels of personal consumption probably rose; and the world economy came to play an ever-larger role in the everyday lives of Ottoman subjects.

The wars of contraction, c. 1683–1798

On the international stage, military defeats and territorial contraction marked the era, when the imperial Ottoman state was much less successful than before. At the outset, it seems worthwhile to make several general points.

First, at bottom, the Ottoman defeats are as difficult to explain as the victories of earlier centuries. Sometime during the early sixteenth century, as the wealth of the New World poured into Europe, the military balance shifted away from the Ottomans; they lost their edge in military technology and using similar and then inferior weapons and tactics, battled European enemies. Moreover, the earlier military imbalance between offensive and defensive warfare in favor of the aggressor had worked to the Ottomans' advantage, but now defenses became more sophisticated and vastly more expensive. Sultan Süleyman the Magnificent, whose reign had seen so many successes, died before the walls of Szigetvar, poignantly symbolizing the difficulty of attacking fortified cities that had become an increasingly common feature of warfare. Further, Western economies could better afford the mounting costs of the new technologies and defensive combat in part because of the vast infusion of wealth from the New World. The story of Ottoman slippage and west European ascendancy is vastly more complicated, of course, and is continued in the subsequent chapters.

Second, during the eighteenth century, absolute monarchies emerged in Europe that were growing more centralized than ever before. To a certain extent, the Ottomans shared in this evolution but other states in the world did not. The Iranian state weakened after a brief resurgence in the earlier part of the century, collapsed, and failed to recover any cohesive strength until the early twentieth century. Still further east, the Moghul state and all of the rest of the Indian subcontinent fell under French or British domination.

Third, the Ottoman defeats and territorial losses of the eighteenth century were a very grim business but would have been still greater except for the rivalries among west, east, and central European states. On a number of occasions, European diplomats intervened in post-war negotiations with the Ottomans to prevent rivals from gaining too many concessions, thus giving the defeated Ottomans a wedge they employed to retain lands that otherwise would have been lost. Also, while it is easy to think of the era as one of unmitigated disasters since there were so many defeats and withdrawals, the force of Ottoman arms and diplomatic skills did win a number of successes, especially in the first half of the period.

A century of military defeats began at Vienna in 1683 and ended with Napoleon Bonaparte's invasion of Egypt in 1798 (map 3). The events immediately following the failed siege in 1683 which turned into a rout were terrible and catastrophic for the Istanbul regime, and include the loss of the key fortress of Belgrade and, in 1691, a military disaster at Slankamen that was compounded by the battlefield death of the grand vizier, Fazıl Mustafa. Elsewhere, the newly emergent Russian foe (the Ottoman–Russian wars began in 1677) attacked the Crimea in 1689 and captured the crucial port of Azov six years later. Yet another catastrophe occurred at Zenta, in 1697, at the hands of the Habsburg military commander, Prince Eugene, of Savoy. The Treaty of Karlowitz in 1699 sealed these losses and began a new phase of Ottoman history. For the first time, an Ottoman sovereign formally acknowledged his defeat and the permanent loss of (rather than temporary withdrawal from) lands conquered by his ancestors. Thus, the sultan surrendered all of Hungary (except the Banat of Temeşvar), as well as Transylvania, Croatia, and Slovenia to the Habsburgs while yielding Dalmatia, the Morea, and some Aegean islands to Venice and Podolia and the south Ukraine to Poland. Russia, for its part, fought on until 1700 in order to again gain

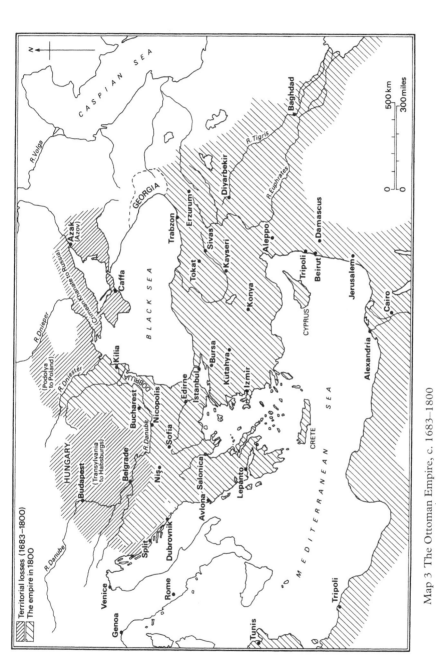

Map 3 The Ottoman Empire, c. 1683–1800
Adapted from Halil İnalcık with Donald Quataert, eds., *An economic and social history of the Ottoman Empire, 1300–1914* (Cambridge, 1914), xxxvii.

Azov (which the Ottomans were to win and then lose again in 1736) and the regions north of the Dniester river.

Two decades later, the 1718 Treaty of Passarowitz ceded the Banat (and Belgrade again), about one-half of Serbia as well as Wallachia. Ottoman forces similarly were unsuccessful on the eastern front and, in a series of wars between 1723 and 1736, lost Azerbaijan and other lands on the Persian–Ottoman frontier. Exactly one decade later, in 1746, two centuries of war between the Ottomans and their Iranian-based rivals ended with the descent of the latter into political anarchy.

The agreement signed at Küçük Kaynarca in 1774 with the Romanovs, similar to the 1699 Karlowitz treaty, highlights the extent of the losses suffered during the eighteenth century. The 1768–1774 war, the first with Czarina Catherine the Great, included the annihilation of the Ottoman fleet in the Aegean Sea near Çeşme by Russian ships that had sailed from the Baltic Sea, through Gibraltar, and across the Mediterranean. In a sense, the vast indemnity paid was the least of the burdens imposed by the treaty. For it severed the tie between the Ottoman sultan and Crimean khan; the khans became formally independent, thus losing sultanic protection. This status left the Ottoman armies without the khan's military forces that had been a mainstay during the eighteenth century, when they partially had filled the gap left by the decay of the Janissaries as a fighting unit (see below). Equally bad, the Ottomans also surrendered their monopolistic control over the Black Sea while giving up vast lands between the Dnieper and the Bug rivers, thereafter losing the north shore of the Black Sea. Other provisions of the treaty were to be of enormous consequence later on. Russia obtained the right both to build an Orthodox Church in Istanbul and protect those who worshiped there. Subsequently, this rather modest concession became the pretext under which Russia claimed the right to intercede on behalf of all Orthodox subjects of the sultan. In another provision of the treaty, Russia recognized the sultan as caliph of the Muslims of the Crimea. Later sultans, especially Abdülhamit II (1876–1909) expanded this caliphal claim to include not only all Ottoman subjects but also Muslims everywhere in the world (see below and chapter 6). Thus, as is evident, the 1774 Küçük Kaynarca treaty played a vital role in shaping subsequent internal and international events in the Ottoman world. The Treaty of Jassy ended another Ottoman–Russian war, that between 1787 and 1792, and acknowledged the Russian takeover of Georgia. Further, the Crimean khanate, left exposed by the 1774 treaty, now was formally annexed by the Czarist state.

Bonaparte's motives for invading Egypt in 1798 long have been debated by historians. Was he on the road to British India, or merely blocking

Britain's path to the future jewel in its crown? Or, as his unsuccessful march north into Palestine seems to suggest, was he seeking to replace the Ottoman Empire with his own? Regardless, the invasion marked the end of Ottoman domination of this vital and rich province along the Nile and its emergence as a separate state under Muhammad Ali Pasha and his descendants. Henceforth, Ottoman–Egyptian relations fluctuated enormously. Muhammad Ali Pasha nearly overthrew the Ottoman state during his lifetime (d. 1848), but his successors kept close ties with their nominal overlords. Nevertheless, during the nineteenth century, except for a tribute payment, Egyptian revenues no longer were at the disposal of Istanbul.

While a review of these battles, campaigns, and treaties makes apparent the pace and depth of the Ottoman defeats, the process was not quite so clear at the time. There were a number of important victories, at least during the first half of the eighteenth century. For example, although Belgrade fell just after the 1683 siege, the Ottomans recaptured it, along with Bulgaria, Serbia, and Transylvania, in their counter-offensives during 1689 and 1690. In fact Belgrade reverted to the sultan's rule at least three times and remained in Ottoman hands until the early nineteenth century. In 1711, to give another example, an Ottoman army completely surrounded the forces of Czar Peter the Great at the Pruth river on the Moldavian border, forcing him to abandon all of his recent conquests. Several years later, the Ottomans regained the lost fortress of Azov on the Black Sea. In a 1714–1718 war with Venice, the Istanbul regime regained the Morea and retained it for more than a century, until the Greek war of independence. Ottoman forces won other important victories in 1737, against both Austrians and Russians. For several reasons, including French mediation and Habsburg fears of Russian success, the Ottomans, in the 1739 peace of Belgrade, regained all that they had surrendered to the Habsburgs in the earlier Treaty of Passarowitz. In the same year, they again obtained Azov from the Russians who withdrew all commercial and war ships from the Black Sea and also pulled out of Wallachia. Even after the disasters of the war that ended at Küçük Kaynarca, the Ottomans won some victories, compelling Russia to withdraw again from the principalities (and from the Caucasus). Catherine did so again in 1792 when she also agreed to withdraw from ports at the mouth of the Danube.

State economic policies

Historians have hotly debated the nature and role of state policies in Ottoman economic change. Some say that in the eighteenth century the state was too controlling, while others argue the opposite. Those in the latter group assert that eighteenth-century regimes in Europe adopted mercantilistic policies that controlled the flow of goods and materials within and across their borders, allowing them to shape the world market in their favor and to become powerful. But, they say, the Ottoman state failed to do so in sufficient measure and, for this reason, it declined in power.

As in the past, the eighteenth-century Ottoman state claimed the right to command and move about economic resources as it deemed necessary. Experience, however, had shown the dangers of such intervention and so, after c. 1600, the state did so only selectively. But, when it did – to provide foodstuffs, raw materials, and manufactured goods for the palace, other state elites, the military, and the inhabitants of the capital city – these interventions powerfully affected producers and consumers. The effects usually were doubly disruptive and negative since the state often paid below-market prices for the goods and, often drained away all or most of a commodity, thus creating scarcities. Crops of entire areas or the manufacturing output of certain guilds were commandeered for particular purposes, for example, to supply the royal household or marching armies. On the Balkan front during the later eighteenth century, for example, nearby regions supplied the army with grain while other supplies, such as rice, coffee, and biscuits flowed from more distant Egypt and Cyprus. The state also devoted considerable energies to the feeding of the population of Istanbul, not from charitable concern but rather fear that food shortages would provoke political unrest. And so innumerable regulations dictated the transport of wheat and sheep to fill the tables of the capital's enormous population.

Whether such policies strangled the economy during the late eighteenth-century era of wartime crisis and had a decisively negative impact on Ottoman economic development, or whether the state foundered because it was not sufficiently rigorous and mercantilist, cannot be known for certain. It is clear, however, that both sides of the debate give the state more power than it actually had. Indeed, global market forces may have affected the eighteenth-century Ottoman economy more powerfully than state policies. It thus seems more useful to look to other factors for a fuller understanding of Ottoman economic change (see chapter 7). More confidently, we can assert that, after c. 1850 (see chapter 4), the state moved away from such so-called provisioning policies and market forces played a greater role than before.

Intra-elite political life at the imperial center

During the eighteenth century, the sultan most often possessed symbolic power only, confirming changes or actions initiated by others in political life. Although the end of the so-called "rule of the harem" closed a famous version of female political control, elite women remained powerful. The dynasty continued to marry its daughters to ranking officials as a means of forging alliances and maintaining authority. Such support may have become even more important as power shifted out of the palace. Since at least 1656, when Sultan Mehmet IV gave over his executive powers to Grand Vizier Köprülü Mehmet Pasha, political rule had rested in the households of viziers and pashas. Also, warrior skills fell out of fashion in favor of administrative and financial skills as the exploitation of existing resources rather than acquisition of new lands became the major sources of state revenues. Hence, the vizier and pasha households furnished most office appointees, providing the now crucial financial and administrative training, and were often bound to the palace through the marriages of Ottoman princesses. Unlike the "slaves of the sultan" who had ruled earlier, these male and female elites did not remain aloof from society but were involved in its economic life through their control of pious foundations and lifetime tax farms and partnerships with merchants. The entourages of these viziers and pashas served as recruiting grounds for the new elites, providing them with employment, protection, training, and the right contacts. By the end of the seventeenth century, most domestic and foreign policy matters rested in these households.

At the beginning of the eighteenth century, however, Sultan Mustafa II unsuccessfully sought to overturn this trend and reconcentrate power in his own hands and that of the palace and the military. Desperately trying to regain power and reposition himself in the political center, Mustafa II somewhat shockingly confirmed hereditary rights to timars, the financial backbone of a cavalry that already was militarily obsolete. But his coup attempt, the so-called "Edirne Event" (*Edirne Vakası*) of 1703, failed. Thereafter the sultan's powers and stature were so reduced that he was required to seek the advice of "interested parties" and heed their counsel. This set of events sealed the ascendancy of the vizier–pasha households and of their allies within the religious scholarly community, the ulema, and set the tone for eighteenth-century politics at the center. And so, at a moment when many continental European states were concentrating power in the hands of the monarch, the Ottoman political structure evolved in a different direction, taking power out of the ruler's hands.

As the sultans lost out in the struggle for domestic political supremacy, they sought new tools and techniques for maintaining their political presence. Beginning in the early eighteenth century, for example, the central state reorganized the pilgrimage routes to the Holy Cities in an effort to enhance its own legitimacy and consolidate power (see chapter 6). (It is, however, unclear if the sultan or other figures at the center initiated this action.) Developments during the so-called Tulip Period (1718–30) more certainly illustrate the subtle means that sultans used to prop up their legitimacy. This Tulip Period, a time of extraordinary experimentation in Ottoman history, was so named by a twentieth-century historian after its frequent tulip breeding competitions. The tulip symbolized both conspicuous consumption and cross-cultural borrowings since it was an item of exchange between the Ottoman Empire, west Europe, and east Asia. Sultan Ahmet III and his Grand Vizier Ibrahim Pasha (married to Fatma, the Sultan's daughter), as part of their effort to negotiate power, employed the weapon of consumption to dominate the Istanbul elites. Like the court of King Louis XIV at Versailles, that of the Tulip Period was one of sumptuous consumption – in the Ottoman case not only of tulips but also art, cooking, luxury goods, clothing, and the building of pleasure palaces. With this new tool – the consumption of goods – the sultan and grand vizier sought to control the vizier and pasha households in the manner of King Louis, who compelled nobles to live at the Versailles seat of power and join in financially ruinous balls and banquets. Sultan Ahmet and Ibrahim Pasha tried to lead the Istanbul elites in consumption, establishing themselves at the social center as models for emulation. By leading in consumption, they sought to enhance their political status and legitimacy as well.

Later in the eighteenth century, other sultans frequently used clothing laws in a similar effort to maintain or enhance legitimacy and power. Clothing laws – a standard feature of Ottoman and other pre-modern societies – stipulated the dress, of both body and head, that persons of different ranks, religions, and occupations should wear. For example, Muslims were told that only they could wear certain colors and fabrics that were forbidden to Christians and Jews who, for their part, were ordered to wear other colors and materials. By enacting or enforcing clothing laws, or appearing to do so, sultans presented themselves as guardians of the boundaries differentiating their subjects, as the enforcers of morality, order, and justice. Through these laws, the rulers acted to place themselves as arbitrators in the jostlings for social place, seeking to reinforce their legitimacy as sovereigns, at a time when they neither commanded armies nor actually led the bureaucracy (see also chapter 8).

Elite–popular struggles in Istanbul

At the political center and in other Ottoman cities were contests not only within the elites for political domination but also between the elites and the popular masses. In this struggle the famed Janissary corps played a vital role. As seen above, the Janissaries once had been an effective military force that fought at the center of armies and served as urban garrisons.

By the eighteenth century, they had become militarily ineffectual but still went to war. Their arms and training had deteriorated so sharply that the Crimean Tatars and other provincial military forces had replaced them as the fighting center of the army. The discipline and rigorous training marking this once elite fire-armed infantry had disappeared by 1700, transforming the corps from the terror of its foreign foes to the terror of the sultans. Already in the later sixteenth century, they had insulted the corpse of Sultan Süleyman the Magnificent and denied his son Selim access to the throne until appropriate gifts of money had been offered. Their proximity to the sultan – serving as his bodyguards – and elite military status placed them in the tempting role of kingmakers, with a ready ability to make and unmake rulers.

Certainly during the eighteenth century if not before, the Janissaries' primary identity shifted from that of soldiers to civilian wage earners. Their ability to live on their military salaries faded as the mounting costs of wars prevented the state from paying Janissary salaries that could keep up with inflation. As garrisons, they physically were part of the urban fabric. To counteract declining real wages, members of the garrisons developed economic connections with the people they were guarding and supervising in Istanbul and other important cities including Belgrade, Sofia, Cairo, Damascus, and points in between. There they became butchers, bakers, boatmen, porters, and worked in a number of artisanal crafts; many owned coffee houses. By the eighteenth century, Janissaries either themselves had entered these trades and businesses or had become mafia-like chieftains protecting trades for a fee. They thus came to represent the interests of the urban productive classes, including corporate guild privilege and economic protectionist policies, and were part and parcel of the urban crowd. And yet their membership in the Janissary corps meant that they were part of the elites. And further, their commander, the agha of the Janissaries, administratively was an important man, sitting on the highest councils of state. As they increasingly became part of the urban economy, the Janissaries began to pass on their elite status. Earlier prohibitions against marriage and living outside the barracks fell away and gradually the sons of city-dwelling Janissaries replaced the peasant boys of the devşirme recruitment (the last devşirme levy was in 1703). By the early eighteenth century, this fire-armed infantry had become hereditary and urban in origin, a position passed from fathers to sons who were Muslim not Christian by birth.

The elite-popular identity of the Janissaries – born among the popular classes and yet part of and linked to the elites – gave them an important role in domestic politics. They repeatedly made and unmade sultans, appointing or toppling grand viziers and other high officials, sometimes as part of intra-elite quarrels but often on behalf of the popular classes. Until their annihilation in 1826, they often served as ramparts against elite tyrannies and a popular militia defending the interests of the people. If we consider them in this role rather than as fallen angels – corrupted elite soldiers and elements of the state apparatus run amok – then the eighteenth century becomes a golden age of popular politics in many Ottoman cities when the voice of the street, orchestrated by the Janissaries, was greater than ever before or since in Ottoman history.

Political life in the provinces

The shifting locus of political power in the center – from the sultans to sultanic households to the households of viziers and pashas to the streets – was paralleled by important transformations in the political life of the provinces. Overall, during the seventeenth and eighteenth centuries, provincial political power seemed to operate more autonomously of control from the capital. Nearly everywhere the central state became *visibly* less important and local notable families more so in the everyday lives of most persons. Whole sections of the empire fell under the political domination of provincial notable families. For example, the families of the Karaosmanoğlu, Çapanoğlu, and Canıklı Ali Paşaoğlu respectively dominated the economic and political affairs of west, central, and northeast Anatolia; in the Balkan lands, Ali Pasha of Janina ruled Epirus, while Osman Pasvanoğlu of Vidin controlled the lower Danube from Belgrade to the sea. And, in the Arab provinces, the family of Süleyman the Great ruled Baghdad for the entire eighteenth century (1704–1831) as did the Jalili family in Mosul, while powerful men such as Ali Bey dominated Egypt.

These provincial notables can be placed in three groups, each reflecting a different social context. The first group descended from persons who had come to an area as centrally appointed officials and subsequently put down local roots, a marked violation of central state regulations to the contrary. Central control, indeed, had never been as extensive or thorough as the state's own declarations had suggested. Officials did circulate from appointment to appointment, but the presence of careful land surveys and lists of rotating officials notwithstanding, not as often or regularly as the state would have preferred. Nonetheless, such appointees to positions of provincial authority, whether governors or timar holders, remained in office for shorter periods in the sixteenth and seventeenth centuries and longer periods during the eighteenth century. That is, by comparison with the sixteenth and seventeenth centuries, the circulation of centrally appointed officials in the provinces slowed considerably during the eighteenth century. Through negotiations with the center, these individuals gained the legal right to stay. Thus, for example, the al Azm family in Damascus and the Jalili family in Mosul had risen in Ottoman service as governors while, from lower-ranking posts, so had the Karaosmanoğlu dynasty in western Anatolia. In each case family members remained in formal positions of provincial power for several generations and longer.

The second group consisted of prominent notables whose families had been among the local elites of an area before the Ottoman period. In some cases the sultans had recognized their status and power at the moment of incorporation, for example, as they did with many great landholding families in Bosnia. Historians likely have underestimated the retention of local political power by such pre-Ottoman elite groups, and more of these families played an important role in the subsequent Ottoman centuries than has been credited. In another pattern, existing elite groups who originally were stripped of power gradually re-acquired political control and recognition by the state.

The third group – that seems to have existed only in the Arab provinces of the empire – consisted of slave soldiers, Mamluks, whose origins went back to medieval Islamic times. Mamluks, for example, had governed Egypt for centuries, annually importing several thousands of slaves, until their overthrow by the Ottomans in 1516–1517. During the Ottoman era, a Mamluk typically was born outside the region, enslaved through war or raids, and transported into the Ottoman world. Governors or military commanders then bought the slave in regional or local slave markets, brought him into the household as a military slave or apprentice and trained him in the administrative and military arts. Manumitted at some point in the training process, the Mamluk continued to serve the master, rose to local pre-eminence and eventually set up his own household, which he staffed through slave purchases, thus perpetuating the system. The powerful Ahmet Jezzar Pasha who ruled Sidon and Acre (1785–1805) in the Lebanon–Palestine region, and Süleyman the Great at Baghdad, each began as a Mamluk in the service of Ali Bey in Egypt.

The evolution of rule by local notables in the areas of Moldavia and Wallachia – modern-day Rumania–was unique. Local princes, at least nominally selected by the regional nobility, had served there as the "slaves and tribute payers" of the sultans, that is, as tribute-paying vassals, until after 1711, when they were removed because they had offered help to Czar Peter during his Pruth campaign. In their stead, the capital appointed powerful and rich members of the Greek Orthodox community, who lived in the so-called Fener/Phanar district of the capital. For the remainder of the century and, in fact, until the Greek war of independence, these Phanariotes ruled the two principalities with full autonomy in exchange for tribute payments. They implemented the most brutal and oppressive rule seen in the Ottoman world, one that closely approximated serfdom. They were centrally appointed (without even nominal input from regional nobles) but ran the principalities with a totally free hand, thus appearing as exceptions in the picture being offered here.

In general, whether these provincial notables originated from central appointees, pre-Ottoman elites, or Mamluks, they built and maintained intimate ties with the local religious scholarly community of the ulema, as well as merchants and landholders. In the case of the first two notable groups – the descendants of central appointees or pre-Ottoman elites – the marriage of women from notable families was part of their process of local power accumulation. In addition, these elite women held considerable properties and tax farms and administered pious foundations in their own names. They thus wielded considerable personal power that also could be used by the family in its negotiations with local elites or with the Ottoman center.

It seems important to stress that a notable family's establishment of authority in an area usually was not a rebellion against Ottoman central authority. Rather, local dynasts recognized the sultan and central authority in general, forwarded some taxes to the center and sent troops for imperial wars – actions that reflected the complex and fascinating interaction of mutual need existing between province and center in the eighteenth-century Ottoman world. Indeed, since the late seventeenth century, the central state had been depending on provincial notables for both the recruiting and provisioning of troops. As seen, this relationship gave considerable leverage and bargaining power to the local elites. On the other hand, the notables despatched provincial troops because they needed the central state for legitimation and, as we now shall see, their economic wellbeing as well.

Beginning in 1695, the central state developed lifetime tax farms (*malikane*), a grant of the right to collect the taxes of an area in exchange for cash payments to the treasury. Very quickly, by 1703, these lifetime tax farms had spread and came into wide use in the Balkan, Anatolian, and Arab provinces alike. *Malikane* are crucial for understanding how the central state maintained some control in the provinces, long after its imperial military troops had vanished from the area. Vizier and pasha households in the capital controlled the auctions of the lifetime tax farms, letting and subletting them to the local elites of the various provincial areas. In this way the Istanbul elites maintained a shared financial interest with notable families while, since they could remove this lucrative privilege, exercising control over them. Thus, in any test of power, notable families ultimately either yielded or risked losing their lifetime tax farms. The existence of these lifetime tax farm links between the capital and the provinces thus helps to explain why the notable groups in fact usually submitted and sent troops when requested.

This pattern of negotiation, mutual recognition, and control predominated between c. 1700 and 1768 but was shaken during the remainder of the eighteenth century. The fighting in the Russo-Ottoman wars of 1768–1774 and 1787–1792 caused massive disruptions in the battle zones and everywhere imposed enormous manpower and financial strains. In this situation, the notables' knowledge of and access to local resources became more important than ever, while the wartime chaos gave them greater latitude of action. Thus, it seems, the *malikane* system partly disintegrated, weakening provincial ties to the center. In this chaotic period, notables such as Jezzar Pasha and the Karaosmanoğlu pursued foreign policies apart from the central state, while others such as Ali Pasha of Janina and Osman Pasvanoğlu undertook separate military campaigns, sometimes against other notables and sometimes against the Russians. Some historians have considered these actions de facto efforts to break away from Ottoman suzerainty. But probably they were not, as the following suggests.

In 1808, one of the notables briefly served as grand vizier, an event that marks the power of provincial groups during this crisis period. Bayraktar Mustafa Pasha, from the Bulgarian areas along the Danube, marched on the imperial capital in an unsuccessful effort to rescue the sultan from his Janissary enemies. Once in Istanbul, he convened an assembly that included many powerful notables from the Balkan and Anatolian provinces. In the ensuing assembly, the notables negotiated with the sultan over the respective rights and power of the contending parties. A formal written document (*sened-i ittifak*) was prepared but, in the end, went unsigned by the sultan and most of the notables. Nonetheless, the incident illustrates the evolution of the Ottoman state to that point. On the one hand, the sultan's need for a document ratifying the notables' willingness to obey him suggests how independent they had become in the context of the late eighteenth-century crisis. On the other hand, the fact that the notables did affirm their support of the sultan, when they collectively held the balance of military power over the central state, suggests the continuing importance of the dynasty in economic and political life, even when the sultanate and central state were very weak. The debate over this 1808 agreement underscores the commitment of provincial notables and central elites to their ongoing reciprocal and mutually profitable relationship. The center badly needed notables' monies, troops, and other services. The notables for their part relied on the central state and the sultan to arbitrate among the provincial elites' competing claims by conferring formal recognition of their political power and access to official revenue sources. These were "local Ottomans" and, in however disguised a manner, sought to be and were part of an Ottoman system.

Religious solutions to political and military weakness

Unlike the notables mentioned so far, the leaders of the Wahhabi movement (and the Saudi dynasty connected to it) categorically rejected the legitimacy of Ottoman rule. The rationale of the Wahhabi emergence must be located in the larger issue of how the non-European world, in this case areas with substantial Muslim populations, sought to deal with the terrible losses being inflicted on them. Muslim states everywhere – in North Africa, the Ottoman lands, Iran, and India – were on the defensive, losing populations and revenues in repeatedly unsuccessful confrontations with one or another European power.

During the eighteenth and subsequent centuries, writers posed the problem of weakness in two distinctly different ways and thus proposed totally dissimilar solutions. On the one hand, the first group viewed the crisis of defeat as a technical problem that could be solved by technical means. Thus, the Ottomans were weak because of technological inferiority to the Europeans. The solution therefore focused on adoption of the best military technology available, as sultans had in the past. In the eighteenth century, this meant borrowing from Europe. And so European military officers were summoned to the capital city; for example, Baron de Tott served from 1755 to 1776 in order to create a modern, rapid-fire artillery corps. Also, the Ottoman Grand Admiral Gazi Hasan Pasha sought to rebuild the fleet according to the highest and most modern standards.

On the other hand, a series of religious activists considered the crisis of defeat as a religious and moral problem, to be resolved through moral reform. This solution was presented more or less simultaneously by the Tijaniyya Sufi order in North Africa, the Wahhabis in Arabia and Shah Waliullah of Delhi on the Indian subcontinent. The three movements each offered a religious answer to the problem posed by the weakness of Islamic states in the world. The Wahhabi movement of concern here aimed to revive society by eliminating all of the allegedly un-Islamic practices that had crept in since the time of the Prophet Muhammad. In central Arabia, Muhammad ibn Abdul Wahhab (1703–1792) preached the need to return to the principles of early Islam as understood by the great medieval jurist ibn Hanbal. Muslims, Abdul Wahhab said, had forgotten the faith that God revealed to the Prophet.

For the Ottomans, this message posed grave risks. Early in the eighteenth century, they already had lost control of parts of the Arabian peninsula, the Yemen and Hadramaut. Followers of Abdul Wahhab then seized control of much of the rest of Arabia and raided deep into Iraq, thus threatening Ottoman sovereignty in those locations. But this Wahhabi threat was far worse than mere territorial occupation. Abdul Wahhab preached that the Holy Cities of Mecca and Medina, under Ottoman protection, were filled with abominations and un-Islamic shrines. These cities, as well as the Islam of the Ottomans, were corrupt, he asserted, and needed cleansing. To do so, Abdul Wahhab allied himself with Muhammad ibn Saud, whose descendants would come to lead the Wahhabi movement, seize, sack, and purify the Holy Cities in 1803 and, more than a century later, found the kingdom of Saudi Arabia. Thus, unlike most other provincial leaders, the Wahhabis denied the legitimacy of the Ottoman regime and sought to replace it with their own reformed Islamic state. And they would base their own legitimacy on these teachings and on their control of Mecca and Medina.

This fundamental challenge to Ottoman legitimacy did not go unanswered. At about the same time that Abdul Wahhab began preaching, the central government began placing greater emphasis on protecting the Holy Places and those making the sacred pilgrimage. And from the later eighteenth century the sultans increasingly articulated their role as caliph, leader of Muslims everywhere. Thus, Wahhabi successes in the late eighteenth and early nineteenth centuries helped trigger Ottoman appropriation of these religious symbols (see chapter 6).

Suggested bibliography

Entries marked with a * designate recommended readings for new students of the subject.
*Abou-El-Haj, Rifaat. *The 1703 rebellion and the structure of Ottoman politics* (Istanbul, 1984).
Aksan, Virginia. *An Ottoman statesman in war and peace* (Leiden, 1995).
Artan, Tülay. "Architecture as a theatre of life: Profile of the eighteenth-century Bosphorus." Unpublished Ph.D. dissertation, Massachusetts Institute of Technology, 1989.
Cuno, Kenneth. *The Pasha's peasants: Land, society and economy in lower Egypt 1740–1858* (Cambridge, 1992).
Duman, Yüksel, "Notables, textiles and copper in Ottoman Tokat, 1750–1840." Unpublished Ph.D. dissertation, Binghamton University, 1998.
Hathaway, Jane. *A tale of two factions. Myth, memory and identity in Ottoman Egypt and Yemen* (Albany, 2003).

*Hourani, Albert. "Ottoman reform and the politics of the notables," in W. Polk and R. Chambers, eds., *The beginnings of modernization in the Middle East: The nineteenth century* (Chicago, 1968), 41–68.

Ivanova, Svetlana. "The divorce between Zubaida Hatun and Esseid Osman Aga: Women in the eighteenth-century Shari'a court of Rumelia," in Amira El Azhary Sonbol, *Women, the family, and divorce laws in Islamic history* (Syracuse, 1996), 112–125.

*Keddie, Nikki, ed. *Women and gender in Middle Eastern history* (New Haven, 1991).

*Khoury, Dina. *State and provincial society in the Ottoman Empire: Mosul 1540–1834* (Cambridge, 1997).

Kırlı, Cengiz. "The struggle over space: coffee houses of Ottoman Istanbul, 1780–1845." Ph.D. dissertation, Binghamton University, 2000.

Masters, Bruce. *The origins of western economic dominance in the Middle East: Mercantilism and the Islamic economy in Aleppo, 1600–1750* (New York, 1988).

*McGown, Bruce. "The age of ayans, 1699–1812," in Halil İnalcık with Donald Quataert, eds., *An economic and social history of the Ottoman Empire, 1300–1914* (Cambridge, 1994), 637–758.

Olson, Robert. "The esnaf and the Patrona Halil rebellion of 1730: A realignment in Ottoman politics," *Journal of the Economic and Social History of the Orient*, 17 (1974), 329–344.

Pamuk, Şevket. "Prices in the Ottoman Empire, 1469–1914," *International Journal of Middle East Studies* (August 2004), 451–468.

Panaite, Viorel. "Power relationships in the Ottoman Empire: the sultans and the tribute-paying princes of Wallachia and Moldavia from the sixteenth to the eighteenth century." *International Journal of Turkish Studies*, 7, 1 & 2 (2001), 26–53.

Raymond, André. *The great Arab cities in the 16th–18th centuries* (New York, 1984).

*Quataert, Donald. "Janissaries, artisans and the question of Ottoman decline, 1730–1826," in Donald Quataert, ed., *Workers, peasants and economic change in the Ottoman Empire, 1730–1914* (Istanbul, 1993), 197–203.

Salzmann, Ariel. "Measures of empire: Tax farmers and the Ottoman *ancien régime*, 1695–1807." Unpublished Ph.D. dissertation, Columbia University, 1995.

*"An *ancien régime* revisited: Privatization and political economy in the 18th century Ottoman Empire," *Politics and society*, 21, 4 (1993), 393–423.

Shaw, Stanford. *Between old and new: The Ottoman Empire under Sultan Selim III 1789–1807* (Cambridge, MA, 1971).

Silay, Kemal. *Nedim and the poetics of the Ottoman court: Medieval inheritance and the need for change* (Bloomington, 1994).

Sousa, Nadim. *The capitulatory regime in Turkey* (Baltimore, 1933).

Wortley Montagu, Lady Mary. *The Turkish Embassy letters* (London, reprint, 1994).

Zilfi, Madeline. "Elite circulation in the Ottoman Empire: Great mollas of the eighteenth century," *Journal of the Economic and Social History of the Orient*, 26, 3 (1983), 318–364.

Politics of piety: The Ottoman ulama in the post-classical age (Minneapolis, 1986).

*"Women and society in the Tulip era, 1718–1730," in Amira El Azhary Sonbol, ed., *Women, the family, and divorce laws in Islamic history* (Syracuse, 1996), 290–303.

*Zilfi, Madeline, ed. *Women in the Ottoman Empire: Middle Eastern women in the early modern era* (Leiden, 1997).

4   The nineteenth century

Introduction

During the long nineteenth century, 1798–1922, the earlier Ottoman patterns of political and economic life remained generally recognizable. In many respects, this period continued processes of change and transformation that had begun in the eighteenth century, and sometimes before. Territorial losses continued and frontiers shrank; statesmen at the center and in the provinces continued their contestations for power and access to taxable resources; and the international economy loomed ever more important. And yet, much was new. The forces triggering the territorial losses became increasingly complex, now involving domestic rebellions as well as the familiar imperial wars. Domestically, the central state became more powerful and influential in everyday lives than ever before in Ottoman history, extending its control ever more deeply into society. Its primary tools of control changed from consumption competitions and tax farms to a much larger and professional military and bureaucracy. As a part of the effort to more fully control its population, the state redefined the status of Muslims and non-Muslims and, after some delay sought, towards the end of the period, to re-order the legal status of women as well. And finally, a new and deadly element evolved in the Ottoman body politic – inter-communal violence among Ottoman subjects – that attested to the power of these accelerating political and economic changes.

The wars of contraction and internal rebellions

By the twentieth century, the Ottoman Empire in Europe had receded to a small coastal plain between Edirne and Istanbul. One measure of the losses: before 1850, a majority of all Ottoman subjects lived in the Balkans while, c. 1906, the European provinces held only 20 percent of the total.

Foreign wars on the Balkan frontiers, sometimes against the Habsburgs but especially against Russia, continued to shred the Ottoman domains.

Within the empire, as we have seen, many provincial notables during the eighteenth century had practiced substantial degrees of autonomy while acknowledging the fundamental legitimacy of the Ottomans' enterprise and their state. Seldom, if ever, had the rebels sought to break out of or destroy the Ottoman imperium. There had been revolts but, generally, these had worked within the system, claiming as their goal the rectification of problems within the Ottoman universe, such as the reduction of taxes or better justice. But in the nineteenth century – in the Balkan, Anatolian, and Arab provinces alike – movements emerged that actively sought to separate particular areas from Ottoman rule and establish independent, sovereign states subordinate to no higher political authority. Further, in almost every instance, one or another of the Great Powers supported these revolts, and their assistance indeed was crucial to the success of the rebels' effort. Thus, the nineteenth century is different in that many of the territorial losses resulted from revolts and rebellions on the part of Ottoman subjects against their suzerain or sovereign. This seems generally new in Ottoman history.

The eighteenth century closed with Napoleon Bonaparte's invasion of Egypt in 1798, that ended with his solo flight back to France in 1799 and the later surrender of the French army to its British and Ottoman foes (see map 3 on p. 39). In the turmoil, an Ottoman military officer from the Albanian region, Muhammad Ali, eventually seized power in 1805 and established himself as master of Egypt. During his remarkable reign (until his death in 1848), Muhammad Ali built up a formidable military that threatened the European balance of power and, it seems, the Ottomans' hold on the sultanate itself. Thanks to his career, Egypt embarked on a separate course for the remainder of Ottoman history. It remained the sultan's nominal possession after the British occupation in 1882. But, in 1914, Egypt formally became part of the British Empire following the Ottoman entry into World War I on the German and Austro-Hungarian side.

In 1804, at about the same moment that Muhammad Ali was seizing control of the southeastern part of the Ottoman Empire, the Serbs in the northwest corner rebelled. Appealing to the Sultan to correct abuses at the hands of the local administration, Serb rebels turned to Russia for aid. A complex struggle evolved, involving the two powers and the Serbs. By 1817, hereditary rule by a Serbian prince had been established and from that date, in reality, Serbia was a state separate from the Ottoman. Legally it became so only in 1878, as a result of the Congress of Berlin. In a sense, this pattern reversed that of the Ottoman conquests, from direct rule to vassalage to independence. Other losses derived from the more familiar pattern of war with Russia, ending with a formal agreement, as instanced by the 1812 Treaty of Bucharest that acknowledged the loss of Bessarabia.

The overall pattern in the Balkans is confusing in its detail but clear in overall direction. Often a local revolt would meet success or the Russians would drive very deep into the southern Balkans. But then a troubled international community, fearful of Ottoman disintegration or Russian success, would convene a gathering, undo the worst results but allow some losses to ensue. Thus, the empire retained its integrity, avoiding a world war of the Ottoman succession, but Russia was placated with some gains. The 1829 Treaty of Adrianople typifies this pattern. In 1828, Russian armies, while winning major victories in eastern Anatolia, drove down through the western Black Sea areas, through Varna, captured the former Ottoman capital of Edirne on the present-day border of Turkey and Bulgaria and seemed poised to attack Istanbul itself. Nonetheless, despite the massive victories, Russia yielded up nearly all of its conquests, settling for a few more pieces of land and actual but not formal Ottoman withdrawal from Moldavia and Wallachia (map 4).

In this fashion, the so-called "Eastern Question" – how to solve the problem posed by the continuing territorial erosion of the Ottoman empire – continued to be addressed over the course of the nineteenth century. On the one hand, many European leaders came to understand the grave risks that total Ottoman collapse posed to the general peace. And so they agreed to seek to maintain its integrity, for example, reversing the potentially devastating results of war at the negotiating table and, in 1856, admitting the Ottoman state into the "Concert of Europe". Thus, the European consensus that the empire should be maintained, tottering but intact, helped preserve the Ottoman state. On the other hand, through their wars and support of the separatist goals of rebellious Ottoman subjects, European states abetted the very process of fragmentation that they feared and were seeking to avoid.

Another hallmark event of the nineteenth century, the 1821–30 Greek war of independence, clearly illustrates the central role of international politics in the revolts against the sultan. After failing to suppress the Greek rebels, Sultan Mahmut II in 1824 invited Muhammad Ali Pasha to intervene with his powerful fleet and army. He did so with great success and the Greek rebellion appeared to be over. But in 1827, the combined British, French, and Russian squadrons annihilated the Egyptian navy at Navarino and three years later, the 1830 Treaty of London acknowledged the formation of a new state, in the southern area of modern Greece.

This sequence of events in turn led to a near takeover of the Ottoman empire by Muhammad Ali Pasha. Believing that his help against the Greek rebels entitled him to the Syrian provinces of the sultan, Muhammad Ali

Map 4 The dismemberment of the Ottoman Empire, 1672–1913
Adapted from Halil İnalcık with Donald Quataert, eds., *An economic and social history of the Ottoman Empire, 1300–1914* (Cambridge, 1994), xxxviii.

sent his son Ibrahim Pasha against the Ottoman Empire in 1832. Conquering Acre, Damascus, and Aleppo, the Egyptian army won another
major victory at Konya in central Anatolia and seemed poised to capture
Istanbul (as Russia had been just three years before). Irony of ironies,
the Russian nemesis landed its troops between Muhammad Ali's army
and Istanbul and became Ottoman saviors. Here, an infamous foreign
foe thwarted a major domestic rebel apparently intent on invading the
city and overthrowing Ottoman rule. Fearing that a strong new dynasty
leading a powerful state would become its neighbor, the Russians backed
the Ottomans and signed the 1833 Treaty of Hünkiar Iskelesi to confirm
their protection.

During the 1830s, Muhammad Ali controlled a section of southeast
Anatolia and most of the Arab provinces and, in 1838, threatened to
declare his own independence. The Ottomans attacked his forces in Syria
but were crushed and again rescued, this time by a coalition of Britain,
Austria, Prussia, and Russia (but not France). These powers stripped
Muhammad Ali of all his gains – Crete and Syria as well as the Holy Cities
of Mecca and Medina – leaving him only hereditary control of Egypt
as compensation. The lesson seemed clear. The Western powers were
unwilling to permit the emergence of a dynamic and powerful Egyptian
state that threatened Ottoman stability and the international balance of
power. Although he may have had the power to do so, Muhammad Ali
did not become the master of the Middle East, in significant measure
because the European states would not allow it.[1]

The separation between the Ottoman Empire and its nominal Egyptian province entered a final phase in 1869, when the Egyptian ruler,
the Khedive Ismail, presided over the opening of the Suez Canal. The
ties which this created between the Egyptian and European economies –
already thick because of cotton and geography – were brought home by
the British occupation of the province in 1882. The final break occurred
as Britain declared a protectorate over Egypt in 1914, nearly 400 years
after the armies of Sultan Selim I had entered Cairo and destroyed the
Mamluk Empire.

In its quintessence, the Eastern Question is exquisitely revealed in the
diplomacy following the Ottoman–Russian war of 1877–1878, that triggered truly major territorial losses. In the first round of negotiations,
Russia forced the Ottomans to sign the Treaty of San Stefano, creating a

---

[1] There is debate over this issue. See Afaf Lutfi Sayyid Marsot, *Egypt in the reign of
Muhammad Ali* (Cambridge, 1984), for the argument that Egypt was on the verge of
major economic development that was destroyed by Europe. This view is being modified
by a number of scholars; see for example, the book by Juan Cole (cited in the bibliography
to this chapter).

gigantic zone of Russian puppet states in the Balkans reaching to the Aegean Sea itself. Such a settlement would have vastly enlarged the Russian area of domination and influence and destroyed the European balance of power. And so the German chancellor, von Bismarck, who probably was the leading politician of the age, proclaimed himself as an "honest broker" seeking peace and no territorial advantage for Germany and convened the powers in Berlin. There the assembled diplomats negotiated the Treaty of Berlin which took away most of the Russian gains and parceled out Ottoman lands as if they were door prizes at some gigantic raffle. Serbia, Montenegro, and Rumania all became independent states, a ratification of long-time realities of separation to be sure, but formal losses nonetheless. Bosnia and Herzegovina were lost in reality but remained nominally Ottoman, under Habsburg administration until their final break in 1908, when they were annexed by the Vienna state. The greater Bulgaria of the San Stefano agreement was much reduced; only one-third became independent and the balance remained under a qualified and precarious Ottoman control. Rumania and Russia settled territorial disputes between them, with the former obtaining the Dobruja mouth of the Danube and yielding south Bessarabia to Russia in exchange. Other provisions ceded pieces of eastern Anatolia to Russia and the island of Cyprus – a great island battleship to protect the Suez Canal and the lifeline to India – to Britain. France was bought off by being allowed to occupy Tunis.

The Treaty of Berlin vividly illustrates the power of Europe during the last part of the nineteenth century, able to impose its wishes on the world, drawing lines on maps and deciding the fate of peoples and nations with seeming impunity. It would do so again on many more major occasions – for example, partitioning Africa in 1884 and the Middle East after World War I. With truly fateful consequences, some inhabitants of both western Europe and the partitioned lands falsely concluded that military strength/weakness implied cultural, moral, and religious strength/weakness.

Between this epochal treaty and World War I, the Ottoman state enjoyed a minor victory against the Greeks in a short 1897–1898 war but suffered additional losses in the 1911–1912 Tripolitanian war with Italy and, more seriously, in the Balkan wars of 1912–1913. In these latter conflicts, the Ottoman successor states of Greece, Bulgaria, and Serbia at first fought against the Ottomans and then among themselves. In the end, the Ottomans lost the last of their European possessions except for the coastal plain between Edirne and the capital city. Possessions that in the sixteenth century had stretched to Vienna now ended a few hours' train ride from Istanbul (map 5).

Map 5 The Ottoman Empire, c. 1914
Adapted from Halil İnalcık with Donald Quataert, eds., *An economic and social history of the Ottoman Empire, 1300–1914* (Cambridge, 1994), 775.

The outbreak of war in 1914 between two grand coalitions – Britain, France, and Russia against Germany and Austria-Hungary – doomed the Ottoman empire. Majority sentiment among the Ottoman elite probably favored a British alliance, but that was not an available option. Britain already had gained Cyprus and Egypt; thus its road to India was well guarded. In any event, it was not able to reconcile a potential Ottoman ally's claims for integrity with its Russian ally's demands for Ottoman lands, especially the waterways connecting the Black and Aegean Seas. Ottoman statesmen well understood that neutrality was not a possibility since it would have made partition by the winning coalition inevitable. And so, with the enthusiastic support of some among the Young Turk leaders who had seized power during the Balkan wars' crisis, the Ottomans entered the war on what turned out to be the losing side.

During the multi-front four-year war, the Ottoman world endured truly horrendous casualties through battles and disease, and the massacre of its own population. As the war ended, British and French troops were in victorious occupation of Anatolian and Arab provinces, as well as the capital city itself. During the war, the two powers had prepared the Sykes–Picot Agreement of 1916 to partition the Arab provinces of the Ottoman empire between them. As the war ended, both sent troops to enforce their claims; subsequent peace conferences confirmed this wartime division. Palestine was the exception, becoming part of the British zone and not, as was originally planned, an international zone. Britain thus obtained much of present-day Iraq, Israel, Palestine, and Jordan while France took the Syrian and Lebanese lands – both remaining in power until after World War II.

In Arabia and Anatolia, independent states emerged from the Ottoman wreckage. After a prolonged struggle, the Saudi state defeated its many rivals in the Arabian peninsula, including the Hashemites of Mecca, finally forming the kingdom of Saudi Arabia in 1932. As World War I was ending, Ottoman resistance forces had formed in various areas, concentrating in the Anatolian provinces that had provided the bulk of the Ottoman soldiers. In the ensuing months and years, as Great Power claims to the Arab provinces of the empire were implemented, general strategies of Ottoman resistance against foreign occupation transmuted into ones for the liberation of Anatolia only. Fighting and defeating the invading forces of the Athens government that claimed western and northern Anatolia for Greece, the resistance leaders gradually redefined their struggle as a Turkish one, for the liberation of a Turkish homeland in Anatolia. That is, the Ottoman struggle became a Turkish war. The concentration of significant resistance forces, Ottoman evolving into Turkish, in Anatolia meant that any British and French occupation would be very costly. The emerging Turkish leadership, for its part, was willing to negotiate on certain issues vital to Great Power interests, such as repayment of outstanding Ottoman debts, the question of the waterways connecting the Black and Aegean Seas, and renunciation of claims to the former Arab provinces. In the end, the Great Powers and the Turkish nationalists agreed to terminate the Ottoman Empire. The sultanate ceased to exist in 1922 while the Ottoman caliphate ended in 1923.

Overview: evolution of the Ottoman state, 1808–1922

From one viewpoint, the nineteenth-century changes simply were additional phases in the ongoing transformation of the Ottoman state since the fourteenth century – part of its ongoing effort to acquire, retain, or modify tools in order to control its subjects and defend the frontiers. The nineteenth-century tool-kit, as we shall see, was quite different from that of the eighteenth century, when it included competitive consumption of goods, the military forces of the provincial notables, the vizier and pasha households at the center, the lifetime tax farm (*malikane*) as the political-financial instrument extracting revenues linking the two, and an important place for the community of religious scholars (ulema).

Overall, the central state – in both its civilian and military wings – vastly expanded in size and function and employed new recruitment methods during the nineteenth century. The number of civil officials that totaled perhaps 2,000 persons at the end of the eighteenth century reached 35,000–50,000 in approximately 1908, virtually all of them males. As the bureaucracy expanded in size, it embraced spheres of activity previously considered outside the purview of the state. Hence, state functionaries once performed a limited range of tasks, mainly war making and tax collecting, leaving much of the rest for the state's subjects and their religious leaders to address. For example, the separate religious communities had financed and operated schools, hospices and other poor relief facilities. Muslim, Christian, and Jewish groups – usually via their *imam*s, priests, and rabbis – had collected monies, built schools, or soup kitchens, or orphanages and paid the teachers and personnel to care for the students, the poor, and the orphans. But, during the second half of the nineteenth century, the official class took on these and many other functions, creating separate and parallel state educational and charitable institutions. During the reign of Sultan Abdülhamit II, for example, the state built as many as 10,000 schools for its subjects, using these to provide a modern education based on Ottoman values. Thus, the state continued its evolution from a pre-modern to a modern form and the numbers of state employees vastly increased. Ministries of trade and commerce, health, education, and public works emerged, staffed increasingly by persons who were trained specialists in the particular area. Ottoman women, moreover, began to be included in the same modernization process.

As the size and functions of government changed, so did recruitment patterns. In the recent past of the eighteenth century, households of viziers and pashas in the capital and of notables in the provinces had trained most of those who administered the empire. During the nineteenth century, however, the central Ottoman bureaucracy gradually formed its own educational network, largely based on west and central European models, and increasingly monopolized access to state service. Knowledge of European languages, that provided access to the sought after administrative and technological skills of the West, became increasingly prized. The personnel of the Translation Bureau (*Tercüme Odası*), formed to provide an alternate source of skilled translators when the Greek war of independence seemed to question the loyalty of the Greek dragomans, were the first wave. Subsequently, officials went to European schools, returned home with both the language and the technical skills, and passed those on to others in newly built schools on Ottoman soil. More and more, knowledge of the West became the key to service and mobility within the burgeoning bureaucracy. The borrowing, it must be cautioned, was no mere copying of Western models but rather a blending of imported knowledge and institutions with existing Ottoman patterns and morality. The infusion of Ottoman practices and principles into Western ones already was occurring early in the nineteenth century. Such recombining may well have become more pronounced during the vast expansion of the educational system under Sultan Abdülhamit II.

The Ottoman military too, came to rely on western technologies and methods while growing vastly in size from 24,000 army personnel in 1837 to 120,000 in the 1880s. Throughout, only males served. As in the civilian sector, recruitment patterns for military service also changed. From the early part of the century, a central state system of conscripting peasants emerged to replace reliance on the forces of the provincial notables. The terms of military service became very long: for most of the nineteenth century, conscripts remained for twenty years in both active service and the reserves.

The central state employed the expanding bureaucracy and military – along with a host of other new technologies such as the telegraph, railroads, and photography – to control, weaken, or destroy domestic rivals. With varying degrees of success, it battled against diverse groups such as the Janissaries, guilds, tribes, religious authorities, and provincial notables – bodies that had mediated between the central state and the subject population – to gain political dominance and greater access to the wealth being generated within Ottoman society. There is no doubt that the late nineteenth-century central state exerted more power over its subjects and competing domestic power clusters than ever before in Ottoman history. The Janissaries were destroyed and the guilds badly weakened and, after the campaigns against them by Sultan Mahmut II during the 1820s and 1830s, local notables in Anatolia and the Arab lands did not raise their hands against the state. Moreover, in the 1830s, state surveillance systems attained new levels of intrusiveness. Networks of spies, at least in Istanbul, began systematically reporting to state agencies on all manner of conversations among the general public.

On the other hand, centralization was hardly a process of mere domination by the capital over the provinces. Thus, Istanbul, while extending itself more deeply into provincial politics, economics, and society, did so through compromises with local groups and elites. Consequently, their autonomy, power, and authority endured until the end of the empire and, indeed, to the present day in places such as modern Turkey, Iraq, Syria and Transjordan. Many tribes retained substantial degrees of autonomy. After all, Kurdish tribes today still act with some independence from the central states of Turkey, Syria and Iraq. Also, while it is likely true that a higher proportion of tax revenues paid from local areas went to the central state than previously, provincial notables kept their status, much of their power and their access to the local surplus. For example, when Istanbul set up provincial administrative councils to directly control the various regions, notables occupied many of the seats and continued to do so until the end of the empire (see chapter 6). A major indicator of the nature of central state power is the persistence of tax farming. Despite all the waste involved, tax farming remained the predominant method of collecting taxes from the agrarian sector, the mainstay of the Ottoman economy. In a historic compromise of vital significance, local notables remained part of the tax farming apparatus and so retained a powerful hand in provincial affairs. Some historians feel this occurred despite the efforts of the central state to impose full control and thus indicates failed centralization. But others argue that it was a deliberate sharing of power among elites at the center and in the provinces and therefore an indicator of the actual nature of the late Ottoman state. Moreover, the state sought but failed to break the political power of the various religious authorities – Christian, Muslim, Jewish – over their constituencies. Despite the efforts of policy-makers, the leaders of religious communities (*millets*), perhaps, particularly, the Christian, retained a powerful voice in the lives of their coreligionists.

Who was in charge of Ottoman politics at the center during the nineteenth century? Until 1826 and Sultan Mahmut's destruction of the Janissaries, it is difficult to say. During the period immediately surrounding the Document of Alliance (1808), provincial notables likely were in charge while in the several decades before and after this event, various individuals and groups contended for and held power. These included the sultan, Istanbul elites and the urban crowd supported by the Janissaries. After the 1826 event, the central state remained exceptionally weak during the 1820s and 1830s. The threatening appearance of the Russian and Egyptian armies quite near the capital attests to this central state weakness against foreign foes, at precisely the moment that Sultan Mahmut II (1808–1839) was destroying his Janissary foes and waging successful campaigns against the provincial notables. The sultan probably was supreme between 1826 and 1839, followed by bureaucratic ascendancy between 1839 and 1876. This sultanic subordination to the bureaucracy subsequent to the apparent consolidation of personal power by the autocratic Sultan Mahmut II is puzzling and not well understood. Sultan Abdülhamit II reversed the pattern and took up the autocratic reins soon after his accession to the throne in 1876. In 1908, the "Young Turk" revolutionaries curbed his autocracy and restored the dormant Constitution of 1876 that placed power in the hands of a parliamentary government. The experiment suffered, however, as yet more Ottoman provinces fell away, making a mockery of the claim that parliamentarianism would halt territorial hemorrhaging. Civilian bureaucrats ran affairs until 1913 when a Young Turk military dictatorship took over, promising to save the state from further losses (quite falsely as it turned out).

Ongoing transformation of Ottoman state–subject and subject–subject relationships

As we have just seen, the nineteenth-century state strove to eliminate intermediating groups – guilds and tribes, Janissaries and religious communities – and bring all Ottoman subjects directly under its authority. In doing so, it sought to radically transform the relationship between itself and its subjects and within and among the subject classes. In earlier centuries, the Ottoman social and political order had been based on differences among ethnicities, religions, and occupations and on notions of an overarching common subordination and subjecthood to the monarchical state. This order had been based on the presumption of Muslim superiority and a contractual relationship in which the subordinate non-Muslims paid special taxes and in exchange obtained state guarantees of religious protection. Non-Muslims legally were inferior to Muslims and, after the first Ottoman centuries, generally were unable to serve in government office or the military (although there were many exceptions). The reality, of course, had been more complicated. For example, many Christian subjects had taken up the protection of various European states and enjoyed immunity from Ottoman laws (and taxes) through the capitulatory system (chapter 5).

In a series of three enactments between 1829 and 1856, the central state aimed to strip away the differences among Ottoman subjects and make all male subjects the same in its eyes and in one another's as well. This was nothing less than a program to radically reconstitute the nature of the state and male Ottoman society. In such actions, the Ottoman elites shared a set of goals with state leaders in many areas of the nineteenth-century globe, such as nearby Austria-Hungary, Russia, and more distant Japan. In the Ottoman world, these enactments were intended to make male subjects equal in every respect: both in appearance as well as matters of taxation, and bureaucratic and military service. The reforms sought, on the one hand, to eliminate the Muslims' legal privileges and, on the other, to bring back under direct Ottoman state jurisdiction its Christian subjects who had become protégés of foreign states.

In 1829, a clothing law undermined the sartorial order based on difference that had existed for centuries. In the past, as seen, clothing laws in the Ottoman Empire, western Europe, and China all had sought to maintain class, status, ethnic, religious, or occupational distinctions among both men and women. In a sweeping enactment, the 1829 law sought to eliminate the visual differences among males by requiring the adoption of identical headgear (except for the ulema and non-Muslim clerics) – see chapter 8. Appearing the same, all men presumably would become equal.

This drive for equality anticipated, by a full decade, the more famous Rose Garden decree (Hatt-i Sherif of Gülhane) of 1839, that usually is seen as the beginning of the Tanzimat era of reform in the Ottoman empire. This 1839 royal statement of intentions spoke of the need to eliminate inequality and create justice for all subjects, Muslim or non-Muslim, rich or poor. It promised a host of specific measures to eliminate corruption, abolish tax farming, and regularize the conscription of all males. In return for equal responsibilities, it promised equal rights. In 1856, another imperial decree (Hatt-i Humayun) reiterated the state's duty to provide equality and stressed guarantees of equality of all subjects, including equal access to state schools and to state employment. And, it also reiterated the call for equality of obligation of Ottoman males, i.e. universal male conscription into military service.

In the Ottoman world, as in France, the United States, and the German Reich after 1870, women only slowly were included in such "modern" notions of equality of subject and citizen. Women simply were not discussed either in the clothing law of 1829 or the imperial decrees of 1839 and 1856. As in the French Declaration of the Rights of Man or the American Declaration of Independence, women were not seen as included in the announced changes that were to occur. Thus, Ottoman women presumably were to continue to wear dress that differentiated by community and class. But, as in the eighteenth century, changes in fashion were the norm during the nineteenth century as well and so women continued to test prevailing communal and class boundaries (also see chapter 8). Ottoman society continued to grapple with the meaning of equality and women perforce, if very slowly, were included. For example, families increasingly began to seek formal education for their daughters. The top elites often sent them to private schools while the aspiring middle ranks sought female mobility in the state schools. As early as the 1840s, women began receiving some formal education in state schools. By the end of the century, perhaps one in three school age girls were attending state primary schools, but the upper-level schools remained all-male domains until just before World War I. Moreover, a very few women entered state service, almost all serving as teachers in the state girls' schools and the Fine Arts School. Otherwise, the religious, military, and civil bureaucracies remained male preserves.

In the end, neither equality of rights nor of obligation prevailed, either for men or women. In the 1880s and later, the state still punished women for publicly wearing clothing that it deemed immodest. Further, many of the property guarantees that women had enjoyed under Islamic law disappeared with the modernizing reforms. The new imperial laws more rigidly defined rights than had local magistrates and, in some ways, women's legal rights to property actually declined under the impact of the reforms. Non-Muslims for their part refused to serve in the military (with the support of their Great Power patrons) and, in fact, did not do so until the 1908 Young Turk Revolution. When the new Ottoman regime put teeth into the conscription law for Christians, many of them voted with their feet and emigrated to the New World. Further, as seen, heads of the Christian religious communities, jealous of their prerogatives, lobbied with the Great Powers to keep the legal distinctions among Ottoman subjects. The state, for its part, failed to live up to its promises and did not proportionately recruit and promote non-Muslims into state service (see chapter 9). Nonetheless, the accomplishments towards equality were real although, as the example of women's property rights suggests, change was not always simply positive.

Here we need to ask why the Ottoman state, or any state, would initiate an emphasis on equality and seek to change its social basis, overthrowing a system that had functioned for many centuries. After all, many states successfully have based their power on the privileges of the few, not the rights of the many. To address this issue we need to look at one universal pattern and then several that relate specifically to the Ottoman case. First, French Revolutionary principles of the rights and obligations of "Man" instantly had made France into the most powerful nation in continental Europe, with its army recruited from the *levée en masse*. The lesson was clear: universal conscription meant vastly enhanced military and political strength. But, to render such conscription palatable, the state had to grant universal rights (to males).

Second, since 1500 if not before, European economic strength had mounted to equal and then surpass that of any other region of the globe, including the Ottoman Empire. And, over time, the European and Ottoman economies became increasingly intertwined and, as they did, the process promoted the economic power of the Ottoman Christians more than the Muslims. Why this is so is not entirely certain. West Europeans' assumptions that Ottoman Christians – because they were Christians – were somehow more trustworthy as business partners than Muslims certainly played a role. As protégés of European merchants, Ottoman Christians obtained powerful tax exemptions (in the form of *berats*, see chapter 7), that allowed them to buy and sell goods more cheaply than Muslim merchants. Also, the pre-nineteenth-century Ottoman state did favor Muslims in granting them employment in the military and state bureaucratic service. With fewer of these job prospects before them, Christians were more likely to engage in risk taking, meaning trade and commerce. As trade with west and central Europe mounted, so did the opportunities for such ventures. And so, numbers of Ottoman Christians profited from the economic ties and acquired, from the eighteenth century onwards, substantial economic power. The nineteenth-century Ottoman state sought to capture and subordinate that success with its enactments in 1829, 1839, and 1856, offering Christians full equality.

Third, the enactments were part of a systematic state program to retain the loyalty of Ottoman Christian subjects in the Balkans. By promising equality, the state aimed to win back or retain the loyalty of its Balkan Christian subjects who were being courted by Russia and the Habsburgs and/or separatist movements. This ideology of Ottomanism – equality of all male Ottoman subjects – remained a policy keystone until the end of the empire in 1922. But, after 1878, while the stress on equality remained, a shading of emphasis developed in favor of the rights of Muslims. This slight shift of emphasis became more noticeable during Abdülhamit's reign but also marked, to a lesser degree, the final Ottoman years as well. It is no coincidence that the shift occurred after the 1878 Berlin treaty and the massive losses of Christian-populated provinces, which left the empire with a Muslim majority population for the first time in many centuries.

Nationalism and the nineteenth-century Ottoman Middle East

Peaceful relations among Ottoman subjects were the norm over most of the period and the Ottoman system worked relatively well for almost all of its history. These statements, true as they are, will be passionately rejected by many. Images of the "Terrible Turk," the "Bulgarian horrors" and the Armenian massacres resonate powerfully today, both in the historical imagination and the politics of the early twenty-first century. My goal here is to demystify the violence of the nineteenth-century Ottoman Empire, which certainly had its share of inter-communal strife, by placing it in its wider historical context (see also chapter 9). Overall, this violence should be understood as part of a global process that has given birth to nation states everywhere, including the Middle East, Europe, the United States, and east and south Asia. By contextualizing this violence, I do not seek to minimize or justify it.

There certainly was plenty of violence within the Ottoman community. In 1822, Ottoman officials killed or deported the entire population of the island of Chios during the Greek rebellion. In 1860, thousands of Damascene Christians died at the hands of fellow Ottoman subjects, Muslims, in a set of incidents that had both class and religious overtones. In 1895–1896, lower-class Muslims, perhaps with official connivance, murdered large numbers of Armenians in the capital. And worst of all, at least 600,000 Armenian civilians perished in 1915–1916, at the hands of Ottoman soldiers and officials as well as Ottoman civilians (see chapter 9).

Ottoman Muslims had no monopoly on bringing death to their neighbors. As early as the 1840s, Maronite Christians and Druze in the Lebanon and Syrian regions began fighting one another. During the initial phases of the Greek war of independence, Orthodox Christian Greeks in 1821 slaughtered Ottoman Muslims in the city of Tripolis. In 1876, Christians in Bulgaria murdered 1,000 Muslims and triggered the Muslim slaughter of 3,700 Christians, the so-called "Bulgarian horrors" when the European press focused on Christian suffering but ignored that of Muslims. Further, Middle East violence was not confined to the nineteenth century. For example, during his early sixteenth-century campaign in eastern Anatolia, Sultan Selim I killed many thousands of suspected supporters of his political rivals, the Safevids.

Likewise, the pages of American and European history are soaked in the blood of innocent, civilian, victims. Embedded in the birth and expansion of the American colonies and the United States were centuries of incalculable violence done to native Americans and African slaves. There are many examples from European history as well, such as the St. Bartholomew's Day Massacre in 1572 when the French monarchy murdered 10,000 of its own Huguenot Protestant subjects, or when the French Terror of 1793–1794 executed 17,000 French citizens. Still more terrible are events of the later twentieth century, such as the slaughter of the Jews in the Jewish Holocaust and the horrors in Bosnia, Kossovo, and Rwanda-Burundi. This recitation of painful and awful atrocities is not meant to explain away or justify the violence of the nineteenth-century Ottoman world or the slaughter of the Armenians in 1915–1916. But it does seek to demonstrate a historic and general connection between the creation and perpetuation of states and nation states and the inflicting of violence on their own subjects and citizens.

Why did already existing differences – religious or ethnic – among Ottoman subjects erupt into violence? It is clear, after all, that inter-subject relations in the nineteenth-century Ottoman Empire were far worse than in the past. The question is why. More specifically, to what extent was the nineteenth-century violence a necessary part of the process by which an area broke away and became a new state separate from the Ottoman Empire? In other words, was violence a necessary and endemic part of nineteenth-century separatist struggles? Historians disagree strongly over the origins of the breakaway movements that occurred in the Balkan, Anatolian (and to a lesser extent the Arab) provinces of the empire. Generally, two types of analysis are presented, respectively based on so-called push and pull factors. In the "push" analysis, stress is placed on the good intentions of the Ottoman state but the incomplete nature of its reform efforts during the nineteenth century. In this view, the state sought to bring about equality between Muslim and non-Muslim subjects and more equitable relations between elites and the lower strata. But, because it was slow to do so, frustrations mounted and revolts ensued. In this view, the state fell victim to its own well-minded policies. "Pull" analysts are less kind about state intentions and instead refer to Ottoman oppression, both political and economic. Deprived of political rights and driven by mounting economic impoverishment under Ottoman maladministration, they say, nationalist sentiments developed among local leaders who led the drive for independence.[2]

Thus, the issue of nationalism, on which there is profound confusion among scholars and the general public, takes center stage. In an older view, nationalism – sentiments of uniqueness, superiority, and the claim for independence – preceded and gave birth to the nation state. Persons felt they were part of an oppressed national group that had been and was being deprived of its economic, political, and cultural rights. And so they demanded the right to a state independent of Ottoman domination. In more recent arguments, the state is said to have come into being first; with nationalism emerging only subsequently. That is, the new state, to preserve itself, sponsored and created national identity formation within its borders.[3]

---

[2] In his many works, Halil İnalcık (see, for example, "Application of the Tanzimat") advocates the "push" theory while L. S. Stavrianos, *The Balkans since 1453* (New York, 1958), is a proponent of the "pull" hypothesis.

[3] L. S. Stavrianos, *The Balkans since 1453* (New York, 1958) argues that the nation came first; Benedict Anderson, *Imagined communities: Reflections on the origins and spread of nationalism* (London, 1983), discusses the invention of national identity.

A better understanding of this nationalism would seem to lead to a fuller appreciation of the factors that gave rise to violence among Ottoman communities that previously had been coexisting fairly well over the centuries. And yet to achieve this is no small task since nationalism in Ottoman history (and elsewhere) is encrusted with mythologies. One popular myth – that now has been debunked – had it that the Balkan economies were dying under oppressive Ottoman misadministration and needed freedom to survive. In fact, recent scholarship has shown the exact opposite to have been true; Ottoman state policies had produced positive economic results. In Ottoman Bulgaria, for example, the reforms had regularized tax burdens, brought greater internal stability, and made life more secure. Thus, a Bulgarian economic expansion ensued during the middle nineteenth century, in the years before the breakaway from Ottoman rule. In the presence of this general upswing in prosperity, Bulgaria became independent. Generally, it turns out, the Balkans on the eve of their separation witnessed growing not declining prosperity. But because the new states then embarked on politically popular but economically disastrous policies, such as ill-advised land re-distribution schemes, the period following independence brought economic decline, so that those economies in fact were worse off after independence than before. Hence, we can no longer use economic decline to explain the emergence of separatist movements.[4]

In sum, to begin to understand nationalism and nineteenth-century violence, we need to break with mythologies and examine the specific manner in which economic, cultural, political, and other variables intersected and interacted at particular points in time. Let me close by putting it this way. There were ancient, age-old differences among Ottoman subjects. But the hatreds between them were not ancient but recent, and created by specific events during the eighteenth and nineteenth centuries. It is our task as historians to uncover and understand the factors newly creating and feeding those hatreds.

Foreign capital and the nineteenth-century Ottoman Empire

The Ottoman state financed the expansion of its bureaucratic and military apparatus partly through rising tax revenues, increases that derived from heavier tax burdens – mainly from the agrarian population – and the overall expansion of the economy, especially after 1840 (see chapter 7). But these sums were inadequate to the task and the state found itself on the horns of a dilemma. The monies could be obtained by loans from

---

[4] See Palairet entry in bibliography to this chapter.

Europe, where economic expansion and wealth from the colonies generated funds for investment abroad. But Ottoman administrators well understood the danger of such loans – that they could lead to European domination or control. Until the mid-century, they rejected this path. But finally, aware of the risks, they took out the first loans, to help finance Ottoman participation in the Crimean war of 1853–1856. Predictably, as feared and anticipated, one loan led to another and, by the mid-1870s, the Ottoman state found itself unable to repay its international debts. (At the same moment, Egypt, Tunisia, and many other states around the globe were experiencing a similar crisis.) Negotiations between the European creditors and Ottoman debtor state followed and, in 1881, the Ottoman Public Debt Administration emerged. The Ottoman state honored its financial obligations and permitted the Debt Administration, a consortium of foreign creditors, to oversee part of the Ottoman economy and use the supervised revenues to repay the debts. The Debt Administration became a vast, essentially independent bureaucracy within the Ottoman bureaucracy, run by the creditors. It employed 5,000 officials who collected taxes that then were turned over to the foreign holders of the debt. Thereafter, foreign loans continued to finance Ottoman bureaucratic and military expansion.

Further, the security that the Debt Administration arrangement gave to would-be foreign investors attracted yet additional European capital, mainly to invest in railroads, ports, and public utilities. Virtually all such facilities that existed in the late Ottoman Empire derived from foreign capital ventures (see chapter 7). And so, needed improvements in transportation, commerce, and urban facilities were made, but at the price of further foreign capital control of the Ottoman economy. The foreign loans to the state and foreign investments in the Ottoman private sector meant that many of the necessary changes in the bureaucratic, military, and economic infrastructures were being implemented. But the price was high. The debt burden became enormous and consumed a sizeable chunk of all Ottoman revenues. Perhaps worse, the mounting international control compromised the authority of the Ottoman state with its own subjects, who paid some of their taxes to the foreign Debt Administration and who watched the works of European capital increase, almost daily, around them.

Suggested bibliography

Entries marked with a * designate recommended readings for new students of the subject.

*Abou-El-Haj, Rifaat. *Formation of the modern state* (Albany, 1991).

Adanir, Fikret. "The Macedonian question: the socio-economic reality and problems of its historiographic interpretations," *International Journal of Turkish Studies*, Winter 1985–6, 43–64.

Ahmad, Feroz. *The making of modern Turkey* (London, 1993).

Akarlı, Engin. *The long peace: Ottoman Lebanon, 1861–1920* (Berkeley, 1993).

*Arat, Zehra F. *Deconstructing images of "The Turkish woman"* (New York, 1998).

Berkes, Niyazi. *The development of secularism in Turkey* (Montreal, 1964).

*Brown, Sarah Graham. *Images of women: The portrayal of women in photography of the Middle East, 1860–1950* (London, 1988).

*Çelik, Zeyneb. *The remaking of Istanbul* (Seattle and London, 1989).

*Cole, Juan. *Colonialism and revolution in the Middle East: Social and cultural origins of Egypt's Urabi movement* (Princeton, 1993).

"Feminism, class, and Islam in turn of the century Egypt," *International Journal of Middle East Studies*, 13 (1981), 394–407.

*Doumani, Beshara. *Rediscovering Palestine: Merchants and peasants in Jabal Nablus, 1700–1900* (Berkeley, 1995).

Findley, Carter. *Ottoman civil officialdom* (Princeton, 1992).

Fortna, Benjamin C. *Imperial classroom. Islam, the state, and education in the late Ottoman Empire* (Oxford, 2000).

Gelvin, James. *Divided loyalties: Nationalism and mass politics in Syria at the close of empire* (Berkeley, 1999).

Gerber, Haim. *Social origins of the modern Middle East* (Boulder, CO, 1987).

Hovannisian, Richard G., ed. *The Armenian people from ancient to modern times. II: Foreign dominion to statehood: The fifteenth century to the twentieth century* (New York, 1997).

İnalcık, Halil. "Application of the Tanzimat and its social effects," *Archivum Ottomanicum*, 5 (1973), 97–128.

*Keddie, Nikki, ed. *Women and gender in Middle Eastern history* (New Haven, 1991).

Makdisi, Ussama. *The culture of sectarianism. Community, history, and violence in nineteenth century Lebanon* (Berkeley, 2000).

*Mardin, Şerif. "Super-westernization in urban life in the last quarter of the nineteenth century," in Peter Benedict *et al.*, eds., *Turkey: Geographical and social perspectives* (Leiden, 1974), 403–445.

Marx, Karl. *The Eastern Question* (London, 1897, printing of letters dated 1853–1856).

Meeker, Michael. *A nation of empire. The Ottoman legacy of Turkish modernity* (Berkeley, 2002).

Orga, Irfan. *Portrait of a Turkish family* (New York, 1950).

*Palairet, Michael. *The Balkan economies c. 1800–1914: Evolution without development* (Cambridge, 1997).

*Quataert, Donald. "The age of reforms, 1812–1914," in Halil İnalcık with Donald Quataert, eds., *An economic and social history of the Ottoman Empire, 1300–1914* (Cambridge, 1994), 759–943.

Rogan, Eugene L. *Frontiers of the state in the late Ottoman Empire. Transjordan, 1850–1921* (Cambridge, 1999).

Seton-Watson, R. W. *Disraeli, Gladstone and the Eastern Question* (London, 1935). (Compare with Marx above.)

Sousa, Nadim. *The capitulatory regime in Turkey* (Baltimore, 1933).

*Zilfi, Madeline, ed. *Women in the Ottoman Empire: Middle Eastern women in the early modern era* (Leiden, 1997).

Zürcher, Erik. *The Unionist factor: The role of the Committee of Union and Progress in the Turkish nationalist movement of 1905–1926* (Leiden, 1984).

Turkey: A modern history, 3rd edition (London, 2004).

5   The Ottomans and their wider world

Introduction

The present chapter focuses on international relations and addresses two complementary aspects of the place of the Ottoman Empire in the wider international community. Thus, it explores the empire's relations with other states, empires, and nations, as well as its diplomatic strategies. The chapter offers a distinctive commentary on the global order through the Ottoman perspective. It first focuses on the changing place of the Ottoman empire in the international order, 1700–1922, as it declined from first- to second-rank status. It then examines the changing diplomatic tools employed in dealing with other states, particularly the shift from occasional to continuous methods of diplomacy. Another diplomatic tool, the caliphate, gave the Ottoman state a special religious instrument that it increasingly used for secular state purposes from the eighteenth century onwards. And finally, the chapter provides an overview of Ottoman relations with Europe, central Asia, India, and North Africa.

The Ottoman Empire in the international order, 1700–1922

The place of the Ottoman state and any political system in the international order is a function of many factors, sometimes demographic and economic power. A large and densely settled population is not always a certain barometer of political importance: consider the vast power of eighteenth-century Prussia with its tiny population and the political weakness of nineteenth-century China, the world's most populous country at the time. In the Ottoman case, a relative decline in the global importance of its population paralleled its fading international political importance. Between 1600 and 1800, the Ottoman population slipped from being one-sixth that of western Europe to only one-tenth and from about one-eighth to one-twelfth that of China. Its relative economic importance fell even more dramatically. Ironically, the Ottomans' peak of political power precisely coincided with the conquest of the New World by western Europe. This event clearly placed Europe on a separate trajectory from the rest of the world and shifted the balance of power westward from the Mediterranean world to the Atlantic economies.

Globally speaking, the Ottoman state in 1500 was one of the most powerful in the world, surpassed perhaps only by China. Then the "Terror of the World," the Ottoman Empire played a crucial role in the lives and deaths of many, quite different, states. The Ottoman Empire destroyed or outlasted the Mamluks of Egypt, the Safevids of the Iranian plateau and the Venetian Republic. It played a vital, formative role (see chapter 1) in the lifecycles of the Vienna Habsburgs and the Russian Romanovs until all three dynastic states vanished in the early twentieth century. The Ottoman state helped to define the kingship of Philip II of the Spanish Habsburgs as a crusading enterprise while exercising a less central but still key influence on the international politics of France. For the English monarchy, the distant Ottoman state was a more marginal concern.

By the eighteenth century, however, the "Terror" had become the Sick Man of Europe. Even so, as we shall see, the Ottomans remained high on the international agendas of Britain, France, Russia, Vienna, and the new states of Italy and Germany during the nineteenth century. In addition, the Ottomans were significant to the interests of many states in the Indian subcontinent, central Asia as well as North Africa. Between the Ottomans and their neighbors, from early times, there existed quite permeable frontiers with habitual diplomatic, social, cultural, and economic exchanges across them. For example, merchants with their goods moved routinely in both directions across these boundaries and the quantities exchanged became increasingly large over time (see chapter 7). European artists, architects, scientists, and soldiers of fortune frequented the Ottoman capital in search of employ in the court of the sultan and ranking notables. To give a fifteenth-century example of these cultural exchanges, recall the fine portrait of Sultan Mehmet the Conqueror by the Renaissance Venetian painter, Gentile Bellini. Three centuries later, Mozart captured this fluidity well in his opera, *Escape from the Seraglio*. His hero, Belmonte, disguised himself as a Spanish architect in order to enter the sultan's palace and find his lost beloved. To the composer's Vienna audiences, west Europeans in Istanbul were a familiar image. Istanbul, Vienna, Rome, and Paris all were attractive destinations for those seeking work and favor in the courts of the great.

Diplomatic activity is another measure of frequent exchanges across frontiers. Emissaries, on missions of greater and briefer durations and importance, commonly crossed the Ottoman frontiers in both directions. During the sixteenth century, for example, representatives of the sultans and of the French and Hapsburg rulers visited one another's courts to seek advantage, redress grievances and negotiate possibilities of peace and war. Two centuries later, we can count the number of diplomatic exchanges as an indicator of the tempo and pace of the cross-frontier contacts in the centuries preceding continuous, "modern" diplomacy. Thus, between 1703 and 1774, the Ottomans signed sixty-eight recorded treaties or agreements with other sovereign entities, each requiring at least a single diplomatic mission in one direction or the other. Hence, during the reign of Sultan Ahmet III (1703–1730), twenty-nine treaties or agreements were signed, including three with the Nogai Tatars and one with Iran, while Sultan Mahmut I (1730–1754) signed thirty agreements, including four with Iran and two with the Dey of Algiers (a nominal vassal of the sultan). Thus, taking the eighteenth century as our example, there clearly were frequent diplomatic contacts between the Ottoman Empire and the wider world prior to the emergence of modern diplomacy.

From occasional to continuous methods of diplomacy

A major, worldwide shift took place in the conduct of diplomacy, beginning in the Italian peninsula during the Renaissance period. While in many respects the Ottoman state participated in the changes in diplomacy from an early date, the turning point probably did not occur until the nineteenth century, when patterns and trends that had been evolving slowly came together. In sum, Ottoman diplomacy became continuous only at a relatively late date.

In the more distant past, diplomacy fairly could be characterized as ad hoc, intermittent, non-continuous, and personally highly dangerous. Seeking to conduct negotiations for a specific purpose, a ruler (in this case the sultan) assembled a specially formed mission, usually consisting of trusted government servants. Gathering the individuals together, the ruler issued directives and letters of introduction as well as the missives to be delivered. The emissaries went on their journey, arrived at the foreign court, negotiated, and returned with the results. When the group left the foreign court, the diplomatic contact between the two states ended. Thus diplomacy between states functioned only sporadically, during the weeks and months of these embassies. To personalize this pattern, consider the career of Ahmet Resmi Efendi (1700–1783). He began state service as a clerk and, after twenty-five years, was sent on a four-month mission to Vienna, on the occasion of the accession of Sultan Mustafa III. His visit ended in 1758, and he returned to Istanbul where he entered the financial offices of the state. He is somewhat unusual in that he went on more than one mission for his ruler. Thus, in 1764–1765, he traveled to Berlin, unsuccessfully offering Frederick the Great an alliance with the Ottoman state. This type of diplomacy personally was highly risky and could result in imprisonment and even execution (but not for Ahmet Resmi). While such methods of diplomacy in general provided no principles of protection for emissaries, those to the Ottoman court received some because the Prophet Muhammad's behavior allegedly provided the precedent for the protection of persons sent on diplomatic missions. Still, diplomats sent to Istanbul were held responsible for their sovereign's behavior and many ended up in the Seven Towers prison (until Selim III, 1789–1807, halted the practice).

During the period of so-called "pre-modern" international relations, the Ottoman state generally employed unilateral diplomacy, that is, at the will of the sultan. There are many examples regarding Venice, the Hapsburg Empire, and Poland in which the sultan unilaterally granted peace or trade concessions at his own discretion. Such unilateral actions were standard practices in "pre-modern" diplomacy; they also can be understood to reflect the Ottoman Empire's power at the time. And yet, Ottoman diplomacy sometimes possessed a certain bilateral quality. Back in the sixteenth century, for example, Süleyman the Magnificent treated King Francis I of France as an equal, addressing him with the title of "padishah." Also, the Ottomans granted certain reciprocal rights in peace settlements that lent them a bilateral character, dependent on the continuing consent of both the Ottoman ruler and the other party, whether it be the Habsburg emperor or the Venetian Senate.

In "pre-modern" diplomacy, a condition of war between nations was assumed to prevail unless specifically stated otherwise. There was no recognized condition of peace, only halts in the fighting. Sultans therefore felt at liberty to resume fighting at will and without warning. In the Ottoman world, this notion of permanent war found its theoretical justification in the Islamic division of the world between the House of War and the House of Islam. It needs to be stressed that the same notion of permanent war prevailed elsewhere, for example, in China and Europe, where it received different legal justifications. Until 1711, agreements to end fighting with European states were limited to one, two, five, seven, eight, twenty, or twenty-five years of peace. Eternal peace first appeared in the 1711 Treaty of Pruth, but the 1739 Peace of Belgrade with Vienna relapsed to the earlier system and limited the peace to twenty-seven moon years.

The so-called capitulations played a vital role in Ottoman international relations, governing the treatment of foreigners who happened to be residing, for however long, within the sultanic domains. The concept of capitulations, based on the idea that each state possessed its own laws too exalted for others to enjoy, was not uniquely Ottoman, and prevailed elsewhere in the world, for example in China. Hence, only Ottoman subjects normally could benefit from Ottoman law. The ruler granted capitulations to foreigners in a unilateral, non-reciprocal, manner. Although Sultan Süleyman the Magnificent usually is credited with initiating the practice, recent scholarship suggests that negotiations during his reign were not completed and it was his son Selim II who likely granted the first capitulations, to France, in 1569. In a unilateral act of generosity, friendship, and favor, and because the sultan wanted or needed certain commodities, he allowed the French king's subjects to travel in the Ottoman lands under the king's own laws, outside of the sultan's legal and fiscal jurisdiction. This act, intended to benefit the Ottoman state, lapsed on the death of the sultan granting it. (Their limited character faded in 1740 when, in gratitude for diplomatic aid, capitulations to the French were made permanent.) A capitulation meant that all subjects of a foreign monarch and citizens of republics such as Venice remained under the laws of their own king or republic once the capitulatory favor had been granted. Otherwise, foreigners inside the empire had no legal protection. Persons with capitulatory status also enjoyed full exemption from Ottoman taxes and customs duties. Not surprisingly, capitulations proved popular and were requested by other Western states, especially England and Holland. Harmless enough in the sixteenth-century era of Ottoman power, they came to dangerously undermine its sovereignty later on.

As the Ottoman Empire weakened, European states twisted the capitulations into something they had never been intended to be. In the sixteenth century, only small numbers of merchants obtained these legal and tax immunities. By the eighteenth century, however, large numbers of foreigners within the empire advantageously did business thanks to these tax exempting privileges. Still worse, many Ottoman non-Muslim subjects obtained certificates (*berats*), granting them the tax privileges and benefits of Europeans who had capitulatory status, including exemption from the jurisdiction of the Ottoman courts. Again and again, Ottoman policy-makers sought to eliminate the capitulatory regime and its abuses, but failed to do so because of European opposition. Finally, during World War I, and over the protests of its German ally, the Young Turk leaders unilaterally suspended the capitulations. These finally were abolished in the Turkish Republic in 1923 but continued in Egypt until the late 1930s.

"Modern diplomacy," a different form of regulating relations among states and of conducting international relations, had emerged during the late Renaissance as a way of dealing with the incessant warfare of the many principalities in the Italian peninsula. From there, modern diplomacy spread to west and central Europe by the time of the Peace of Westphalia in 1648 and thereafter to the rest of the world. This mode of inter-state relations and diplomacy is continuous and reciprocal and rests on notions of reciprocity, extraterritoriality, and equality of sovereignty: no matter how weak or strong, each state is equal to the next when they meet on matters of international relations. The emergence of modern diplomacy coincided, more or less, with the decline in Ottoman military power and, in the later centuries, became an important tool in the Ottoman arsenal of survival.

During the negotiations for the Karlowitz treaty in 1699 and again in 1730, the Ottomans accepted French mediation on their behalf. By the late eighteenth century, Ottoman policy-makers not only accepted but actively sought mediation as well as defensive treaties of alliance. Examples include the 1798 Russian, British, and Ottoman alliance against Bonaparte, as well the 1799 tripartite defensive alliance with Britain and France. Until the nineteenth century, however, permanent diplomacy remained unidirectional as west, central, and east European states, but not the Ottoman, sent resident legations. The Istanbul government accepted European diplomats (whose reports back home are a marvelous source of Ottoman history) virtually from the time that resident missions were first developed in Europe. This refusal to send permanent emissaries may have reflected the older attitude, pre-dating permanent embassies, that only weaker princes should send a standing representative, not rulers of more powerful states. In any event, for a long time the Ottomans did not feel they needed permanent representation abroad. As seen above, reciprocity long had been present in Ottoman diplomacy and often existed on an ad hoc basis. For example, when an Ottoman subject was poorly treated in a state to which capitulatory privileges had been granted, there may have been consequences. More specifically, following the signature of the 1774 Küçük Kaynarca treaty, emissaries from the two sides traveled to their adversaries' capital conveying letters ratifying the treaty.

During the eighteenth century, as in the past, the Ottoman court treated foreign ambassadors as guests, paying their expenses and assigning them escort officers. This behavior has been interpreted as a refusal to recognize some aspects of the new state system, saying these guests were present by invitation and on sufferance but not by right. If so, the early eighteenth-century French government also was guilty of the same reluctance since the French court in 1720 paid for the transportation and the entire six-month stay of the Ottoman emissary to Paris, one Yirmisekiz Çelebi.

Sultan Selim III is credited for initiating reciprocal and continuous relations. Beginning in 1793, he established a permanent embassy in London and counterparts in Paris, Vienna, and Berlin within a few years. He also appointed consuls to look after commercial interests (such consulates apparently already had existed in different places after 1725). For a variety of reasons, Sultan Selim's efforts failed and diplomatic service at the ambassadorial (but perhaps not the consular) level was suspended in the 1820s.

The "modern" Ottoman diplomatic service began taking its definitive shape in 1821. In their dealings with foreigners, the Ottoman rulers had been dependent on translators, the so-called dragomans. These dragomans mainly were recruited from the Ottoman Greek community, which possessed considerable multilingual skills because substantial Greek trading communities did business in the Mediterranean, Black Sea, Atlantic, and Indian Ocean worlds. To a lesser extent, other diaspora communities with international commercial links, notably the Armenian, possessed similar language capabilities and supplied dragomans. With the Greek war of independence, the loyalty of Ottoman Greeks generally became suspect. The Greek Patriarch of Constantinople was hung and the Greek dragomans, who had been in positions of power and sensitivity, were seen as potentially disloyal. And so, in 1821, the Ottoman government established the Translation Bureau (*Tercüme Odası*) to develop a new source for the recruitment of translators and end its dependence on the dragomans. This Translation Bureau, which remained very small until 1833, assumed responsibility for translations from European languages. A seemingly minor office, it quickly became the major site of political prestige and mobility within the Ottoman bureaucracy. Personnel of the Translation Bureau rose to become among the most important bureaucrats of the nineteenth-century Ottoman Empire, as it increasingly integrated into the international state system of continuous diplomacy. Knowledge of European languages, especially French, became a key qualification for advancement in Ottoman state service and the best place to learn was in the Translation Bureau. For many, but not all elites, proficiency in French served not merely as a symbol of cultural modernity but became virtually its content. In the eyes of such individuals, modernity meant knowledge of European languages and the lack of such tools of knowledge (incorrectly) spelled backwardness and reaction.

Sultan Mahmut II (1808–1839) formally created the Foreign Ministry and, in 1834, set up the diplomatic apparatus to allow for permanent missions abroad. The timing seems crucial for the capital city had just escaped occupation by the Russians in 1829 and by the forces of Muhammad Ali Pasha in 1833. In this crisis, the armies had failed and only diplomacy remained to save the state. Thus, the group of full-time, salaried persons – dedicated solely to conducting diplomacy on behalf of the Ottoman state in foreign lands – owed its emergence to both long-term evolutionary patterns and the immediate crisis of the early 1830s. By the early 1870s, there were Ottoman embassies in Paris, London, Vienna, and St. Petersburg, legations in Berlin, Washington, and Florence/Rome and consulates in a number of states in North and South America, Africa, and Asia. In 1914, the central offices of the Foreign Ministry in Istanbul held about 150 officials. By then, there were eight embassies – in Berlin, Paris, Rome, St. Petersburg, Tehran, London, Washington, and Vienna. In addition, lower ranking diplomats served in eight legations – in Athens, Stockholm, Brussels, Bucharest, Belgrade, Sofia, Madrid, and The Hague – while more than 100 staffed the Ottoman consular service, not including commercial agents.

Most Ottoman diplomats derived from elite backgrounds. A school named Galatasaray Lycée (*Mekteb-i Sultani*), established in 1868, became the most important single source of Foreign Ministry officials. Instructors offered lessons, mostly in French, from a curriculum based on that of a French *lycée*. Students came from wealthy families, both Muslim and non-Muslim, and their attendance at the school served as a key vehicle for entry into Ottoman elite life.

Thanks to their privileged backgrounds and training, more than two-thirds of all Foreign Ministry officials commanded two or more foreign languages. As the century wore on, their knowledge of French became more important and that of Persian less so, while Arabic language skills remained stable. Thus, the content of elite education changed considerably and exposure to west European culture eroded mastery of Islamic Arabo-Persian culture.[1]

Service in the Foreign Ministry was a prestigious and much sought after career, a reflection of the importance of diplomacy in the life of the empire. The best and the brightest of those who entered state service chose the Foreign Ministry. Not coincidentally, the three leading Tanzimat Grand Viziers – Mustafa Reşit, Fuat, and Ali Pashas – who dominated the era had all been foreign ministers. And, within the foreign service, the west European posts – particularly Paris and London – were most prestigious, higher ranking than those in Iran, the Black Sea littoral, the Balkans, or central Asia. This hierarchy says a great deal about the values of the time and where cultural as well as political power resided.

Despite the dragoman crisis surrounding the Greek Revolution, Ottoman Greeks and Armenians remained important within the Foreign

---

[1] For a more nuanced view of the Galatasaray school, see Benjamin C. Fortna, *Imperial classroom. Islam, the state, and education in the late Ottoman Empire* (Oxford, 2000), 99–112.

Ministry. The same factors that had propelled them into the dragoman corps – the heavy engagement of the Armenian and Greek diaspora communities in commerce in Iran, the Mediterranean and Black Sea worlds, Europe, and South and North America – continued in force. Hence, they constituted a significant minority, some 29 percent, of all Foreign Ministry officials, a participation rate that is somewhat larger than the non-Muslims' share of the total Ottoman population during the later nineteenth century. Slightly over-represented in the Foreign Ministry as a whole, these Ottoman Christians nonetheless did poorly, in proportion to their numbers, in terms of holding the better positions. While some did head major embassies, they mainly ended up in the minor consular posts despite the fact that they were the best-educated group. In sum, they readily entered the Foreign Ministry but did not have equal access to promotion opportunities.

The caliphate as a special tool of Ottoman diplomacy

The Ottomans possessed an unusual tool – the caliphate – in conducting diplomacy. The position of caliph originated in the seventh century CE, when the title was bestowed on political leaders – at first elective and then hereditary – of the new Islamic states after the death of the Prophet Muhammad. By 1000 CE, the caliphs had lost their political power but the position continued. During the 1000–1258 period, the caliphs served in a highly prestigious but mainly symbolic role that bound the Muslim community together, regardless of who actually held real political power in the various areas of the Islamic world. In the eyes of most Muslim jurists, the caliphate had ended in 1258 when the Mongols sacked Baghdad and murdered the last caliph. In the Ottoman era, sultans occasionally used the title of caliph but the title had ceased to carry any real significance.

In the eighteenth century, however, a different kind of caliphal position came to occupy a minor place in the Ottoman diplomatic arsenal. The latter-day caliphate began to emerge during the negotiations over the Küçük Kaynarca treaty of 1774. At that time, Russia recognized the Ottoman sultan as caliph of the Crimean Tatars. This token gesture, implying a vague kind of Ottoman religious suzerainty, was meant to camouflage the actual severing of the centuries-old tie between the sultans and the Crimean khans. That is, the Ottoman–Crimean connection was broken but not totally since the caliphal title remained, however ambiguous it may have been. The Russians in return received recognition of their own form of religious claim, the right to build and protect an Orthodox church in Istanbul, a bridgehead they later used to massively interfere in Ottoman domestic affairs (see chapter 3). Other forces were working that promoted Ottoman usage of the new caliphal tool. On a general level, the Ottomans' military and political power abruptly and visibly collapsed in the 1768–1774 war, one of the worst defeats in their history. Equally dangerously, the growing Wahhabi state in Arabia offered a spiritual as well as military threat that jeopardized Ottoman administration of these distant provinces. Both the spiritual claims of the Wahhabi reformers as the heirs of true Islam and their early nineteenth-century seizure of Mecca and Medina seemed to undermine Ottoman legitimacy. Thus, the treaty of 1774, the continuing decline of Ottoman military power, and the Wahhabi threat all worked to fashion the caliphal position into a negotiating tool and means of bolstering the sultans' prestige. Essentially, the Ottoman rulers were able to make this claim to the caliphate because of their military prowess in past centuries, their longevity as a dynasty, their possession of the Muslim Holy Cities of Mecca and Medina, and because they remained the most powerful Islamic state to survive in the age of European imperialism. By the nineteenth century, large numbers of Muslims had fallen under British, Russian, and French domination in India, central Asia, and North Africa. The sultan began appealing to them and to his own subjects as caliph, as a rallying point for resistance and for loyalty. The caliphal idea – with all of its historic prestige and honor and evocation of earlier, better, Islamic times – indeed was most popular among central Asian and Indian Muslims, communities under attack by both Britain and Russia. Sultan Abdülaziz (1861–1876) already had adopted a pan-Islamic approach in his relations with other Muslim countries, appealing to a shared Islam as the basis for concerted action under his own caliphal leadership. But it was Sultan Abdülhamit II, ruling an empire that had become more Muslim than Christian in population since 1878, who most emphasized the caliphate.

Abdülhamit II first used the caliphal instrument during the Ottoman–Russian war of 1877–1878. The Russians earlier had crushed the central Asian Muslim states of Bukhara, Khiva, and Khokand, leaving the Afghans as a buffer between them and the British. After the Ottoman–Russian war began, the sultan sent a high level mission to Afghanistan to obtain help against their common Russian enemy. The emissary also visited British India where, in Bombay, Muslims gave him an enthusiastic welcome. For the rest of his reign, Sultan Abdülhamit II sent agents to work within these communities and strengthen his own position in this arena of Great Power politics.

Many Muslim heads of state, including the Uzbek khans, the Crimean khans, and the sultans of Sumatra in the East Indies acknowledged the Ottoman ruler as caliph. And they sometimes also recognized the

Ottomans as their temporal leaders. For example, the ruler of Kashgar in central Asia is said to have issued coins bearing the Ottoman sultan's name during the nineteenth century, while the Afghan emirs, acknowledging the sultan as successor of the true caliphs, agreed to read his name at the Friday prayer.

Although we cannot know how effectively the caliphate cemented the sultan's hold on his own subjects, it is clear that the caliphal appeal ultimately did not have a major impact on the loyalties of Muslims under the domination of Britain, France, and Russia. In 1914, the Ottoman caliph/sultan issued a call for a holy war (*jihad*) against his French, British, and Russian enemies, appealing to their Muslim subjects to revolt. In the end they did not, despite three decades of propaganda. Indeed many served, if sometimes unwillingly, in the armies of the caliph's enemies.

Ottoman relations with states in Europe, Iran, central Asia, India, and North Africa: relations with Europe

The Ottoman relationship with Europe changed considerably over time. It certainly was one characterized by war: between c. 1463 and 1918, the Ottomans fought at least forty-three wars and thirty-one of them were with the various European states. And yet, during this time of warfare, other, co-operative relationships existed, often hidden by the ideological divisions of the age. In the sixteenth century, the Pope and other Christian theologians still thought of the broader European world as being divided into the lands of Islam under the Ottomans and the Christian world, the *respublica Christiana*. The latter term meant that all Latin Christian states, but not including those of Orthodox Christianity, were part of a single, theoretically unified community, despite the fact they spoke different languages and were under the rule of different monarchs. This *respublica Christiana* notion was dying in the sixteenth century, alive only in the minds of theologians and a few others, being replaced by the concept of nation states, loyalty to which became more important than vague sentiments of Christian unity. For example, in the sixteenth century, the French king pursued policies to enhance the power of his state, at the expense of the rest of the Christian world. And so Francis I synchronized his foreign policy with that of the Ottomans, but very carefully avoided entering into an official alliance. One season, when it was battling with the Habsburgs who were also his enemy, Francis allowed the Ottoman fleet to winter on his south coast, the present day Riviera. For that he was roundly but ineffectually vilified. (Recall that during Süleyman the Magnificent's reign occurred the first negotiations for granting a capitulation to the King of France.) Compare Francis' caution in dealing with his *de facto* Ottoman ally and events that occurred a century and a half later. In 1688, another French king, Louis XIV, felt able to attack a fellow European Christian state, the Habsburg, at the very moment it was fighting the Ottomans. Louis received some mild rebukes but generally his actions were seen as the normal business of state. His decision marks a turning point in the evolution of the inter-state system, in Ottoman–west European relations, and the final collapse of the *respublica Christiana* ideal. Louis had shifted his policies abruptly. Just a few years before, he had sent troops to help the Habsburgs *against* the Ottoman forces at the battle at St. Gotthard (1664) and similarly had aided Venice in its fight against the Ottomans on Crete. So, 1688 clearly marks the presence of *raison d'état*, the principle that any behavior to protect a state was justified, as well as the more visible role of the Ottomans in the European balance of power, and the disappearance of the *respublica Christiana*.

Thus, in the Karlowitz negotiations of 1699 and those for the 1730 Peace of Belgrade, the French actively mediated on behalf of the Ottomans to prevent the Habsburgs from becoming too successful and upsetting the European balance of power. As the eighteenth century proceeded, west European–Ottoman relations evolved still further. The Ottomans signed formal alliances and actively fought in Egypt with one west European state, Britain, against another, France. By the mid nineteenth century, active military co-operation no longer seemed strange and during the Crimean war of 1853–1856 the Ottomans, British, and French all fought together against Russia. In 1856, the Ottoman Empire entered the "Concert of Nations," a formal recognition of their transformation from antagonist to participant in the European state system.

One final word: while in a true sense the Ottoman state operated as one among many, using diplomacy and war in the European political arena, it nonetheless remained unique. As other states on the continent came to define themselves, they increasingly considered the Ottoman Empire to be an alien body, an "encampment on European soil." But at the very same moment, some of them were allied with the Ottomans in a war. The legacy survives to the present; in part for this reason, I believe, the European Union continues to struggle with the application of Turkey, an important Ottoman successor state, for full membership (see chapter 10).

Relations with Iran and central Asia

West, central and east Europe, although certainly an important and intense site of Ottoman diplomacy, were not the only regions in which Ottoman diplomats conducted their business. Active diplomacy persisted for centuries with states in central Asia, Iran, India and, to the west,

North Africa. For example, between 1700 and 1774, Iranian monarchs sent embassies to the Ottoman state on eighteen separate occasions. Despite their frequency and their importance, these relationships largely have been overlooked in scholarly publications on Ottoman history.

As in earlier times, the Ottoman sultans during the eighteenth century intermittently established diplomatic ties with the rulers at Samarkand, Bukhara, Balkh, and Khiva in the borderlands between Iran and central Asia. Often, the one or the other sent emissaries on the occasion of an accession to the throne or to discuss attacks on common enemies, first the Iranians but in later centuries, the Russians. Very often, the emissaries of Muslim states to the Ottoman court included pilgrimage to the Holy Cities in their itinerary. For example, an Uzbek khan sent an ambassador to Sultan Mustafa II who in the meantime had been dethroned. So the emissary presented his credentials and gifts to Sultan Ahmet III in 1703, went on the pilgrimage and in 1706 returned home. Another emissary quickly followed, sent by the succeeding khan to announce his own accession and congratulate Ahmet III. This person also made the pilgrimage before returning. During the early 1720s there were two additional Uzbek embassies but then none until 1777. Diplomatic contacts with the Khiva Uzbek khans of the Aral Sea area dated from the second half of the sixteenth century. The 1683 debacle at Vienna prompted an embassy to discuss the possibility of aid, while there were other embassies in 1732, 1736, and 1738. The catastrophe of Küçük Kaynarca in 1774 also sparked a flurry of diplomacy between the Ottoman and central Asian rulers, who all feared continued Russian expansion. The Uzbek khan at Bukhara sent two emissaries in 1780; one died in Konya after making the pilgrimage but the other returned safely. Sultan Abdülhamit I sent valuable gifts along with his credentials (in Persian) to the Bukhara ruler. This mission and several to the Kazakh khans and to the Kirgiz were part of his grand diplomatic offensive to gain support for the retaking of the Crimea. One of the sultan's emissaries to Bukhara, in 1787, then traveled to Afghanistan and, in 1790, re-established relations between the Ottoman and Afghan rulers.

Relations with rulers in India

Rulers from various states in the Indian subcontinent regularly dispatched emissaries to Istanbul during the fifteenth to seventeenth centuries, often on the occasion of their accession. There is a famous, perhaps apocryphal, story of a letter from the great Moghul Emperor Humayun to Süleyman the Magnificent in 1548. Many states in India, including the Moghul, sent emissaries during the eighteenth century, for example, in

1716, 1722, and 1747, often to obtain Ottoman aid in wars against Iran. A ruler on the Malabar coast ordered an emissary to Istanbul in 1777, seeking help against local Zoroastrian enemies. He sent two elephants as a gift, via Suez. One died en route but the other was presented to the sultan and lived out its days in the Ottoman capital. In 1780, the sister of a south Indian ruler arrived, asking for Ottoman help against the Portuguese and the English. Sultans Abdülhamit I and Selim III both concluded frequent political and commercial agreements with the Mysore sultanate in southern India, then enmeshed in the middle of the French–British struggle for the subcontinent. On one occasion, the Mysore ruler, Tipu Sultan, requested Ottoman intercession since, temporarily, they were allies of the British against Bonaparte in Egypt. Thus, at a moment at the end of the eighteenth century, Ottoman–British diplomacy was working both in the eastern Mediterranean and in the Indian subcontinent.

Relations with North African states

Political relations between Istanbul and the western North African states changed considerably over time. In the sixteenth century, the areas just east of Morocco had been provinces under direct control, but after local military commanders seized power during the seventeenth century, they became vassal states of varying sorts. Overall, Ottoman diplomacy in the region either sought to regulate the behavior of their nominal vassals or mediate in struggles among the vassals or between one of these and the neighboring sultanate of Fez, in modern Morocco. The North African states had found an important source of income in piracy and made their livings preying on shipping. The 1699 Karlowitz treaty, however, required Istanbul to more energetically protect signatories' ships from attacks by North African corsairs. Thus forced to take action against his own vassals, Sultan Ahmet III in 1718 coerced the Dey of Algiers into halting his attacks on Austrian shipping. As mediators, the Ottomans often intervened in disputes between Fez and the Algerians, for example, in 1699. To obtain military supplies and political aid, the Moroccan sultan sent gifts to Istanbul in 1761, 1766, and 1786. In 1766, he was seeking support against French attacks but in 1783 he inquired as to what kind of aid he might offer in the Ottomans' own struggle against the Russians. At this same moment, his Algerian rivals also were sending gifts to Sultan Abdülhamit I.

A fascinating example of Ottoman diplomacy in the western Mediterranean occurred in the late eighteenth century. Recall that in the 1768–1774 war, the Russians had sailed from the Baltic Sea, into the Mediterranean, and into the Aegean Sea, to destroy the Ottoman fleet at Çeşme.

(They also burned Beirut.) When the second war with Czarina Catherine erupted, the sultan appealed to the Moroccan ruler to block Gibraltar and keep out the Russians while, in 1787–1788, an Ottoman legation negotiated with Spain to achieve the same goal.

Suggested bibliography

Entries marked with a * designate recommended readings for new students of the subject.

*Aksan, Virginia. "Ottoman political writing, 1768–1808," *International Journal of Middle East Studies*, 25 (1993), 53–69.

Anderson, M. S. *The Eastern Question* (New York, 1966).

Cassels, Lavender. *The struggle for the Ottoman Empire, 1717–1740* (New York, 1967).

*Deringil, Selim. *The well protected dominions* (London, 1998).

Farooqhi, Naimur Rahman. *Mughal–Ottoman relations* (Delhi, 1989).

Findley, Carter. *Ottoman civil officialdom* (Princeton, 1992).

Heller, Joseph. *British policy towards the Ottoman Empire, 1908–1914* (London, 1983).

Hurewitz, J. C. *The Middle East and North Africa, a documentary record. I: European expansion, 1535–1914*, 2nd edn (New Haven and London, 1975).

Itzkowitz, Norman and Max Mote. *Mübadele: An Ottoman–Russian exchange of ambassadors* (Chicago, 1970).

Langer, William. *The diplomacy of imperialism* (New York, 2nd edn, 1951).

Marriott, J. A. R. *The Eastern Question* (Oxford, 1940).

*McNeill, William. *Europe's steppe frontier* (Chicago, 1964).

Panaite, Viorel. *The Ottoman law of war and peace. The Ottoman Empire and tribute payers* (Boulder: distributed by Columbia University Press, New York, 2000).

"Trade and merchants in the Ottoman-Polish 'Ahdnames (1489–1699)." *The great Ottoman–Turkish civilisation*, II (Ankara, 2000), 220–229.

Parvev, Ivan. *Habsburgs and Ottomans between Vienna and Belgrade* (New York, 1995).

Vaughan, Dorothy M. *Europe and the Turk: A pattern of alliances, 1350–1700* (Liverpool, 1951).

Wasit, S. Tanvir. "1877 Ottoman mission to Afghanistan," *Middle Eastern Studies* 30, 1 (1994), 956–962.

6 Ottoman methods of rule

Introduction

In its essence, the Ottoman state was a dynastic one, administered by and for the Ottoman family, in cooperation and competition with other groups and institutions. In common with polities elsewhere in the world, the central dynastic Ottoman state employed a variety of strategies to assure its own perpetuation. It combined brutal coercion, the maintenance of justice, the co-option of potential dissidents, and constant negotiation with other sources of power. This chapter examines some of the obvious as well as the more subtle techniques of rule that it employed to domestically project its power over the centuries. Significantly, it explores the actual power of the central government in the provinces. It suggests that the older narratives stressing an extensive amount of administrative centralization are overstated.

The Ottoman dynasty: principles of succession

At the heart of Ottoman success lay the ability of the royal family to hold onto the summit of power for over six centuries, through numerous permutations and fundamental transformations of the state structure. Therefore, we first turn to modes of dynastic succession and how the Ottoman dynasty created, maintained, and enhanced its own legitimacy.

Globally, royal families have used principles of both female and male or exclusively male succession. In common with early modern and modern monarchical France (where the Salic law prevailed), but unlike the modern Russian and British states, the Ottoman family used the principle of male succession, considering only males as potential heirs to the throne. Many dynasties employed a second principle of succession, primogeniture, by the eldest son of the ruler. The Ottoman dynasty departed sharply from the usual inheritance practices for almost all of its history. From the fourteenth through the late sixteenth centuries, the dynasty employed a brutal but effective method of hereditary succession – survival of the fittest, not eldest, son. From an early date, following central Asian tradition, reigning sultans sent their sons to the provinces in order to gain administrative experience. There, as governors, they were accompanied by their retinues and tutors. (Until 1537, various Ottoman princes also served as military commanders.) In this system, all sons possessed a theoretically equal claim to the throne. When the sultan died, a period between his death and the accession of the new monarch usually followed, when the sons jockeyed and maneuvered. Scrambling for power, the first son to reach the capital and win recognition by the court and the imperial troops became the new ruler. This was not a very pretty method; nonetheless it did promote the accession of experienced, well-connected, and capable individuals to the throne, persons who had been able to win support from the power brokers of the system.

This method of succession changed abruptly when Sultan Selim II (1566–1574) sent out only his eldest son (the future Murat III, 1574–1595) to a provincial administrative post, Manisa in western Anatolia. Murat III in turn sent out only his eldest son (the future Mehmet III, 1595–1603), again as governor of Manisa. Mehmet III in fact was the last sultan who actually administered as a governor (for another fifty years, eldest sons were named as governors of Manisa but never served). Thus, during those reigns, the Ottomans *de facto* conformed to the practice of primogeniture.

During part of the time that survival of the fittest operated as a principle of succession, so too did the bloody practice of fratricide. Sultan Mehmet the Conqueror (1451–1481) was the first to employ fratricide, ordering the execution of all his brothers. This requires some explanation since Ottoman society and Islamic societies in general vigorously condemned murder (as did contemporary Christian Europe). Yet in both Europe and the Middle East, an act that would have been immoral if committed by an individual person was permissible to rulers. Private persons couldn't murder but rulers could. Here, clearly, is the face of *raison d'état*. Machiavelli would have recognized himself in the following regulation (*kanunname*) that Sultan Mehmet issued to justify his fratricidal actions: "And to whomsoever of my sons the Sultanate shall pass, it is fitting that for the order of the world he shall kill his brothers. Most of the Ulema allow it. So let them act on this."[1] Thus, private individuals could not kill but the ruler could murder, even his own brothers, for the sake of order and stability in the realm. For more than a century, the practice of fratricide continued and, in 1595, after gaining the throne, Mehmet III ordered the execution of his nineteen brothers! The custom of fratricide really

[1] A. D. Alderson, *The structure of the Ottoman dynasty* (London, 1956), 25.

ended in 1648; thereafter, it happened only once again. In 1808, Sultan Mahmut II executed his brother, the only other surviving male, Mustafa IV, in order to preserve his own rule.

As the dynasty abandoned fratricide, it also shifted away from survival of the fittest to succession by the oldest male of the family. This practice (called *ekberiyet*) began in 1617 and prevailed to the end of the empire. Accordingly, on the death of the sultan, the oldest male – often an uncle or brother of the deceased sultan – assumed the throne. As succession of the eldest developed, the "gilded cage" (*kafes*) system began, in 1622. When the eldest male became sultan, the rest of the males were allowed to live, to assure continuity of the royal family. Accordingly, princes were kept alive, not actually in a cage but rather within the palace grounds, particularly the harem, where they were shielded from public view and under the eye and control of the reigning sultan. The royals, however, rarely received any administrative education or experience; typically but not always, time in the cage was not devoted to preparation for eventual rule. Moreover, only a reigning ruler was allowed to beget children. Sultan Mehmet III was the last ruler who, as prince, fathered children. Rule by the eldest male meant that a potential ruler might wait a long time in the cage before becoming sultan: thirty-nine years is the record. During the nineteenth century, those who ruled typically waited fifteen years and longer before ascending the throne.

It is crucial to connect these changes in the succession practices – survival of the fittest, fratricide, and rule of the eldest – to our earlier discussions of where power actually rested at particular moments in Ottoman history. The radical step of fratricide emerged just when the sultans had shed their status as *primus inter pares*, having won their long power struggles against the Turcoman notables and border beys. The later sixteenth-century policy shift from sending all the sons to just the eldest one, in order to acquire administrative experience, occurred as power was passing out of the personal hands of the sultan to that of his court. The adoption of rule of the eldest and the cage system, in turn, coincided with the transition of power away from the palace to the vizier and pasha households. Thus, Ottoman principles of dynastic succession changed along with the locus of power from the aristocrats, to the sultan, to his household, and then to the households of viziers and pashas. Sultans were needed less and less as warriors or administrators but remained essential as symbols and legitimators of the ruling process itself. The royal women played an indispensable role in maintaining and building alliances throughout the Ottoman elite structures and often were key players in the wielding of political power. In a sense it was irrelevant that so many sultans were deposed – nearly one-half of the total – since their position but no longer their person functioned as the indispensable component in the working of the system. In other words, sultans were needed to reign: ruling became the prerogative of others.

Means of dynastic legitimation

As the actual or symbolic leaders of the Ottoman state, the sultans employed a host of large and small measures to maintain their hold over Ottoman society and the political structure. The many daily reminders of their presence which they carefully and continuously offered suggests that their power derived not merely from the troops and bureaucrats they commanded but also from a constant process of negotiation between the dynasty, its subjects, and other power holders, both in the center and the provinces.

The Ottoman rulers used a host of legitimizing instruments to enhance their position, ranging from public celebrations of stages in the lifecycle of the dynasty to good works. At the moment a new sultan ascended the throne, an acknowledgment ceremony was held inside the Topkapi palace complex, where most Ottoman sultans resided between the fifteenth and nineteenth centuries. The new ruler then proceeded to the Imperial Council (*Divan*), presented gifts to this inner circle and ordered the minting of new coins, a royal prerogative. Within two weeks, a vital ceremony – the girding of the sword of Osman, the dynastic founder – took place at the tomb complex at Eyüp, on the Golden Horn waterway in the capital city. With much pomp and circumstance, the sultan left the palace and boarded a boat for the short journey up the Golden Horn. The tomb complex commemorated a companion of the Prophet Muhammad named Eyüp Ansari, who had died before the walls during the first Muslim siege of Byzantine Constantinople, 674–678. In 1453, the troops of Sultan Mehmet the Conqueror miraculously found the body of Eyüp and, on the spot, the sultan erected a tomb, mosque, and attendant buildings. On these sacred grounds occurred the sword girding, the Ottoman coronation, that linked the present monarch both to his thirteenth-century ancestors and to the very person of the Prophet.

The circumcision of a sultan's sons marked another milestone event in the lifecycle of the dynasty since it represented the successful coming of age of the next generation of royal males. Over the centuries, sultans celebrated these events with fireworks, parades, and sometimes very lavish displays. Frequently, to associate their own sons with those of the general populace, the dynasts, including Ahmet III in the early eighteenth century and Abdülhamit in the late nineteenth century, paid for the circumcision of the sons of the poor and other residents of the capital. In 1720,

Sultan Ahmet III held a famous sixteen-day holiday for the circumcision of his sons, celebrated in Istanbul and in towns and cities across the empire. The Istanbul event included the circumcision of 5,000 poor boys as well as processions, illuminations, fireworks, equestrian games, hunting, dancing, music, poetry readings, and displays by jugglers and buffoons. This same sultan, in 1704, held grand festivals to celebrate the birth of his first daughter, an event that recognized women's leadership role in the politics of the royal family.[2] In other ceremonies, the dynasty linked itself to the spiritual and intellectual elite of the state. For example, in the late seventeenth century, young Mustafa II's formal education under the tutelage of the religious scholars (ulema) was celebrated in a ceremony that demonstrated his memorization of the first letters of the alphabet and sections of the Quran. On other occasions, sultans sponsored reading competitions among leading ulema, thus further associating themselves with the intellectual life of these scholars.

Other devices weekly and daily reminded subjects of their sovereign and of his claim on their allegiance. Every Friday, at the noon prayer, the name of the ruling sultan was read aloud in mosques across the empire – whether in Belgrade, Sofia, Basra, or Cairo. Thus, subjects everywhere acknowledged him as their sovereign in their prayers. In the capital city, Sultan Abdülhamit II (1876–1909) marched in a public procession from his Yildiz palace to the nearby Friday mosque for prayers, as his official collected petitions from subjects along the way. Subjects were reminded of their rulers in the marketplace and whenever they used money. Ottoman coins celebrated the rulers, noting their imperial signature, accession date and, often, the regnal year. During the nineteenth century, new devices appeared to remind subjects of their rulers' presence. Postage stamps appeared, imprinted with the names and imperial signatures of the ruler and even, in the early twentieth century, a portrait of the imperial personage himself, Sultan Mehmet V Reşat (1909–1918). And, after the appearance of newspapers, large headlines and long stories proclaimed important events in the life of the dynasty, such as the anniversary of the particular sultan's accession.

In earlier times, artists had celebrated a sultan's prowess in paintings, depicting his victories in battle or otherwise courageously on the hunt or in an archery display. While these are familiar motifs well into the seventeenth century, the palace workshops producing them vanished, perhaps because the sultans were less heroic and more palace bound. The purpose and effect of such paintings, usually placed in manuscripts, is uncertain

[2] Tülay Artan, "Architecture as a theatre of life: profile of the eighteenth-century Bosphorus," Unpublished Ph.D. dissertation, Massachusetts Institute of Technology, 1989, 74.

Plate 1 Fountain of Sultan Ahmet III (1703–1730), Istanbul
Personal collection of author.

since, after all, they remained within palace walls, viewed by only the palace retinue.

The dynasty, using its personal funds, constructed hundreds upon hundreds of buildings for public use, all of them serving to remind subjects of its beneficence. Recall here that rich and powerful persons, not the state, provided for the institutions of health, education, and welfare until the later nineteenth century, when the transforming Ottoman state assumed this responsibility. Sultans and members of the royal family over the centuries routinely financed the building and maintenance of mosques, soup kitchens, and fountains – often in the capital but also everywhere in the empire. They financed these not from state monies but their own private purses (until the nineteenth century, however, the treasury of the sultan and of the state were really not distinguishable). They did so as pious acts and also to reaffirm their right to rule and thus retain the approval, gratitude, and finally obedience of the subject populations. Sultan Ahmet III, in 1728, financed the building of a grand fountain, outside of the first gate of the imperial Topkapi palace (plate 1). In the distant small town of Acre in northern Palestine, Sultan Abdülhamit II constructed a clocktower for the local population and placed his name on it as a reminder of his generosity. Also, during his reign, this sultan engaged in philanthropy to an unprecedented extent, widely distributing small-scale charitable contributions as a means of reinforcing the loyalties of his (presumably) grateful subjects. Sultans also financed the extraordinary imperial mosques that still dominate the skyline of Istanbul and other former Ottoman cities, for example, the sixteenth-seventeenth century Istanbul mosques of Süleyman the Magnificent and of Ahmet I and of Selim II in Edirne – taking care to name these after themselves. Thus, the dynasty inextricably was linked to the greatest places of worship in the Ottoman Muslim world. In the nineteenth century, Sultan Mahmut II continued this tradition, naming his newly built (1826) mosque "Victory" (*Nusretiye*) to commemorate his recent annihilation of the Janissary corps (plate 2). Royal energies and monies went in many other directions as well, for example, to build and support hundreds of bridges, fountains, and inns for travelers across the empire.

The sultans, who professed and maintained Sunni Islam, also took care to address the needs of their Shii Muslim subjects, competing with the Safevids to decorate the Karbala and Nejef shrines (that commemorated crucial events in Shii Islamic history) during the later sixteenth century, and continuing such support later on. In addition, the dynasty energetically asserted its physical presence in the Holy Cities of Mecca and Medina, reminding all of the connection between the dynasty and the Holy Places. There, prominent inscriptions proclaimed Ottoman largesse in repairing structures already nearly a millennium old, giving the dynasty a prominent place in the life of these Holy Places that it jealously guarded. In the late nineteenth century, for example, Sultan Abdülhamit II prevented other Muslim rulers from decorating the Holy Places, just as his predecessors had competed with the Moghul emperors in the sixteenth century. Similarly, the Ottomans sought to monopolize the provisioning of the local population in Mecca. The sultans also took considerable pains to assure the safety of the pilgrims traveling to Mecca and Medina to fulfill the sacred duties. As Ottoman military power continued to weaken, the regime emphasized its identity as a Muslim state in an unprecedented manner. As seen (chapter 5), the title and role of caliph began to emerge as an instrument of international politics in the later eighteenth century. During the first half of the eighteenth century, the sultans began taking particularly careful measures to protect and fortify the pilgrimage route from Damascus to the Holy Cities, building forts and bolstering garrisons. Wahhabi revolutionaries from Arabia, deliberately seeking to undermine Ottoman legitimacy, disrupted the pilgrimage during the

Plate 2 Interior view of Nusretiye (Victory) Mosque of Sultan Mahmut II
(1808–1839)
Personal collection of author.

eighteenth century and, in 1803, captured Mecca itself. Sultan Mahmut II then asked Muhammad Ali Pasha in Egypt to send his own troops, who temporarily broke Wahhabi power. Abdülhamit II, to enhance his caliphal title, facilitate pilgrims' travel, and bind the Syrian–Arabian provinces to Istanbul, built the Hijaz Railroad at the end of the nineteenth century. During World War I, British efforts to capture Mecca and Medina and disrupt the railroad aimed to undermine Ottoman prestige in the larger Islamic world, as had the Wahhabi attacks more than a century before (see chapter 5).

And yet, no reigning Ottoman sultan ever made the pilgrimage and visited the Holy Cities. Indeed, fewer than half a dozen members of the dynasty ever performed the pilgrimage.[3] Four were royal women, several of them wives of sultans. While in Cairo in 1517, Sultan Selim I received the keys to the Holy Cities from the Sharif of Mecca but, although quite nearby, did not visit the sacred places. In the early seventeenth century, Sultan Osman II announced his intent to make the pilgrimage but soon thereafter was killed. Shortly after his deposition in 1922, Sultan Mehmet VI Vahideddin visited Mecca, perhaps the only male Ottoman ever to have done so, but withdrew before performing the pilgrimage rites. How are we to understand this dynastic neglect of such a fundamental duty, one incumbent on all Muslims with suitable health and finances? In the time of Sultan Osman II, the ulema issued a formal religious opinion, saying that sultans needed to stay at home to dispense justice rather than leave the capital to go on pilgrimage.[4] At the time, the ulema opposed his rule and feared that Osman might have a secret agenda in planning a pilgrimage. So, this opinion in favor of a sultan not making the pilgrimage may have been quite idiosyncratic. In the end, the absence of the dynasty from the pilgrimage seems remarkable.

The Topkapi palace – residence of sultans from the fifteenth until the mid-nineteenth century – loomed as a closed place of power and mystery, projecting the awesome majesty that the dynasty sought to convey. It was a forbidden city, not dissimilar from that in Beijing but on a smaller scale. It was built as a series of concentric circles, one inside the other, with in-creasingly restricted access as persons passed through gates from the outer to the inner circles. The general public entered through the main gate of the palace into the first courtyard but no further. Those on official busi-ness passed into the second court to present matters before the imperial council (*Divan*), but no further. The third court was reserved for officials only while other sections were exclusively for the sultan, the royal family,

[3] Alderson, *Structure*, 125.
[4] My thanks to Hakan Karateke for his observations on this point.

and the necessary personal servants and retainers. As the state structures changed, so did the palaces. The Tanzimat sultan Abdülmecit abandoned Topkapi in 1856 for his extravagantly open Dolmabahçe Palace on the Bosphorus shores. The Yildiz palace of Sultan Abdülhamit II, further up the Bosphorus, in turn reflects that monarch's more private and reclusive nature.

Resting within the Topkapi palace (to this day) are sacred relics, the possession of which was intended to bring dignity and honor to their Ottoman guardians. Brought from Cairo in 1517 by Sultan Selim I, these included the mantle of the Prophet, hairs from his beard, his footprint, and other sacred objects, such as his bow. Also present are the swords of the first four caliphs of Islam. Significantly, the relics are situated inside the palace, a seat of political power. Here we have no less than the equivalent of a European monarch proudly owning a piece of the body of John the Baptist, or of the True Cross which the Byzantine emperor allegedly had found and brought to Constantinople.

Aspects of Ottoman administration

The *devşirme* method of recruiting administrators and soldiers – the "child levy" – was long gone by 1700 but deserves discussion here for the light it sheds on the stereotyping that remains all too prevalent in popular perceptions of the Ottoman past. The stereotype overemphasizes the importance of the *devşirme* and asserts that Christian converts to Islam were responsible for Ottoman greatness. As most overgeneralizations, this stereotyping emerges out of some realities. During the fifteenth and sixteenth centuries, *devşirme* conscripts indeed were an important source of state servants and many became grand viziers and other high administrators. Gradually, however, the *devşirme* was abandoned. Sultan Osman II tried to abolish it in 1622, indicating that it was becoming obsolete and dysfunctional. His successor, Sultan Murat IV, suspended the levy and it essentially had disappeared from Ottoman life by the mid-seventeenth century. The stereotyping comes from the coincidence of this diminishing use of the levy with another fact, namely, that the empire was declining in military power during these same years.

In fact, there are several false assumptions present here: the first surrounds the role of changes in domestic political structures in the observable weakening of the Ottoman Empire after c. 1600. For many years, observers falsely concluded that the evolution of the domestic institutions, the shift in power away from the sultan, *caused* the weakening of the empire in the international struggle for power. Historians, however, now have concluded that domestic political structures in the Ottoman

Empire were undergoing change between the sixteenth and the eighteenth centuries, a process that is better described as the evolution of Ottoman institutions into new forms. In their new forms, the institutions certainly differed from those of the past: sultans now merely reigned while viziers and pashas actually ran the state. But these differences in domestic institutions constituted a transformation, not a weakening, between the sixteenth and eighteenth centuries. The charges of weakness and decline stem from the international front where the Ottomans indeed were losing wars and territories. Internationally, the Ottoman system of 1750 was certainly less powerful than it had been in 1600; the relative international position of the empire had fallen quite sharply. Here is the real story of decline. Falling further and further behind Europe, the Ottomans shared a fate with the entire world but for Japan (and its rise of world power after 1853). The west (and some east and central) European states had become immeasurably stronger; the Ottoman Empire, which c. 1500 had been among the most powerful, fell to second-rank status during the eighteenth century. The transfer of power out of the sultan's hands occurred at the same time as but did not cause this international decline.

The second false assumption revolves around the now abandoned notion that the source of Ottoman state strength had been the (converted) Christians running it. When the *devşirme* faded, the argument went, so did the power of the state because Muslims and no longer the ex-Christians now were in charge. In this argument, the conclusion is drawn, quite mistakenly, that the one caused the other – Ottoman greatness derived from the *devşirme* and its abandonment triggered the decline of the Ottoman Empire. In this blatant example of cultural and religious prejudice, Christians are seen as innately superior to Muslims who falsely are seen as incapable of managing a state.

The decline of the *devşirme* and the transformation of the Ottoman state – which both occurred between c. 1450 and 1650 – more productively can be considered as a function of the dynamics of the Ottoman political system in two distinct but related ways. First of all, the early Ottoman state exhibited an extreme social mobility, with few barriers to the recruitment and promotion of males. Growing rapidly, the state military and administrative apparatus desperately needed staffing and offered essentially all comers the opportunity for wealth and power. As a part of that fluid process, the *devşirme* brought in recruits fully dependent (theoretically) on the ruler, at least during the first few generations. Over time, the growing ranks of state servants were drawn from a number of sources. Some derived from the first generation of *devşirme* recruits; others came from the descendants of recruits from earlier generations who had aged in Ottoman service, fathered families, and arranged for the entry of their sons into the military or bureaucracy; and, third, there were many soldiers and bureaucrats who had entered via other channels, for example, the households of Istanbul-based viziers and pashas. Over time, the latter two groups numerically increased in importance; that is, as the political system matured, it furnished its own replacements from within, rendering the *devşirme* unnecessary.

Second, consider the gradual abandonment of the *devşirme* as a part of the process in which power shifted away from the person of the sultan, to his palace, and then to the vizier and pasha households of Istanbul, respectively during the periods c. 1453–1550, 1550–1650, and after 1650. Since only sultans had access to the recruits of the *devşirme* system, its decline derived from the sultans' loss in power within the system. This shift away from the *devşirme* and from the education of recruits in the sultanic palace already was visible in the mid-sixteenth century, at the height of the sultan's personal power. At that time, some state servants already were training palace pages in their own households; these later entered the imperial household and subsequently became high-ranking provincial administrators (*sancakbeyi* or *beylerbeyi*). In the seventeenth century, young men more usually entered palace service via patrons who were ranking persons in the civil or military service. Thus, the *devşirme* and palace system declined and households of viziers, pashas, and high level ulema arose with organizational structures closely resembling the sultan's household. These latter, however, could not recruit *devşirme* – a sultanic prerogative – and instead recruited young slaves or the sons of clients, or allies, or others wanting to enter. Such vizier, pasha, and high ulema households slowly gained prominence, providing persons with varied experiences in the many military, fiscal, and governing responsibilities needed for administrative assignments. Offering recruits with more flexible and varied backgrounds than the *devşirme*, they successfully competed with the palace. By the end of the seventeenth century, vizier–pasha household graduates held nearly one-half of all the key posts in the central and the provincial administration.

To shore up their own power throughout the eighteenth, nineteenth, and twentieth centuries, the sultans routinely married their royal daughters, sisters, and nieces to important officials in state service. In this way, they maintained alliances and reduced the possibility of rival families emerging. Sometimes the daughters were adults and on other occasions infants or young children. Often, when the husbands died, the royal women quickly remarried, allying with another ranking official, thus continuing to help the dynasty. Marriage alliances continued as standard dynastic practice until the end of the empire. For example, in 1914, a

niece of the reigning sultan married the powerful Young Turk leader En-
ver Pasha.[5]

Center–province relations

The present section offers two different geographic examples of the relationship between the capital and the provinces during the eighteenth
and nineteenth centuries: the first from Damascus, 1708–1758, and the
second from Nablus, in northern Palestine, c. 1798–1840. While both
examples are drawn from the Arab provinces, they are intended to be
illustrative of the empire as a whole, suggesting the complex processes of
constant negotiation between imperial and local officials.

By way of background to the Damascus example, first recall the general
flow of events during the eighteenth and early nineteenth centuries. In the
international arena, until c. 1750, the central state enjoyed some successes
on the battlefield, winning back the Morea, defeating Peter the Great and
then the Venetians, and regaining the fortress center of Belgrade. Thereafter, disasters ensued, notably the Ottoman–Russian War of 1768–1774
and the defeats at the hands of Russia and Muhammad Ali Pasha during the 1820s and 1830s. In the domestic political area, Istanbul early
in the eighteenth century enacted some vigorous programs to gain better
control of the provinces, only to yield more power to the local notables
after c. 1750. In this latter period, Istanbul gave its provincial governors
more discretion, increasingly relying on notables as intermediaries with
the populace. Throughout the eighteenth century, however, shared financial benefits bound together the interests of the central and provincial
authorities. And then, near the turn of the nineteenth century, important changes in the visible instruments of control began to occur. Sultan
Selim III and, more successfully, Mahmut II, began to amass power at the
center and build a more centralized political system that sought greater
control over day-to-day life in the provinces.

Also, we need to touch upon the territorial divisions of the empire. In
the early centuries, Ottoman lands had been divided rather simply into
two great administrative chunks – the *beylerbeylik*s of Anatolia (the Asian
areas) and that of Rumeli (the Balkans), each under the eye of a *beylerbeyi*,
with subdivisions of districts (*sancak*s). By the sixteenth century, the administrative system that, speaking very generally, prevailed until the end,
was in place. Provinces constituted the major administrative divisions,
each with its own districts (*sancak*s) and sub-districts (*kaza*s). In each
unit were a variety of officials, each reporting upwards through the chain

---

[5] Artan, "Architecture," 75ff.

of command, finally to the provincial governors at the top of the pyramid. Generally, this administrative pattern prevailed until the end of the empire although, while the names remained the same, the size of each administrative unit decreased over time (map 6).

Center–province relations: Damascus, 1708–1758[6]

Damascus was a key Ottoman place and for this reason it became a center of Istanbul's attention during the first half of the eighteenth century. The story begins in 1701, following massive Ottoman defeats on the European frontier and a disaster in which 30,000 pilgrims on the Damascus–Mecca pilgrimage route died in bedouin attacks. Thus, the Treaty of Karlowitz and the destruction of the pilgrimage caravan made the need for change shockingly clear, both locally and in the center.

Istanbul then moved to revitalize the administration of Damascus in a number of ways. First, it entrusted the governor of Damascus with a number of powers that it previously had spread around among the various provincial administrators – granting him the right to collect taxes, maintain security, prevent revolts, and maintain urban life. The governor was to restore harmony to the Ottoman system, better protecting the subject populations so that they, in turn, could better finance the state and its military. In common with contemporary states everywhere, the Ottoman state's basic task was to assure a prosperous population in order to support the army which in turn defended the population.[7] Second, the capital dispatched a new governor in 1708, who originated in Damascus and possessed strong local connections, a member of the al-Azm family (which to the present has retained an influential voice in Damascene and Syrian politics). At the time of his appointment, he was recognized both as a part of the imperial elite in Istanbul and also of the local elite in Damascus. His connections to Istanbul were crucial and the capital considered the al-Azm appointee as its instrument. The al-Azms for their part pursued their own local interests but also functioned as part of an Ottoman circle, needing the patronage and protection of Istanbul to maintain their hold as governors. These Damascus events reflected part of a larger pattern in which the central state no longer generated its own elites to rule over the provinces but co-operated with local elites, sending them back to their home area to rule, on behalf of the central state. Thus, the al-Azm appointment marked the continuing evolution of Ottoman administration and the growing importance of local connections over palace training.

[6] Karl K. Barbir, *Ottoman rule in Damascus, 1708–1758* (Princeton, 1980).
[7] Ibid., 19–20.

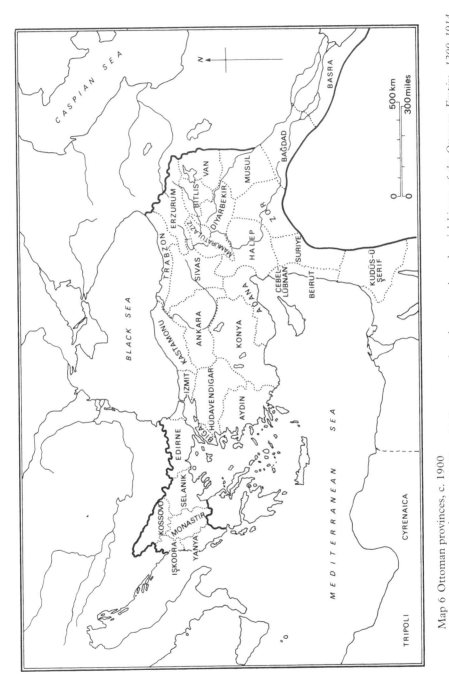

Map 6 Ottoman provinces, c. 1900
Adapted from Halil İnalcık with Donald Quataert, eds., *An economic and social history of the Ottoman Empire, 1300–1914* (Cambridge, 1994), xxxix.

This appointment represents other administrative changes as well, to turn to our third point. After 1708, the governor of Damascus no longer needed to serve in imperial wars and bring troops under his command to the frontiers. This redefinition of responsibility reflected the new eighteenth-century realities of an empire no longer expanding territorially and seizing new revenues. Rather, it acknowledged the new need to consolidate and more effectively exploit existing resources. Without military service, the governor thus lost an important path of promotion. Now marked as an administrator rather than warrior, the governor possessed more direct control and authority over a larger part of the province than ever before. Primarily sworn to keep law and order at the local level, and explicitly ordered not to go away on campaign, the governor became a localized figure in a novel and profound way. As a corollary, the rotation of governors in the empire overall decreased sharply in the early eighteenth century, an indication of the emphasis being placed on their successful discharge of local duties.

Four, with his knowledge of local conditions, the new governor, as part of Istanbul's effort to prevent the growth of autonomous structures in the provinces, sought to create more effective checks and balances among local notables, Janissary garrisons, bedouins, and tribes. He achieved this in a number of ways, including manipulation of the local judiciary. Ottoman law recognized four schools of Islamic law but the state officially had adopted the Hanafi rite. In Damascus, ulema of the Hanafi school increasingly obtained favor at the expense of the Damascus religious establishment, which followed the locally more prevalent Shafii school. Indeed, while the Damascus ulema until c. 1650 derived from the Shafii, Hanafi, and Hanbali schools of law, almost all were Hanafi by 1785. In this way, the state aimed to create a more homogeneous legal administration, more in line with principles being followed in Istanbul.

Fifth, the new governor acted to create greater safety for the *haj* pilgrims, a task given a much higher priority than in the past. And so he posted more garrisons, provided stronger escorts, and built more forts along the route to the Holy Cities. After 1708 and until 1918, the Damascus governor served officially as commander of the pilgrimage, part of the greater imperial commitment to solving problems within the region as well as to raising the profile of the state in matters of religion.

These programs of closer central control in Damascus province more or less worked until 1757, when bedouins plundered the returning pilgrimage and 20,000 pilgrims died of heat, thirst, and the attacks. This ended, until the nineteenth-century reforms, centralization efforts in the area of Damascus. Thereafter, local notables rose to greater prominence in the area. Famed among them, Zahir ul Umar launched and Jezzar

Pasha further expanded a mini-state in the area from north Palestine to Damascus. (Jezzar Pasha's beautiful mosque can still be seen in Acre, as can the nearby aqueducts that he built to boost Palestinian cotton production for sale to Europe.) Similarly, powerful provincial notables emerged almost everywhere during the later eighteenth century. For example, the Karaosmanoğlu ruled west Anatolia for most of the eighteenth century while, near modern-day Albania, Tepedelenli Ali Pasha controlled the lives of 1.5 million Ottoman subjects.[8]

Center–province relations: Nablus, 1798–1840[9]

Unlike Damascus, Nablus was not an important center but rather a hill town of modest regional significance. The Nablus story has two parts: the first centering on the period c. 1800 and the second dating from the 1840s. In its first part, we learn much about the nature of provincial life in many regions during the later eighteenth century when notable autonomy reached new levels and the writ of the central state sometimes was scarcely felt. And second, the case of Nablus reflects the intrusion of the nineteenth-century reforms beginning in c. 1840 into provincial life. Thus, it reveals the nature of political power during the early nineteenth century, the manner in which the state then operated. At Nablus (and across the empire), the central state fused with the local notables in a new way, making their power a part of its own authority. Here and elsewhere, Istanbul legitimated local elites by making them part of the new, centrally created institutions at the local level, and vice versa. The central government was being legitimated on the local scene (as the Damascus example also illustrates) *because* of the co-operation of the local elites who joined in centrally organized institutions, giving these credibility in the eyes of the local population. Here, then, is the mutually beneficial arrangement between capital and province that lay at the heart of Ottoman rule.

The first part of our Nablus story begins at the moment when Napoleon Bonaparte, after invading Egypt, marched northward into Syria and attacked Acre in 1799. To defend his provinces, Sultan Selim III sent repeated decrees ordering local military forces to gather and attack the invader. In this atmosphere, a local official in Jenin, near Nablus, wrote a poem exhorting his fellow leaders in the region to resist Bonaparte. Enumerating each one of the ruling urban and rural households and families, he praised them for their courage and military strength. However, not

---

[8] Also see above, pp. 46–50.
[9] Beshara Doumani, *Rediscovering Palestine: Merchants and peasants in Jabal Nablus, 1700–1900* (Berkeley, 1995).

once in this poem of twenty-four stanzas did he mention the sultan or Ottoman rule, "much less the need to protect the empire or the glory and honor of serving the sultan."[10] Instead, he referred to local elites, and to the threat to Islam and to women. As for the flood of imperial decrees into the area calling for action, he mentioned them only in passing, by saying that they came "from afar." How remote seem the awesome towers and walls of Topkapi.

How much control did the state have in this region? Seemingly little. It had such trouble collecting taxes in the Palestine area that it used the tour system. This method had been initiated by the al-Azm appointee to the Damascus governorship in 1708. Thus, a few weeks before the Ramadan month of fasting, the governor annually led a contingent of troops to specified locations in the Nablus area, physically and personally appearing to remind the inhabitants of their fiscal obligations to the state. Even so, the taxes were rarely paid fully or in time.

Within Palestine at large, autonomy varied considerably. When Istanbul called for soldiers to fight Napoleon, the leader of districts near Jerusalem appeared before its court and promised that he would provide a certain number of troops or pay a fine. But in more distant Nablus, leaders dragged their feet. See the frustration of the faraway Sultan Selim III:

Previously we sent a . . . [decree] . . . asking for 2,000 men from the districts of Nablus and Jenin to join our victorious soldiers . . . in a Holy War. Then you signed a petition excusing yourselves, saying that it was impossible to send 2,000 men due to planting and plowing. You begged that we forgive you 1,000 men . . . and in our mercy we forgave you 1,000 men. But until now, not one of the remaining 1,000 has come forward . . . [Therefore] we will accept instead the sum of 110,000 piasters . . . If you show any hesitation . . . you will be severely punished.[11]

In the end, the central state received neither the troops nor the money. But, it is important to note, Nablus leaders were not challenging Ottoman rule and, indeed, they fought against the French. But they were not going to surrender their autonomy and sought to guard their own economic, social, and cultural identity and cohesion against interference from the capital. Clearly, as this example shows, Istanbul in 1800 was no powerful force in the everyday affairs of Nablus.

To better understand the impact of central policies on Nablus life beginning around 1840, the second part of the story, we need first to consider the host of measures promulgated to extend state control into the

---

[10] Ibid., 17.
[11] Ibid., 18.

countryside across the empire. These included steps to increase its military presence, keep the population disarmed, revive conscription, and maintain the head tax. In the Anatolian (and some other) areas of the empire during the mid-1840s, survey teams enumerated the size and wealth of every household, including a staggering variety of livestock – sheep, goats, horses, cattle, as well as the income from agriculture, manufacturing and other activities. More broadly, the state launched efforts to count the population in the late 1840s (and, in 1858, codified the existing land legislation). By the end of Sultan Mahmut II's reign in 1839, local notables generally no longer acted independently of the center. Indeed, Istanbul often appointed formerly autonomous dynasts to other corners of the empire, for example, sending the powerful Karaosmanoğlu of west Anatolia to be governors of Jerusalem and Drama. Thanks to such changes, the central state became a more important element in local politics almost everywhere in the empire.

But the social, economic, and political influence of most notables remained substantial if not intact (also see chapter 4). The same local families who had dominated regional politics and economics in the eighteenth century continued in power, remaining until the early twentieth century and sometimes later. Former notables and their descendants continued to serve as regional officials, frequently on the new local councils created by the state. Later on, when other administrative changes made these posts unpaid, the continued domination by local elites was guaranteed since none but the wealthy could afford to serve. Also, recall that tax farming prevailed until the end of the empire, thus continuing local notables' sway in maintaining a crucial role in the local economy. They dominated the agrarian sector in other ways, for example, maintaining a choke hold on credit, both informal and formal, including the state-financed Agricultural Bank. Local and central elites thus both competed and co-operated in the extraction of taxes. In the later nineteenth century, cultivators' taxes supported local elites as they previously had and, to a greater extent than in the past, the central state elites as well. Thus, the negotiated compromise between central and provincial elites likely increased the overall tax burden of the average cultivator.

In 1840, Istanbul inaugurated a series of changes in the formal provincial administrative organization in order to win over the local notables and rule the provinces with and through them. Imperial legislation established a council for each province (*vilayet*) and district (*sancak*). Each respectively consisted of thirteen members, seven representing the central government and six elected by and from among local notables. The subdistrict (*kaza*) council would have five members, chosen from the local notables, including non-Muslims. Electors at the lowest, *nahiye*, level, were to be chosen by lot. Over each of the four levels, Istanbul appointed supervisory officials. In these provisions, Istanbul offered official recognition of local notables' participation in the new central administrative structures while seeking to gain more control over them. Thus, the 1840 changes did not break with the past but rather tried to redefine the terms of notables' involvement in governing.

In Nablus, the 1840 imperial edict concerning the councils touched off a prolonged round of intense negotiations over issues of central control and local autonomy, part of a long-standing tug of war between the center and the local elites. In this case, members of the local ruling group, who were the Nablus advisory council, negotiated with the central state as they had in the past. But there was a difference: the central state had become more aggressive and intrusive than before. The Jerusalem governor wrote to Nablus and asked the existing local council to nominate persons who would serve in the next council, asserting these must be drawn from both the Muslim and non-Muslim communities. The Nablus Muslim notables, who were running local affairs, asserted that the present membership of the council was the natural leadership of the area and so should continue without change. Moreover, they explicitly rejected the right of the state to help name the council and its leaders. Discussions dragged on for several months and ended in a negotiated compromise; the Nablus notables kept most of their autonomy but agreed to the inclusion of some new members. In this case of Nablus, council members did not seek to challenge the legitimacy of the new councils since it was a vehicle by which they, a (new) class of merchants and manufacturers in the town, had been given a formal voice in the political process. Thus, the centralizing state was able to insinuate itself more than before into local structures while local elites successfully warded off most of the effects of the centralization program.

These tense, sometimes combative, yet symbiotic and mutually beneficial relationships between the Istanbul regime and the local elites defined the new age of growing centralization. The trends displayed at Nablus in 1840 accelerated throughout the remainder of the Ottoman epoch, everywhere in the empire. Thus state control and interference in everyday life increased over the course of the century; the central bureaucracy grew by leaps and bounds and, in the age of Sultan Abdülhamit II truly was present in most corners of the empire. And yet, as a final example of Ottoman rule in Transjordan again reminds us, local groups successfully resisted these imperial encroachments. There, as a 1910 revolt clearly demonstrated, the writ of Istanbul remained limited. On the one hand, villagers and bedouin finally were compelled to pay taxes, at a level basically satisfactory to the capital. But, on the other hand, they successfully continued to refuse any form of registration and outright rejected military conscription as well as state efforts to take away their personal firearms.

Suggested bibliography

Entries marked with a * designate recommended readings for new students of the subject.

*Abou-El-Haj, Rifaat. *The 1703 rebellion and the structure of Ottoman politics* (Istanbul, 1984).

*Alderson, A. D. *The structure of the Ottoman dynasty* (London, 1956).

Artan, Tülay. "Architecture as a theatre of life: profile of the eighteenth-century Bosphorus." Unpublished Ph.D. dissertation, Massachusetts Institute of Technology, 1989.

*Atıl, Esen. *Levni and the surname. The story of an eighteenth century Ottoman festival* (Istanbul, 1999).

Barbir, Karl K. *Ottoman rule in Damascus, 1708–1758* (Princeton, 1980).

Barkey, Karen. *Bandits and bureaucrats: The Ottoman route to centralization* (Ithaca, 1994).

Bonner, Michael, Mine Ener, and Amy Singer, eds. *Poverty and charity in Middle Eastern contexts* (Albany, 2003).

*Doumani, Beshara. *Rediscovering Palestine: Merchants and peasants in Jabal Nablus, 1700–1900* (Berkeley, 1995).

*Faroqhi, Suraiya. *Pilgrims and sultans: The hajj under the Ottomans* (London, 1994).

*Fattah, Hala. *The politics of regional trade in Iraq, Arabia and the Gulf, 1745–1900* (Albany, 1997).

*Gavin, Carney E. S. *et al.* "Imperial self-portrait: the Ottoman Empire as revealed in the Sultan Abdul Hamid II's photographic albums." Published as a special issue of the *Journal of Turkish Studies*, 12 (1988).

*Hourani, Albert. "Ottoman reform and the politics of the notables," in W. Polk and R. Chambers, eds., *The beginnings of modernization in the Middle East: the nineteenth century* (Chicago, 1968), 41–68.

*Khoury, Dina. *State and provincial society in the Ottoman Empire: Mosul 1540–1834* (Cambridge, 1997).

*Özbek, Nadir. "Philanthropic activity, Ottoman patriotism and the Hamidian regime, 1876-1909." *International Journal of Middle East Studies*, 37, 1 (2005), 59–81

*Peirce, Leslie. *The Imperial harem: Women and sovereignty in the Ottoman Empire* (Oxford, 1993).

Penzer, N. M. *The harem* (London, 1965 reprint of 1936 edition).

Rogan, Eugene L. *Frontiers of the state in the late Ottoman Empire. Transjordan, 1850–1921* (Cambridge, 1999).

Zarinebaf-Shahr, Fariba. "Women, law, and imperial justice in Ottoman Istanbul in the late seventeenth century," in Amira El Azhary Sonbol, ed., *Women, the family and divorce laws in Islamic history* (Syracuse, 1996), 81–95.

The Ottoman economy: population, transportation, trade, agriculture, and manufacturing

Introduction

As the following chapter makes clear, history is not merely about leaders and politics but also the masses of people and their everyday lives. In the following pages, I tell about the ways Ottoman subjects earned livelihoods in the various sectors of the economy. This overview of the Ottoman economy is not a lesson in elementary economics, overflowing with statistics at micro- and macro-levels. Rather, it is designed to demonstrate how people in the Ottoman Empire made their livings and how these patterns changed over time. To achieve this goal, the chapter emphasizes a complex matrix that relates demographic information on population size, mobility, and location with changes in the significant sectors of the economy. After reviewing population changes, the chapter turns to the first sector, agriculture that, in 1700, was the dominant economic activity, as it was virtually everywhere else in the world. The chapter then turns to each of the other economic sectors in which people worked – manufacturing, trade, transport, and mining – in the rank order of importance just listed. As will become evident, although the economy remained basically agrarian, agriculture itself changed dramatically, becoming more diverse and more commercially oriented. In addition, Ottoman manufacturing struggled first with Asian, then with European competitors, yet obtained surprising levels of production. If these transformations did not lead to anything approaching an industrial revolution, they nonetheless did sustain improving levels of living until the end of the empire.

Population

The Ottoman state, before the late nineteenth century, counted the wealth of its subjects but not the people themselves. When examining its human resources, it enumerated only those responsible for the payment of taxes (household heads, usually males) or likely to be of military use (young men). Therefore, population size for a given area or the empire as a whole can only be approximated until the 1880s, when the first real censuses appear. But, while the actual numbers of people cannot be known, the general patterns of demographic change can be seen, and so let us begin with these.

In the early eighteenth century, about all that can be said with certainty is that the aggregate Ottoman population was smaller than it had been towards the end of the sixteenth century. It seems quite likely that the overall population declined in the seventeenth century, part of a general Mediterranean population trough. Moreover, as seen, the empire was declining in global demographic importance (chapter 5). Further, by 1800, the populations of the Anatolian and Balkan provinces were about the same whereas, in the seventeenth century, that of the Balkan provinces had been greater. And finally, it seems safe to say that, in the eighteenth century, the population of the Arab lands was declining, with very sharp drops after c. 1775. In the nineteenth century, by contrast, the population of all three regions – the Balkans, Anatolia, and the Arab lands – increased.

A few numbers here might be useful: the total population may have equaled some 25–32 millions in 1800. According to one estimate, there were 10–11 millions in the European provinces, 11 millions in the Asiatic areas, and another 3 millions in the North African provinces. Another estimate indicates the Balkan regions accounted for one half or more of a total 30 millions during the seventeenth and eighteenth centuries. In 1914, more certainly, Ottoman subjects totaled some 26 millions. To understand these figures, we need to consider that the territorial size of the empire had been much reduced – from a total area of 777,000 to 337,000 square miles (3.0 to 1.3 million square kilometers). Thus, while population totals in 1800 and 1914 were about the same, the densities approximately had doubled since the same number of inhabitants were squeezed into less than half the area they had occupied. Further, the demographic center of the empire remained in Europe, until quite near the very end. Population densities in Rumeli (the Balkans) were double those in Anatolia, while these latter were triple the densities in Iraq and Syria and five times those in the Arabian peninsula. To realize the demographic importance of the Balkan provinces, consider the following figures. In the 1850s, Rumeli held about one-half the total Ottoman population while, in 1906, the tiny Balkan fragments remaining in Ottoman hands still accounted for a full one-quarter of the total Ottoman population. Demographically, the Balkan provinces were crucial and their loss was a terrible economic blow for the Ottoman economy and state.

Ottoman subjects did not live very long: Muslims in Anatolia in the final decades of the empire averaged, from birth, a lifespan of twenty-seven to thirty-two years. If they managed to survive until the age of five, then forty-nine years was the norm. Similarly, inhabitants of early nineteenth-century Serbia lived an average of twenty-five years from birth.

In Istanbul, Anatolia (and perhaps the Balkans), Ottoman subjects did not live in multiple households of three generations of family – grandparents, parents, and children. Rather, they dwelt in simple or nuclear families, that is, with parents and children together and only rarely, the grandparents. Rural households in Anatolia were five to six persons in size. Households in three cities in the Danubian areas of the Balkans averaged 4.5 persons (in 1866). Istanbul households, at the end of the nineteenth century, averaged about four persons, probably the smallest in the empire. But (equally), fragmentary evidence suggests different patterns in the Arab provinces. Households in Aleppo and Tripoli (in Lebanon) were much larger than the urban figures just seen and held 7.5 and 5.5 persons (in c. 1908). And, at Damascus, one of the larger cities of the empire, residential patterns differed greatly from those in Istanbul. Four-fifths of Damascene households contained at least two generations and one-third of these held more than three generations! At the end of the nineteenth century, houses in Damascus often were quite large and more than one-half of these residences contained more than one family. Indeed, the Damascus multiple-family household averaged nearly three persons more than Istanbul households. The differences between the two likely derive from several factors. Notably, in Istanbul and Ottoman Anatolia, households generally divided on the death of the father while many Damascene households containing siblings continued after the parents' deaths. There were other factors. Polygyny rates were much higher at Damascus although, overall, polygyny among Muslims was not nearly as common as stereotypes would suggest. In the small Arab town of Nablus, 16 percent of the men maintained polygynous relationships while 12 percent of the Muslim men in Damascus did but only 2 percent in Istanbul. Overall, it may be the case that households in Anatolia, Istanbul (and perhaps the Balkans) were smaller and less complex than those in the Arab provinces.

As an example from Aleppo (and likely elsewhere) suggests, there was no visible difference in the structure of households among Muslims, Jews, and Christians, except for the fact that the latter two legally practiced neither concubinage nor polygyny. Divorce was permitted and not uncommon among Ottoman Muslims (and likely the other communities). Because of the need to maintain political ties and property, upper-class Muslim men and women divorced less frequently than did their counterparts lower down in the political and economic order.

A host of factors affected mortality rates, positively and negatively. Knowledge of birth control was widespread but its actual extent remains uncertain. The state passed laws against it in the later nineteenth century but this may have reflected growing official concerns as much as increasing usage. In Aleppo during the eighteenth century, abortion as a form of birth control was practiced but apparently not very frequently. To postpone pregnancies, extended nursing, lactation, commonly was employed while delayed marriage was frequent in late nineteenth-century Istanbul and likely other locations as well. Better sanitation and hygiene played a positive role in extending longevity thanks, in part, to a more activist state that, for example, established quarantine stations and hospitals during the later nineteenth century. Epidemic diseases were grave afflictions. Plague remained a major event in Ottoman society until the second quarter of the nineteenth century. In the capital, for example, plague struck repeatedly during the later 1820s, undermining resistance to Russian invaders not far from the city. In 1785, one-sixth of the population of Egypt died from plague. From the standpoint of disease, the clusters of people concentrated in cities were loci of infection that regularly were devastated. In most areas, urban dwellers formed perhaps 10–20 percent of the total population while, in Ottoman Macedonia, the proportion was an unusually high 25 percent. Plague-devastated cities were refilled by immigration from the countryside. Izmir, because it was a great port city in constant contact with the wider world, perhaps suffered more than average, with plagues recurring in more than half the years of the eighteenth century. Salonica, another port city, endured major eruptions of plague during twelve years of that same century. But how are we to understand a report that, in 1781, plague killed some 25,000 persons there? Such figures surely are incorrect since these represent 50 percent of the population of Salonica at the time. Instead of 25,000 dead, we should understand the report as saying simply that a lot of people died. More accurate death rates exist for the city of Aleppo because a European physician lived in the city during the later eighteenth century and personally counted and recorded plague deaths. Aleppo, an important center on the caravan routes, suffered eight major eruptions of plague, that lasted for fifteen years in the eighteenth century, and four more between 1802 and 1827. According to this physician's figures, deaths from plague, also called the black death, equaled 15–20 percent of the population of Aleppo in the late 1700s. Cities remained dangerous places not merely because of disease. Fire routinely ravaged entire neighborhoods because, in many regions of the empire, wooden houses prevailed. For example, in the capital city during the mid 1820s, a series of fires occurring in just over a week destroyed 21,000 homes!

Famines also took a severe toll. Famines often do not derive merely from natural causes such as bad weather and voracious insects. Quite often, perhaps most of the time, man-made factors that interfere with the distribution of food – including politics, bad transportation, and war – cause famine. Egypt suffered six famines between 1687 and 1731. But, thanks to improvements in transport and communication, they declined in frequency everywhere in the empire during the nineteenth century. Famine faded from many Balkan provinces in the 1830s while the last killing famine in Anatolia occurred four decades later, during the mid 1870s. Thereafter, crop failures in an area usually were offset by shipments of food from outside, thanks to steamships, railroads, and telegraph lines. During wars and other political crises, however, famine re-emerged as supply systems sagged and collapsed. Wars were terrible killers of Ottomans and vast numbers died on the battlefield and away from it as well, of wounds and disease. In this way, wars helped to reduce the male proportion of the population and upset the demographic balance between males and females. Wars, however, killed not only the fathers of the next generation but also its mothers, and vast numbers of noncombatant grandparents and children. Death came with the bullets and also malnutrition and its accompanying diseases. Wars appeared all too frequently in Ottoman history. These terrible killers raged in a full 55 percent of all the years of the eighteenth century and in 45 percent of all the years between 1800 and 1918. And finally, emigration also reduced the overall population. Over one million Ottoman subjects emigrated to the New World between c. 1860 and 1914. The vast majority, 80–85 percent, were Christians and many of these left after 1909, when conscription of Ottoman Christians was enacted. Moreover, the evidence suggests that since more males than females emigrated, the sex ratio of those remaining tilted still more heavily in favor of females.

During the nineteenth century, some clustering of population occurred in coastal areas, thanks to the rise of port cities to serve the growing international trade of the empire. Demographically, port cities grew far faster than the overall population. Most of them were deep-water harbors and closely linked to their hinterlands, at first by caravans and later by railroads. Three examples of port city population growth will suffice – one each from the Balkan, Anatolian, and Arab provinces. In the area of modern-day Greece, the port of Salonica rose from 55,000 persons in 1800 to 160,000 in 1912. On the western Aegean coast of Anatolia, the superlative port of Izmir held c. 100,000 inhabitants in 1800 (double the number of the late sixteenth century) and some 300,000 in 1914. Beirut, in modern Lebanon, grew from a small town of 10,000 in 1800 to a staggering 150,000 in 1914.

By contrast, the population of inland towns and cities often stagnated or declined. Sometimes the causes were political, such as in Belgrade where the population fell by two-thirds, from 25,000 to 8,000, during the civil strife of the early nineteenth century that accompanied the rise of the Serbian state. The number of Diyarbekir dwellers declined from 54,000 to 31,000 between 1830 and 1912 as its trade routes dwindled in importance. Ankara, also in the Anatolian interior, had been an important manufacturing center of mohair wool, cloth, and yarn. During the early nineteenth century, however, its monopoly faded and these activities disappeared because of international competition. But then Ankara became a railhead, the terminus of the Anatolian Railway from Istanbul, and its fortunes revived. And so, its population in 1914 was about the same as a century before, although it surely had dipped sharply during the years in between. Thus bare population statistics mask different stories of rising or falling populations of particular places.

Migrations affected population distribution throughout Ottoman history. These movements of peoples occurred for a host of reasons, economic as well as political. Among migrations for economic opportunity can be counted those to coastal Izmir by Ottoman subjects from interior regions and from the nearby islands in the Aegean Sea. There, and at Beirut, Alexandria, and Salonica, the new arrivals joined migrants from across the Mediterranean world – Malta, Greece, Italy, and France. Thanks to them, the port cities developed a cosmopolitan, multi-lingual "Levantine" culture, more a part of the general Mediterranean world as a whole than the Ottoman Empire in particular. Generally, economic migration to urban centers was a normal and important feature of Ottoman life. Workers often traveled vast distances to work in cities and, after several or more years, returned home, as did, for example, the masons and other construction workers who built the great imperial mosques of Istanbul during the sixteenth and later centuries. Also, to build railroads in the Balkan, Anatolian, and Arab provinces during the later nineteenth century, workers by the thousands came from afar as well as from nearby areas. And, in patterns that date back centuries and continued until the end of the empire, men trudged on foot for months from humble villages in eastern Anatolia to work as porters and stevedores in far away Istanbul, there setting up communal bachelor quarters. Others came from central and north Anatolian towns to serve as the capital's tailors or laundrymen. Like the porters, these remained for several years and were replaced by others from the same village. In the nineteenth century, ethnic Croats and Montenegrins traveled from their northwest Balkan homes to the coalmines at Zonguldak on the Black Sea, bringing along their long traditions of mining skills, and often settling permanently in the region.

In common with economically driven migrations, those for political reasons often were dramatic and still affect the area today. Take, for example, the demographic impact of the Habsburg–Ottoman wars, dating from the late seventeenth century and continuing into the eighteenth century. To escape the fighting, Orthodox Serbs migrated from their homes around Kossovo (southern modern-day Yugoslavia) in an intermittent stream northward. Until then, the Kossovo area had been heavily Serb but after they left, Albanians gradually migrated in, filling the empty spaces. Some Serbs moved into eastern Bosnia, where, consequently, a Muslim majority gave way to an important Christian presence. Other Serbs continued north and crossed over into the Habsburg lands, for example, after the Ottoman victories in the 1736–1739 war. Here, then, is the Ottoman background to the Bosnian and Kossovo crises of the 1990s.

Many of the other politically compelled migrations elsewhere in the Ottoman world were different in their origins and vastly greater in magnitude. These were triggered by two sets of events. In the first, Czarist Russia conquered Muslim states around the northern and eastern Black Sea littoral; the Crimean khanate was among them but there were many others. In the second, the Russian and Habsburg states annexed Ottoman territories or promoted the formation of independent states in the western Black Sea littoral and in the Balkan peninsula overall. As these processes unfolded, some Muslim residents fled, not wishing to live under the domination of new masters. Many more, however, suffered forcible expulsion by the Czars and the governments of the newly independent states. For both, the Muslims were enemies, undesirable "others," to be removed by whatever means necessary. As a result, Muslim refugees began flooding into the Ottoman world in huge numbers, beginning in the late eighteenth century. Between 1783 and 1913, an estimated 5–7 million refugees, at least 3.8 million of whom were Russian subjects, poured into the shrinking Ottoman state. For example, between 1770 and 1784, some 200,000 Crimean Tatars fled to the Dobruja, the delta of the Danube. Still more fled during the period around World War I; in 1921, for example, up to 100,000 refugees overwhelmed Istanbul, most of them from Russia. Many refugees fled once, then again, settling elsewhere in the Ottoman Balkans, only to leave again when that area became independent. Another example: some 2 million people left the Caucasus region, for destinations in the Ottoman Balkans (some 12,000 at Sofia alone), Anatolia, and Syria. The refugees either went voluntarily or by government design, for example, to populate the frontiers or the empty lands along the new railroads. In 1878 alone, at least 25,000 Circassians arrived in south Syria and another 20,000 came to the areas around Aleppo. In Anatolia, the government settled refugees, often with incentives, to people the areas along the developing Anatolian railroad. These refugees endured enormous sufferings: perhaps one-fifth of the Caucasian migrants died on the journey of malnutrition and disease. Between 1860 and 1865, some 53,000 died at Trabzon on the Black Sea, a major point of entry.

These migrations have left a profound mark, not the least of which are the bitter memories of expulsion that still can inflame relations between modern-day countries like Turkey and Bulgaria. Today, the descendants of refugees occupy important leadership positions in the economies and political structures of countries such as Jordan, Turkey, and Syria. The migrations acted like a centrifuge in southern Russia and the Balkans, reducing previously more diverse populations to a simpler one, and depriving the original economies of skilled artisans, merchants, manufacturers, and agriculturalists. The societies of the host regions, for their parts, became ethnically more complex and diverse while both the originating and host societies became religiously more homogeneous. Thus, the Balkans became more heavily Christian than before (although Muslims remained in some areas) while the Anatolian and Arab areas became more Muslim. Subsequently, following the expulsion and murder of Ottoman Armenians and Greeks during and after World War I, the population of Anatolia became more homogeneous in religion.

Over the 1700–1922 period, some urbanization occurred, and the proportion of the total populace living in towns and cities increased. There is fragmentary evidence of an earlier increase in urban populations during the seventeenth century and perhaps part of the next century, partly because of the flight to towns and cities that were safer than the countryside in politically insecure times. Also, as seen above, port cities grew sharply in the eighteenth century but especially during the nineteenth century. Further, ongoing improvements in hygiene and sanitation generally made cities healthier and more attractive places to live during the nineteenth century.

The population also became more sedentary and less nomadic between 1700 and 1922. During the eighteenth century, nomads dominated the economic and political life of some regions in central and east Anatolia and in the Syrian, Iraqi, and Arabian penninsula areas as well. On several occasions, nomads pillaged the pilgrimage caravans on their way from Damascus to Mecca and, generally, dominated the steppe zones of central and east Syria and points east and south. During the nineteenth century, the state successfully broke the power of many tribes. For example, it forcibly settled tribes in southeast Anatolia where vast numbers of them died in the malarial heat of their new homes. Elsewhere, too, it sedentarized tribes, forcing them into agricultural lives and reducing or altogether eliminating their ability to move about at will. Moreover, when the state settled the immigrant refugees, it often used them to create buffer zones of population between the older areas of agrarian settlement and the nomads, forcing these deeper into the desert. There is no doubt that the nomads' numerical importance fell sharply after 1800 (see also under "Agriculture" below). But, it is also true that tribes in some areas, including the Transjordanian frontier, eastern Anatolia and the region of modern-day Iraq continued to exercise considerable autonomy.

Transportation

A comparison of transportation methods during the more distant and recent pasts powerfully evokes the incredible changes that have taken place in the modern era. Until the development of the steam engine in the later eighteenth century, transport by water was the only realistic form of shipping goods in bulk. Sea transport by oared galleys in the Mediterranean world had given way to sailing vessels as the eighteenth century opened. Shipment via sailing vessels was vastly cheaper and almost always faster than land transport. Shipment by land had been prohibitively expensive because – except for the shortest distances – the fodder the animals consumed cost more than the goods they carried. Even the smallest ships of the early modern period carried 200 times more weight than the most efficient forms of land transport. But, unlike that by land, sea transport was wildly unpredictable because of changing weather, currents, and winds. Once embarked on a sea journey, there was no way to predict the day or even the week of arrival, never mind the hour. Under the sailing technologies that prevailed in the eighteenth century, the 900-mile journey between Istanbul and Venice, one of the main trade arteries, could take as short a time as fifteen days with favorable winds. But, in adverse conditions, that same journey lasted eighty-one days. Similarly, the 1,100-mile Alexandria–Venice voyage could go quickly, seventeen days, but it also could last eighty-nine days, five times as long. Thus in the pre-modern period, great uncertainty prevailed about shipping dates and arrival times. Moreover, sailing vessels were very small, tiny by modern standards. The typical merchant ship of the day was 50–100 tons, staffed by a half dozen crew members.

During the nineteenth century, water transport underwent a radical transformation thanks to the emplacement of steam engines that pushed ships through currents, tides, and winds. Predictability increased to the point that timetables appeared, noting exactly the scheduled departure and arrival of ships. Steamships first appeared in the Ottoman Middle East during the 1820s, not long after their development in Western Europe. Steam also brought about a vast increase in the size of the ships. By the 1870s, steamships in Ottoman waters reached 1,000 tons, some ten to twenty times larger than the average size of ships in the sailing era.

(By modern standards, however, these were tiny: the *Titanic* was 66,000 tons while the *Queen Mary 2* displaces 76,000 tons.)

This sea-borne transportation revolution, however, did not take place overnight. During the 1860s, sailing vessels remained commonplace and four times as many sailing as steam vessels called on the port of Istanbul. But, by 1900, the transformation was complete: sails accounted for only 5 percent of the ships visiting the capital city. Nonetheless, astonishingly, this 5 percent represented more sailing vessels than had visited Istanbul in any preceding year during the nineteenth century, a measure of the extraordinary increase in shipping taking place.

Steamships also revolutionized river transport. Until their appearance, river voyages typically were one way, down river only, with the current. The Nile was the great exception: there the current flows south to north while the prevailing winds are north to south, thus making sailing ship transport both down *and* upriver routinely possible. This situation, however, is very rare in Middle Eastern waters. Normally, vessels floated down river with their goods; on arrival, the ships were broken up and the timber sold since moving upriver against the current was next to impossible. And so, transport on the great rivers of the Balkan provinces, such as the Danube, or on smaller ones, such as the Maritza river through Edirne, was uni-directional from the interior to the Black Sea. In the Arab provinces, similarly, goods only flowed down the Tigris on the 215-mile trip from Diyarbekir to Mosul and Baghdad. This particular journey, despite the inefficiency of one-way transport, cost one-half as much as the cheapest land transportation. With steam power, ships traveled both up as well as down rivers, enormously impacting the interior regions of the Danubian and Tigris–Euphrates basins.

Steamships both resulted from and promoted the vast rise of commerce during the nineteenth century (see below). This increase could not have occurred but for the technological revolution in transportation which in turn facilitated still greater upward movements in the volume of commerce. The additional effects were equally important. For example, Western economic penetration of the empire intensified: Europeans owned almost all – 90 percent of the total tonnage – of the commercial ships operating in Ottoman waters in 1914. These ships also accelerated the growth of port cities with harbors deep and broad enough to accommodate the ever-larger ships. Also, the steamships' regularity and dramatically lower costs made possible the vast emigrations to the New World from the Ottoman Empire (and west, central, and eastern Europe as well).

Steamships also prompted construction of the Suez Canal in 1869, an event that helped bring about the European occupation of Egypt (see map 5 p. 60). Further, the all-water route of the canal drastically reduced shipping times and costs. The Iraqi lands thus prospered as the canal made it possible for their produce to be routed through the canal to European consumers. But other Ottoman towns and cities suffered grave losses as the canal diverted overland trade routes. Damascus, Aleppo, Mosul, even Beirut and Istanbul, all lost business because of the diversion of the trade of Iraq, Arabia, and Iran to the canal.

The changes in land transport equaled in drama and scope those of the sea-borne revolution. Until the middle of the nineteenth century, animate transport, human and animal – horse, camel, donkey, mule, and oxen – totally monopolized the shipment of goods over land. The use of human power quite likely was restricted to local, quite short, shipments of goods within villages. Land transport was so laborious, slow, and irregular that journeys were measured not in miles or kilometers but in the time that they would take, depending on the season and the terrain. Take, for example, an 1875 guide book that described trips foreign visitors might take in Ottoman Anatolia, an early indication of the emerging tourist industry. The trip for a horse-mounted traveler from Trabzon to Erzurum – 180 miles distance – was fifty-eight hours long, to be done in eight stages, each stage ranging from four to ten hours.

In terms of transport, the Ottoman world generally divided into two parts – the wheeled zone of the European provinces and the unwheeled world of the Anatolian and Arab provinces. This division more or less coincided with another: horses dominated the Balkan transport routes while camels tended to prevail in the Arab and Anatolian lands. To this general rule, there were exceptions. Ottoman armies had used massive numbers of camels to transport goods up the Danubian basin while horses, mules, and donkeys dominated the important Tabriz–Trabzon trade routes. But the general rule nonetheless held. In the early nineteenth century, the Salonica–Vienna journey took fifty days and involved horse caravans of 20,000 animals. In the 1860s, long caravans of carts trekked from the Bulgarian hill town of Koprivshtitsa on a one-month journey bringing manufactured goods to Istanbul for resale in the Arab lands. But east of the waterways separating the European from the Asian provinces, camels generally prevailed. Superior to all other beasts of burden, the camel could carry a quarter-ton of goods for at least 25 kilometers daily, 20 percent more weight than horses and mules and three times more than donkeys. Mules, donkeys, and horses, however, often were preferred for shorter trips and on the great Tabriz–Erzurum–Trabzon caravan route because of their greater speed. This famed trail annually used 45,000 animals, three caravans per year, each with 15,000 animals carrying a total of 25,000 tons. But nearly everywhere else in the Asian provinces, long strings of camels were the more familiar sight. In the early nineteenth century, 5,000 camels worked the twenty-eight-day Baghdad–Aleppo route while the Alexandretta–Diyarbekir journey of 250 miles required sixteen days. The Aleppo–Istanbul caravan route stretched 500 miles and forty days, and four great caravans annually made the trip during the eighteenth century. Because their carrying capacity comparatively was limited, caravans almost always carried high-cost, low-bulk goods such as textiles and other manufactured goods, as well as relatively expensive raw materials such as spices. Caravan shipments of foodstuffs, on the other hand, were rare because the transport costs usually exceeded their selling price. For example, caravan shipment of grain from Ankara to Istanbul (216 miles) would have raised its price 3.5 times and that from Erzurum to Trabzon (188 miles) three times. These pre-railroad realities meant that fertile lands not near cheap sea transport supported the needs of the local population and the rest was left fallow or for animal raising.

There were several minor changes in the existing, animal-based, land-transport technologies during the nineteenth century. First, in a relatively significant way, wheeled vehicles were re-introduced into the Anatolian and Arab provinces (they largely had disappeared during the fall of the Roman Empire) by Circassian refugees and by European Jewish settlers in Palestine. Also, as commerce increased, there was some improvement of a few so-called metaled roads. Across the width of these roads, strips of metal were laid to reduce the mud. One such highway between Baghdad and Aleppo was built in 1910 and cut the travel time from twenty-eight days to twenty-two days.

Railroads – steamships on land – revolutionized land transport in a profound way. Based on a principle of hauling large numbers of cars – each of which carried as much grain as at least 125 camels – on a low friction track, railroads offered incredibly cheap and more regular transport, especially for bulk goods such as cereal grains. For the very first time in history, the potential of fertile interior regions – such as central Anatolia or the Hawran valley in Syria – could be realized. When railroads were built into such areas, market agriculture immediately developed because the products could be sold at competitive prices. Within just a few years, cultivators in newly opened regions were growing and the railroads were shipping hundreds of thousands of tons of cereals. Overall, by volume, cereals formed the overwhelming majority of goods shipped by rail (map 7).

For a number of reasons, including very low population densities and the lack of capital, the Ottoman lands contained a relatively small railroad network. (In Egypt, by contrast, dense populations concentrated in a narrow strip of rich soils prompted the appearance of a very thick system of trunk and feeder lines by 1905.) The first Anatolian lines were

Map 7 Railroads in the Ottoman Empire, c. 1914, and its former European possessions
Adapted from Halil İnalcık with Donald Quataert, eds., *An economic and social history of the Ottoman Empire, 1300–1914* (Cambridge, 1994), 805.

built in the 1860s. But the biggest development by far occurred in the more heavily settled European provinces that, in 1875, contained 731 miles of track. With just a few exceptions, foreign capital built the lines that accelerated economic development, thus increasing foreign financial control. German capital, for example, financed the Anatolian railway and brought a boom to inner Anatolia. In 1911, Ottoman railroads overall transported 16 million passengers and 2.6 million tons of freight on some 4,030 miles of track. Lines in the Balkans contained 1,054 miles of track and carried 8 million passengers while those in Anatolia held 1,488 miles with 7 million passengers. By contrast, the 1,488 miles of track in the Arab provinces carried only 0.9 millions, a reflection of the scant population (plates 3–4).

Plate 3 Bond certificate of the "Anatolian Railway Company," second series, 1893
Personal collection of author.

Plate 4 Third class coach on the Berlin–Baghdad railway, 1908. Stereo-
Travel Company, 1908
Personal collection of author.

Railroads created a brand new source of employment and, by 1911,
more than 13,000 persons worked on Ottoman railroads. Also noteworthy are the new social horizons opened up both by railroad employ and
travel. The 16 million passenger trips physically brought many Ottoman
subjects to places they had never been before, promoting more communication than ever between and among regions and forever changing
rural–urban relations. Dangerous trips that once had taken months on
foot now took place in safety, over just a few days.

Railroads affected earlier forms of land transport in ways that are sometimes surprising. Relatively dense networks of feeder railroads – smaller
lines leading to a larger main line – emerged in the hinterlands of port
cities such as Beirut and Izmir and to a lesser extent in the Balkan
provinces. But these were an exception. More generally, the Ottoman
railroads evolved as a trunk system – for example, the Istanbul – Ankara
and Istanbul–Konya and Konya–Baghdad railroads – characterized by
main lines with few rail links feeding into them. In the absence of rail
feeders, animal transport was needed to bring goods to the main lines.
As the volume of crops grown for export in the railroad areas boomed,
the number of animals bringing the goods to the trunk lines increased
enormously. In the Aegean area, some 10,000 camels worked to supply
the two local railroads. At the Ankara station, terminus of the line from
Istanbul, a thousand camels at a time waited to unload the goods they had
brought. Hence, even though caravan operators on routes parallel to the

railroads soon went out of business, those servicing the main lines found new work. Thus, like the sailing vessels in Istanbul, traditional forms of land transport were invigorated at least temporarily by the vast increases in commerce prompted by steam engine technologies.

Commerce

Commerce in the Ottoman system took many forms but generally can be divided into international and domestic – that is, trade between the Ottoman and other economies and that within the borders of the empire. Throughout the 1700–1922 period, international trade was more visible but *less* important than domestic trade, both in volume and value.

World wide during the eighteenth and nineteenth centuries, international trade increased enormously but less so in the Ottoman lands. Whereas, for example, international commerce globally grew sixty-four times during the nineteenth century, it increased a comparatively meager ten- to sixteen-fold in the Ottoman Empire. Thus, it is not surprising to learn that while, in 1600, the Ottoman market was a crucial one for the West Europeans, this no longer was true in 1900. The global commercial importance of the Ottoman empire had declined. The Ottoman economy was not shrinking – to the contrary – but it was declining in relative significance. It is also true that it remained among the most important trade partners of the leading economic powers, such as Britain, France, and Germany.

As the preceding section indicated, transportation improvements in steamships and railroads played a major role in the development of Ottoman commerce after their introduction in the early and middle parts of the nineteenth century. Railroad lines, extensive port facilities and harbors were constructed because international demand already was present for the products they would ship, while the new facilities themselves further stimulated the trade.

Let me begin this section by discussing two of the more important additional factors affecting both domestic and international commerce, namely wars and government policies. Wars disrupted commerce not only during the times of fighting, when it was dangerous to move goods across borders and sometimes within the empire. Even worse, they brought territorial losses that ripped and tore apart the fabric of Ottoman economic unity, weakening and often destroying marketing relationships and patterns that had endured for many centuries. Here are two examples. First, when Russia conquered the northern Black Sea shores, it wrecked an important trading network for Ottoman producers. That is, it annexed a major market area in which Ottoman textile producers from Anatolia long

had been selling their goods. Thereafter, the new imperial frontiers between Russia and the Ottoman Empire impeded or choked off altogether
the longstanding flow of goods and peoples between two areas that had
been part of one economic zone but now were divided between two empires. The other example is the fate of Aleppo following World War I, the
conflict that ended the Ottoman Empire and, among other things, gave
birth to the Turkish republic and a French-occupied state of Syria. Aleppo
had been a major producer of textiles, shipping these mainly to Anatolia,
that is, from one point to another within a single Ottoman imperial system. With the disappearance of the Ottoman Empire, the producers were
in one country – Syria – while the customers were in another – Turkey.
Seeking to remold its new Syrian colony into an economic appendage,
France prevented the textiles from being shipped and thus triggered a
collapse in Aleppo textile production. Thus, the Russian and Aleppo examples show the disastrous effects of border shifts on economic activity.

The role of government policy on commerce and the economy in general is hotly debated. Some argue that policy can have a major impact, a
position supported by the example of French actions regarding Aleppo
textiles. Others assert that policy merely formalizes changes already taking place in the economy. The capitulations, for example, are said to
have played a vital important role in Ottoman social, economic, and political history. But did they? Without them, is it possible to imagine that
the Ottomans would have maintained political and economic parity with
western Europe? Or, consider the coincidence of massive state interference and economic recession during the late eighteenth century – which
is the chicken and which the egg (see chapter 3)? Subsequent nineteenth-
century state actions in favor of free trade include the 1826 destruction
of the Janissary protectors of monopoly and restriction, the 1838 Anglo-
Turkish Convention, and the two imperial reform decrees of 1839 and
1856. As a result, most policy-promoted barriers to Ottoman international and internal commerce disappeared or were reduced sharply. But,
whether or not these decisions played a key role in Ottoman commercial
and, more generally, economic development, remains an open question.

The importance of international trade is easy to overstate because it is
so well documented, easily measured and endlessly discussed in readily
accessible western-language sources. The overall patterns in international
commerce seem clear enough. During the eighteenth century, international trade became more important, especially after c. 1750. From improved but still low levels, it then sharply rose in importance during the
early nineteenth century, following the end of the Napoleonic wars. The
balance of trade – the relation of exports to imports – often fluctuated
in the short run but overall moved against the Ottomans. The aggregate

value and nature of the goods being traded certainly changed a great deal. Trade was really quite limited during the early eighteenth century. The Ottoman economy re-exported high-value luxury goods, mainly silks from lands further east, and exported a host of its own goods, such as Angora wool cloth and, later on, cotton yarn. In exchange, imports such as luxury goods arrived. As the eighteenth century wore on, however, Ottoman exports shifted over to unprocessed goods including raw cotton as well as cereals, tobacco, wool, and hides. At same time, Ottomans increasingly imported commodities from the colonies of western Europe in the New World and East Asia. These "colonial goods" – sugar, dyestuffs, and coffee, produced by slave labor and thus lower in price – undercut the sugar from the Mediterranean, the coffee from Arabia (mocha) and the dyestuffs from India. Ottoman consumers also imported quantities of textiles, mainly from India and to a secondary degree from Europe. According to some scholars, a favorable balance of trade still existed at the end of the eighteenth century.

Although, as seen, the volume of international trade rose ten- to sixteen-fold between 1840 and 1914, the pattern of exports in agricultural commodities resembled that of the eighteenth century. Ottomans generally exported a mixed group of foodstuffs and raw materials including wheat, barley, cotton, tobacco, and opium. After 1850, however, some manufactured goods exports appeared, notably carpets and raw silk. In a way, these export manufactures replaced those of mohair cloth and luxury silks that had been important in the eighteenth century and before. While the basket of exported agricultural goods remained relatively fixed, the relative importance of the particular goods in the basket changed considerably over the eighteenth and nineteenth centuries. By way of example, take cotton exports: these boomed and collapsed during the eighteenth century, boomed during the American Civil War, subsequently collapsed again and then soared in the early twentieth century. Regarding the basket of imports: colonial goods remained high on the list while those of finished goods – notably textiles, hardware, and glass – became far more important than during the eighteenth century.

Domestic trade, although not well documented, in fact vastly exceeded international trade in terms of volume and value throughout the entire 1700–1922 period. The flow of goods within and between regions was quite valuable but direct measurements are available only rarely. Consider the following scattered facts as suggestive of the importance of Ottoman domestic trade. First, the French Ambassador in 1759 stated that total textile imports into the Ottoman Empire would clothe not more than 800,000 persons per year, at a time when the overall population exceeded

20 millions. Second, in 1914, not more than 25 percent of total agricultural output was being exported, meaning that domestic trade accounted for the remaining 75 percent. Third, during the early 1860s, the trade in Ottoman-made goods within the province of Damascus surpassed by five times the value of all foreign-made goods sold there. Fourth and finally, among the rare data on internal trade are statistics from the 1890s concerning the domestic commerce of three Ottoman cities – Diyarbekir, Mosul, and Harput. None of these three ranked as a leading economic center. And yet, during the 1890s, the sum value of their interregional trade (1 million pounds sterling) equaled about 5 percent of the total Ottoman international export trade at the time. This is an impressively high figure when we consider their minor economic status. What would the total figure be if the internal trade of the rest of Ottoman cities and towns and villages were known? The domestic trade of any single commercial center such as Istanbul, Edirne, Salonica, Beirut, Damascus, and Aleppo was far greater than these three combined. Consider, too, that the domestic trade of literally dozens of medium-size towns also remains uncounted; similarly unknown is the domestic commerce of thousands of villages and smaller towns. In sum, domestic trade overwhelmingly outweighed the international.

The increasing international trade powerfully impacted the composition of the Ottoman merchant community. Ottoman Muslims as a major merchant group had faded in importance during the eighteenth century when foreigners and Ottoman non-Muslims became dominant in the mounting foreign trade. At first, the international trade was nearly exclusively in the hands of the west Europeans who brought the goods. By the eighteenth century, these merchants had found partners and helped growing numbers of non-Muslim merchants to obtain certificates (*berats*) granting them the capitulatory privileges which foreign merchants had, namely lower taxes and thus lower costs. In 1793, some 1,500 certificates were issued to non-Muslims in Aleppo alone. Although foreigners still controlled the international trade of the empire in 1800, their non-Muslim Ottoman protégés replaced them over the course of the nineteenth century. The best illustration of the new prominence of the non-Muslim Ottoman merchant class might be an early twentieth-century list of 1,000 registered merchants in Istanbul. Only 3 percent of these merchants were French, British, or German, although their home countries controlled more than one-half of Ottoman foreign trade. Most of the rest were non-Muslims. Nonetheless, Muslim merchants still dominated the trade of interior towns and often between the interior and the port cities on the coast. That is, for all the changes in the international merchant community, it seems that Ottoman Muslims controlled most of the domestic trade, plus much of the commerce in international goods once these had passed into the Ottoman economy from abroad.

Agriculture

Throughout its entire history, the Ottoman Empire remained overwhelmingly an agrarian economy that was labor scarce, land rich, and capital poor. The bulk of the population, usually 80–90 percent, lived on and drew sustenance from the land, almost always in family holdings rather than large estates. Agriculture generated most of the wealth in the economy, although the absence of statistical data prevents meaningful measurements until nearly the twentieth century. One indicator of this sector's overall economic importance is the significance of agriculturally derived revenues to the Ottoman state. In the mid-nineteenth century, two taxes on agriculture – the tithe and the land tax – alone contributed about 40 percent of all taxes collected in the empire. Agriculture indirectly contributed to the imperial treasury in many other ways – for example, customs revenues on exports that, in the eighteenth and nineteenth centuries, were mainly agricultural commodities.

Most Ottoman subjects therefore were cultivators. The majority of these in turn were subsistence farmers, living directly from the fruits of their labors. They cultivated, overall, small plots of land, growing a variety of crops for their own consumption, mainly cereals, and also fruits, olives, and vegetables. Quite often they raised some animals, for the milk and wool or hair. Most cultivating families lived on a modest diet, drinking water or a form of liquid yoghurt, eating various forms of bread or porridge and some vegetables, but hardly ever any meat. The animals were beasts of burden and gave their wool or hair which the female members spun into thread and often wove into cloth for family use. In many areas, both in Ottoman Europe and Asia, family members also worked as peddlers, selling home-made goods or those provided by merchants. Some rural families, as we shall see, also manufactured goods for sale to others: Balkan villagers traveled to Anatolia and Syria for months to sell their wool cloth. In western Anatolia, women and men spun yarn for town weavers. And, as just noted, village men in some areas left for work in Istanbul and other far away places. In sum, cultivator families drew their livelihoods from a complex set of different economic activities and not merely from growing crops.

The picture presented above was largely true in 1700 and remained so in 1900: the economy was agrarian and most cultivators possessed small landholdings, engaging in a host of tasks, with their crops and animal products mainly dedicated to self-consumption. But enormous changes over time occurred in the agrarian sector.

To begin with, take the rising importance of formerly nomadic populations in Ottoman agricultural life. The rural countryside, after all, held pastoral nomads as well as sedentary cultivators. Nomads played a complex and important role in the economy, providing goods and services such as animal products, textiles, and transportation. Some nomads depended solely on animal raising while others also grew crops, sometimes sowing them, leaving them unattended for the season and returning in time for the harvest. And it is also true that they often were disruptive of trade and agriculture. For the state, nomads were hard to control and a political headache, and long-standing state pacification programs thus acquired new force in the nineteenth century. As seen above, these sedentarization programs took place at the same time as the massive influx of refugees, a combination that reduced the lands on which nomads freely could move. In the aggregate, animal raising by tribes likely declined while their cultivated lands increased.

A second major set of changes concerns the rising commercialization of agriculture – the production of goods for sale to others. Over time, more and more people grew or raised increasing amounts for sale to domestic and international consumers, a trend that began in the eighteenth century and mounted impressively thereafter. At least three major engines increased agricultural production devoted to the market, the first being rising demand, both international and domestic. Abroad, especially after 1840, the levels of living and buying power of many Europeans improved substantially, permitting them to buy a wider choice and quantity of goods. Rising domestic markets within the empire also were important thanks to increased urbanization as well as mounting personal consumption (see below). The newly opened railroad districts brought a flow of domestic wheat and other cereals to Istanbul, Salonica, Izmir, and Beirut; railroads also attracted truck gardeners who now could grow and ship fruits and vegetables to the expanding and newly accessible markets of these cities. With their rising cash incomes, moreover, the consumption of goods by cultivators in the railroad districts increased.

The second engine driving agricultural output concerns cultivators' increasing payment of their taxes in cash rather than kind. Some historians have asserted that the increasing commitment to market agriculture was a product both of a mounting per capita tax burden and the state's growing preference for tax payments in cash rather than kind. In this argument, such governmental decisions forced cultivators to grow crops for sale in order to pay their taxes. Such an argument credits state policy as the most important factor influencing the cultivator's shift from subsistence to the market. In this same vein, some have asserted that the state's demand for cash taxes from Ottoman Christians had a crucial role in Ottoman history. Namely, Ottoman Christians and Jews for many centuries had been required to pay a special tax (*cizye*) in cash, that assured them state protection in the exercise of their religion. Because of this cash tax, Ottoman Christians supposedly became more involved in market activities than their Muslim counterparts. Such an argument, however, does not explain why Ottoman Jews, who also paid the tax, were not as commercially active. The more relevant variable explaining economic success was not cash taxes but rather the Great Power protection that Ottoman Christians but not Jews enjoyed. This protection won Ottoman Christians capitulatory-like benefits, tax exemptions, and the lower business costs that help to explain their rise to economic prominence.

Cultivators' rising involvement in the market was not simply a reactive response to state demands for cash taxes. Other factors were at work. There was a third engine driving increasing agricultural production – cultivators' own desires for consumer goods. Among Ottoman consumers, increasingly frequent taste changes, along with the rising availability of cheap imported goods, stimulated a rising consumption of goods. This pattern of mounting consumption began in the eighteenth century, as seen by the urban phenomenon of the Tulip Period (1718–1730), and accelerated subsequently. Wanting more consumer goods, cultivators needed more cash. Thus, rural families worked harder than they had previously, not merely because of cash taxes but because of their own wants for more consumer goods. In such circumstances, leisure time diminished, cash incomes rose, and the flow of consumer goods into the countryside accelerated. The railroad districts are an excellent example of rising consumption desires promoting increased agricultural production. Given the opportunity to produce more crops for sale, cereal growers responded immediately, annually shipping one – half million tons of cereals within a decade of the inauguration of rail service.

Increases in agricultural production both promoted and accompanied a vast expansion in the area of land under cultivation. At the beginning of the eighteenth century and indeed until the end of the empire, there remained vast stretches of uncultivated, sometimes nearly empty, land on every side. These spaces began to fill in, a process finally completed only in the 1950s in most areas of the former empire. Many factors were involved. Families frequently increased the amount of time at work, bringing into cultivation fallow land already under their control. They also engaged in sharecropping, agreeing to work another's land, paying the person a share of the output. Often such acreage had been pasturage for animals but now farmers plowed the land and grew crops. The extraordinarily fertile lands of Moldavia and Wallachia, for example, had been among the least populated lands of the Ottoman Empire in the eighteenth century. There, in an unusual, perhaps unique development, local notables brutally compelled more labor from local inhabitants and brought more land under the plow. Elsewhere, millions of refugees brought into production enormous amounts of untilled land. While some settled in populated areas, a process that often caused tensions, vast numbers went to relatively vacant regions, bringing lands under cultivation for the first time (in many centuries). As seen, the empty central Anatolian basin and steppe zone in the Syrian provinces, between the desert and the coast, were frequent refugee destinations. There, government agencies parceled out the land in small holdings of equal size.

Overall, significant concentrations of commercial agriculture first formed in areas easily accessible by water, for example, the Danubian basin, some river valleys in Bulgaria and the coastal areas of Macedonia, as well as the western Aegean coast of Anatolia and the attendant river systems. During the nineteenth century, expansion in such areas continued and interior regions joined the list as well.

Many virginal holdings became large estates, which formed an ever-larger but nonetheless minority proportion of the cultivated land during the 1700–1922 era. On empty lands, large estate formation was made easier because there were no or few cultivators present defending their rights. Such processes occurred in Bulgaria, Moldavia, and Wallachia in the eighteenth century and a century later, on the vast Çukorova plain in southeast Anatolia, as these zones fell under the plow for the first time. By 1900, the Çukorova plain had become a special area of great estates with massive inputs of agricultural machinery. Further east and south, the Hama region of Syria also developed a large landholding pattern. But, in most areas of the empire, severe shortages of labor and the lack of capital hindered the formation of large estates and thus they remained rare. Small landholdings instead prevailed as the Ottoman norm almost everywhere.

There were some increases in productivity – the amount grown on a unit of land. Irrigation projects, one form of intensive agriculture, developed in some areas. More significantly, the use of modern agricultural tools increased during the nineteenth century. By 1900, tens of thousands of iron plows, thousands of reapers, and other examples of advanced agricultural technologies such as combines dotted the Balkan, Anatolian, and Arab rural lands. But more intensive exploitation of existing resources remained comparatively unusual, and most of the increases in agricultural production derived from placing additional land under cultivation.

Rising agricultural production for sale also prompted important changes in the rural labor relations of some areas. Waged labor appeared in some regions of large commercial cultivation. Hence, in west and in southeast Anatolia, gangs of migrant workers harvested the crops for cash wages. Sharecropping rather than wage labor, however, remained more common on large holdings. In Moldavia and Wallachia, as stated above, a form of sharecropping led to near serfdom and some of the worst conditions in the empire. There, eighteenth-century market possibilities had led large holders to rent lands to peasants who paid increasingly heavy rents, taxes, and labor services. At first, for example, peasants owed twelve days of labor but, by the mid-nineteenth century, they worked between twenty-four and fifty days per year – conditions far worse than in the neighboring Habsburg and Romanov empires. Forms of communal exploitation of land, where all worked and shared the produce, prevailed in some Ottoman areas. For example, in some parts of Palestine and in the Iraqi provinces, communal lands were worked jointly, often by tribal members under the direction of their sheikh who supervised distribution of the proceeds.

And finally, foreign ownership of land remained quite uncommon, despite the political weakness of the Ottoman state. While legally permitted to acquire land after 1867, foreigners could not overcome the difficulties posed by the opposition of segments of Ottoman society, including an intact local notable group jealously guarding its privileges, and persistent labor shortages. This seems noteworthy and provides a further indication of the character of the Ottoman Empire during the age of imperialism. While no longer fully independent (see, for example, the discussion of the Public Debt Administration), the Ottoman state still maintained sovereignty over most of its domestic affairs.

Manufacturing

Despite visible increases in mechanization during the later nineteenth century, most Ottoman manufactured goods continued to be made by manual labor until the end of the empire. Manufacturing in the countryside, increasingly by female labor, became more important and that by urban-based, male, often guild-organized, workers less so. Further, the global place of Ottoman manufacturing diminished; most of its international markets dried up and production focused on the still vast but highly competitive domestic market. And yet, selected manufacturing sectors for international export significantly expanded production.

The mechanized production of Ottoman goods, at its peak, remained a growing if still minor portion of total manufacturing output. After

c. 1875, a small number of factories emerged, mainly in the cities of Ottoman Europe, Istanbul, and western Anatolia, with additional clusters amidst the cotton fields in southeast Anatolia (for cotton spinning) and in various silk raising districts for silk reeling, especially at Bursa and in the Lebanon. Big port cities like Salonica, Izmir, Beirut, and Istanbul held the most concentrated collections of mechanized factories. Most Ottoman factories processed foods, spun thread and occasionally wove cloth. One measure: in 1911, mechanized factories accounted for only 25 percent of all the cotton yarn and less than 1 percent of all the cotton cloth then being consumed within the empire. As in agriculture, the lack of capital deterred the mechanization of production.

While it did not significantly mechanize, the Ottoman manufacturing sector nonetheless successfully underwent a host of important changes as it struggled to survive in the age of the Industrial Revolution in Europe, where technology and the greater exploitation of labor produced a host of cheap and well-made goods. Until the later eighteenth century, goods made by hand in the Ottoman Empire were highly sought after in the surrounding empires and states. The fine textiles, hand-made yarns, and leathers of the eighteenth century, however, gradually lost their foreign markets. By the early nineteenth century, almost all of the high quality goods formerly characterizing the Ottoman export sector had vanished. But, after a half-century hiatus, production for international export re-emerged c. 1850, in the form of raw silk, a kind of silk thread and, more importantly, Oriental carpets. Steam-powered silk reeling factories emerged in Salonica, Edirne, and west Anatolia and in the Lebanon. Particularly in west and central Anatolia, factory-made yarns and dyes combined with hand labor to make mind-boggling numbers of carpets for European and American buyers. The two industries together employed 100,000 persons in c. 1914, two-thirds of them in carpet making. Most workers were women and girls, receiving wages that were the lowest in the entire Ottoman manufacturing sector. In addition, several thousands of other female workers hand made Ottoman lace that imitated Irish lace, finding important markets in Europe.

The overwhelming majority of producers focused on the Ottoman domestic market of 26 million consumers, who sometimes lived in the same or adjacent regions as the manufacturer but also, sometimes, in distant parts of the empire. Producing for a domestic market that itself is difficult to examine and trace, these manufacturers are nearly invisible to the historian's scrutiny because most did not belong to organizations or firms that left records. Quite to the contrary, they were widely dispersed in non-mechanized forms of production, either working alone or in very small groups located in homes and small workshops, in urban areas and in the countryside. For example, cotton and wool yarn producers, an essential part of the textile industry, worked in numerous locations (some of which are noted on map 8). While there were yarn factories in places like Izmir, Salonica, and Adana, handwork accounted for the yarn in most of the places noted.

During the 1700–1922 period, the importance of guilds in the manufacture of goods fell very sharply but they did not disappear entirely. The evolution, nature and role of guilds (*esnaf, taife*), however, is not well understood and neither is their prevalence. The economic crisis of the later eighteenth century, with its persistent ruinous inflation, may have accelerated the formal organization of guilds as a self-protective act by producers. Workers banded together to collectively buy implements but often, as in southern Bulgaria, fell under the control of wealthier masters better able to weather the crisis.[1] Thus, ironically, labor organizations may have been evolving into a new phase, towards guilds, as Ottoman manufacturing was hit by the competition of the Industrial Revolution.

Guilds generally acted to safeguard the livelihood of their members, restricting production, controlling quality and prices. To protect their livelihoods, members paid a price – namely, high production costs. (Some historians, however, incorrectly have argued that guilds primarily served as instruments of state control.) After reaching agreement among the members, guild leaders often went to the local courts and registered the new prices to gain official recognition of the change. The presence of a steward indeed is one mark of the existence of a guild. At least some guilds had features such as communal chests to support members in times of illness, pay their funeral expenses, or help their widows and children (plate 5).

Guilds in the capital city of Istanbul were very well developed, perhaps more so than anywhere else in the empire. They likewise existed in many of the larger cities such as Salonica, Belgrade, Aleppo, and Damascus. Smaller towns and cities, such as Amasya often also contained guilds, but their overall prevalence, form, and function remain uncertain. There seems to be a correlation between the size of a city and the likelihood that it held a guild – but not every urban center had them.

Janissaries, until 1826, played a vital role in the life of the guilds. Prior to and throughout the eighteenth century, in every corner of the empire and in its capital city, many, perhaps most, Muslim guildsmen had become Janissaries. This was true, for example, in Ottoman Bulgaria, Serbia, Bosnia, Macedonia, as well as Istanbul. In some cities, the Janissaries themselves were the manufacturing guildsmen but in others,

---

[1] This is the conclusion of Suraiya Faroqhi who presently is studying the evolution of guilds.

Map 8 Some cotton and wool yarnmaking locations in the nineteenth century
Donald Quataert, *Ottoman manufacturing in the age of the Industrial Revolution* (Cambridge, 1994), 28.

Plate 5 Procession of guilds (*esnaf*) in Amasya, nineteenth century
Raymond H. Kevorkian and Paul B. Paboudjian, eds., *Les Arméniens dans l'empire ottoman à la veille du génocide* (Paris, 1992).
With permission.

such as Aleppo and Istanbul, they functioned as mafia-like protectors of such workers. At Istanbul and some other big cities, they dominated the building and carrying trades. Time after time and in many cities besides the capital, the Janissaries mobilized to defend popular interests, either as guildsmen or in co-operation with them. Terrorizing governors and deposing grand viziers and sultans, these potent popular coalitions fought for guild privilege and protection, seeking to maintain prices and restrictive practices. In Bulgaria, for example, the Janissaries struggled to protect urban guilds against the rural manufacturing that threatened their jobs.[2]

Hence Sultan Mahmut II's destruction of the Janissaries in 1826 also was a terrible blow for the guilds. It fell precisely at the moment when international competition was mounting rapidly in the aftermath of the Napoleonic wars. Bereft of protectors in an age when their restrictive practices kept costs too high, the guilds began to disappear. They failed to compete because of what they were: restrictive organizations seeking high prices to benefit members. In Damascus, for example, masters allowed journeymen's wages to fall so steadily in the 1830s to 1870s that the latter could not accumulate enough capital to open their own shops. Whatever importance they may have possessed before, the guilds' role as an organizing unit of Ottoman manufacturing declined during the nineteenth century. In some areas, such as Bulgaria and Aleppo, they indeed survived until very late in the period. But often their form evolved from monopolistic producer to a chamber of commerce-like body that merely registered the names of local manufacturers.

It is important to reiterate that manufacturing guilds declined but Ottoman manufacturing did not. Instead, production shifted to work-ers outside of a guild framework. Sometimes these were nonguild shops in urban areas. In Istanbul, for example, shoemaking flourished at the end of the nineteenth century but as home production and no longer a guild-organized activity. In many regions of the empire, rural manufacturing in homes and workshops played a key role in the survival of manufacturing. The flight to the countryside – to reduce costs by cutting wages – was well underway in the eighteenth century in a number of areas. During the later part of the century, for example, producers began moving out of the north Anatolian city of Tokat, a major manufacturing center, and set up business in nearby smaller cities and villages. Similar patterns have been documented for areas as dissimilar as Bulgaria and the city of Aleppo.

---

[2] Donald Quataert, "Janissaries, artisans and the question of Ottoman decline, 1730–1826," in Donald Quataert, ed., *Workers, peasants and economic change in the Ottoman Empire, 1730–1914* (Istanbul, 1993), 197–203.

Strikingly, women and girls – Muslim, Christian, and Jewish alike – came to play an ever-more important role. Their participation in the workforce hardly was new to the eighteenth and nineteenth centuries but their level of involvement mounted impressively. In many urban and rural homes, women wove, spun, and knitted goods for merchants who paid piece-work wages. In the Ottoman universe, as everywhere else in the world, women obtained less money for equal work than men. And so, a vital part of the story of Ottoman manufacturing centers on the shift from male, urban, guild-based production to female, unorganized, rural and urban labor.

Suggested bibliography

Entries marked with a * designate recommended readings for new students of the subject.

Akarlı, Engin Deniz. "Gedik implements, mastership, shop usufruct, and monopoly among Istanbul artisans, 1750–1850," *Wissenschaftskolleg Jahrbuch*, 1986, 225–231.

*Beinin, Joel. *Workers and peasants in the modern Middle East*. Cambridge, 2001.

Blaisdell, Donald. *European financial control in the Ottoman Empire* (New York, 1929).

*Braudel, Fernand. *The Mediterranean and the Mediterranean world in the time of Philip II*, 2 vols. (New York, 1973).

*Doumani, Beshara, ed. *Family history in the Middle East. Household, property and gender* (Albany, 2003).

Duman, Yüksel. "Notables, textiles and copper in Ottoman Tokat, 1750–1840." Unpublished Ph.D. dissertation, Binghamton University, 1998.

Erdem, Hakkan. *Slavery in the Ottoman Empire and its demise, 1800–1909* (New York, 1996).

*Faroqhi, Suraiya. "Agriculture and rural life in the Ottoman Empire (c. 1500–1878)," *New Perspectives on Turkey*, Fall 1987, 3–34.

Faroqhi, Suraiya and Randi Deguilhem, eds. *Crafts and craftsmen in the Middle East: fashioning the individual in the Muslim Mediterranean* (London, 2005).

*Gerber, Haim. *The social origins of the modern Middle East* (Boulder, CO, 1987).

*Goldberg, Ellis, ed. *The social history of labor in the Middle East* (Boulder, CO, 1996).

Gould, Andrew Gordon. "Pashas and brigands: Ottoman provincial reform and its impact on the nomadic tribes of southern Anatolia 1840–1885." Unpublished Ph.D. dissertation, University of California, 1973.

Hutteroth, Wolf-Dieter. "The influence of social structure on land division and settlement in Inner Anatolia," in Peter Benedict, Erol Tümertekin and Fatma Mansur, eds., *Turkey: geographic and social perspectives* (Leiden, 1974), 19–47.

İnalcık, Halil. "The emergence of big farms, *çiftliks*: State, landlord and tenants," in Keyder and Tabak, cited below, 17–53.

Karpat, Kemal. *Ottoman population, 1830–1914: Demographic and social characteristics* (Madison, 1985).

"The Ottoman emigration to America, 1860–1914," *International Journal of Middle East Studies*, 17 (2) (1985), 175–209.

Keyder, Çağlar and Faruk Tabak, eds. *Landholding and commercial agriculture in the Middle East* (Albany, 1991).

Khalidi, Tarif, ed. *Land tenure and transformation in the Middle East* (Beirut, 1984).

Lewis, Norman. *Nomads and settlers in Syria and Jordan, 1800–1980* (Cambridge, 1987).

*Marcus, Abraham. *The Middle East on the eve of modernity* (New York, 1989).

Mears, Eliot Grinnell. *Modern Turkey* (London, 1924).

Meriwether, Margaret L. "Women and economic change in nineteenth-century Aleppo," in Judith E. Tucker, ed., *Arab women* (Washington, 1993), 65–83.

Owen, Roger. *The Middle East in the world economy, 1800–1914* (London, 1981).

*Palairet, Michael. *The Balkan economies c. 1800–1914: Evolution without development* (Cambridge, 1997).

*Pamuk, Şevket. *The Ottoman Empire and European capitalism, 1820–1913* (Cambridge, 1987).

A monetary history of the Ottoman Empire (Cambridge, 2000).

*Quataert, Donald. *Social disintegration and popular resistance in the Ottoman Empire, 1881–1908* (New York, 1983).

Ottoman manufacturing in the age of the Industrial Revolution (Cambridge, 1993).

Salzmann, Ariel. "Measures of empire: tax farmers and the Ottoman *ancien régime*, 1695–1807." Unpublished Ph.D. dissertation, Columbia University, 1995.

Shields, Sarah. *Mosul before Iraq: Like bees making five-sided cells* (Albany, 2000).

Toledano, Ehud. *The Ottoman slave trade and its suppression, 1840–1890* (Princeton, 1982).

*Vatter, Sherry. "Militant journeymen in nineteenth-century Damascus: implications for the Middle Eastern labor history agenda," in Zachary Lockman, ed., *Workers and working classes in the Middle East: Struggles, histories, historiographies* (Albany, 1994), 1–19.

Zilfi, Madeline. "Elite circulation in the Ottoman Empire: great mollas of the eighteenth century," *Journal of the Economic and Social History of the Orient*, 26, 3 (1983), 318–364.

Politics of piety: The Ottoman ulama in the post-classical age (Minneapolis, 1986).

Women in the Ottoman Empire: Middle Eastern women in the early modern era (Leiden, 1997).

8   Ottoman society and popular culture

Introduction

This chapter continues the emphasis presented in chapter 7, a depiction of the everyday lives of Ottoman subjects. To do so, it draws on an unusual body of literature to look at social organization, popular culture, and forms of sociability and it offers a cultural investigation into various forms of meaning. Societies as complex as the Ottoman are to be understood not only in terms of administrative decrees, bureaucratic rationalization, military campaigns, and economic productivity. They structure spaces within which people think about the common issues of life, death, celebration, and mourning. Often those spaces are highly gendered and at other times they bring men and women of certain classes together.

An overview of social relations among groups

All societies, including the Ottoman, consist of complex sets of relationships among individuals and collections of individuals that sometimes overlap and interlock but at other times remain distinct and apart. Persons assemble voluntarily or gather into a number of often distinct groups. On one occasion, they might identify themselves or be identified by others as belonging to a particular group, yet at other times another identity might come to the fore. At a very general level, the Ottoman world may be described as holding the ruling and subject classes and also divisions by religious affiliations such as Sunni Muslim or Armenian Catholic. There were also occupational groups, sometimes but not always organized as corporate groups (*esnaf, taife*) that we call guilds, as well as huge groups such as women, peasants, or tribes. In all cases, each social group was hardly homogeneous and varied vastly in terms of wealth and status.

We should not straitjacket the Ottoman individual or collective into one or another fixed identity but rather we need to acknowledge the ambiguity and porosity of the boundaries between and among such individuals and groups. On one occasion or another, a particular expression of identity might come to the fore, such as being female but at another time, being a weaver or a Jew might emerge to take precedence over the female identity. Religion, to use another example, functioned as one but not the only means of differentiation. It alone did not confer status but did so in combination with other forms of identity. Nor should we assign a necessarily negative value to differentiation. Difference is a marker distinguishing individuals and groups but it need not be negative, a source of conflict, simply because difference exists. Indeed, in most societies most of the time, differences are merely that. Unusually, they become sources of violence, a theme examined later (chapter 9).

Consider the assertion, too popular in Middle East literature, that by the mere fact of their religious allegiance, Muslims enjoyed a legally superior status to non-Muslims. A glance at the historical records quickly shows that vast numbers of Ottoman Christians and Jews were higher up the social hierarchy than Muslims, enjoying greater wealth and access to political power. For example, in many circumstances, a wealthy Christian merchant possessed greater local prestige and influence than an impoverished Muslim soldier. That is, the category of Muslim or Christian or of being part of the subject or the military class alone did not encompass a person's social, economic, and political reality. Rather, such a quality was but one of several attributes identifying that individual.

To give another example of the many components that constituted identity, take the religious scholars, the ulema, who supposedly formed a particular social category. How meaningful is it to attach a single identity label, in this case "ulema," to a very heterogeneous collection of individuals. Some members of the ulema trained for decades at the feet of teachers in the great and prestigious educational institutions such as al-Azhar in Cairo or the Süleymaniye in Istanbul. But others were scarcely literate. At Istanbul during the seventeenth and eighteenth centuries, rich and powerful ulema families intermarried and formed a distinct upper class group. But, at the same time, lower ranking ulema served in poor neighborhoods and in rural areas. These poor or rural religious scholars, although ulema and thus in one sense part of the same category as the Istanbul elites, had more in common socially, culturally, and economically with their artisan and peasant neighbors than the lofty ulema grandees. In sum, while "ulema" is a useful concept, it alone does not describe the place of the individual in Ottoman society.

Changing social mobility and clothing laws

Let us now turn to the specific issue of social mobility, the extraordinary movement within and between collectivities during the period. Until the eighteenth century, social mobility mainly occurred via the state apparatus. In earlier years, until perhaps the mid seventeenth century, the expansion of the empire had offered enormous opportunities for advancement. The *devşirme*, with its administrator and Janissary graduates, had meant that thousands of Christian peasants' sons rose to high positions of military and political power, enabling the acquisition of wealth and social prestige. Similarly, poor Turkish nomads routinely became the commanders of armies and rulers of provinces, or more modestly, unit leaders, with all the accompanying social and economic privilege. But, as territorial expansion slowed, so did mobility via military channels. Nonetheless, the vizier and pasha households offered graduates ready avenues along other career trajectories. Also, as seen, new civil members of the political elite, sometimes ulema, found sources of wealth outside the state, for example, in pious foundations.

Clothing laws since early times served as important indicators of social mobility and marked out the differences among officials, between officials and the subject classes and also among the subjects. The laws denoted the particular headgear and robes reserved for persons of each particular rank, emphasizing headgear but making distinctions in terms of types and colors of clothing, shoes, belts and other apparel. These laws were intended to divide people into separate groups, each with specific attire, and create a social order in which all knew their limits and gave respect to the notables (plates 6–8). Sometimes the state initiated the clothing laws or their enforcement. But on other occasions subjects did; fearing the erosion of their place in society, they appealed to the state for action. Clothing laws had prevailed in many areas of the "pre-modern" world, and historians have noted the close correlation between fashion changes and changes in the social structure. It seems important that Sultan Süleyman the Magnificent (1520–1566) passed a massive set of regulations governing sartorial behavior, just as the empire was completing an era of great social mobility and fluidity. Thereafter, clothing laws remained basically unchanged for more than 150 years, until c. 1720. During this period, one no longer of territorial expansion but rather state consolidation, there were relatively few fashion changes and comparatively little social mobility. But then, starting in the early eighteenth century, a steady stream of clothing laws flowed. At this time, everywhere in the world – in Europe, the Americas, East Asia, and the Ottoman Empire – new groups were emerging which challenged the economic, social, and political power of ruling dynasties and their supporters. In the Ottoman world, status derived from wealth increasingly competed with status gained from office holding, a process begun c. 1650 with the vizier and pasha households based on pious foundations. In the early eighteenth century, two new

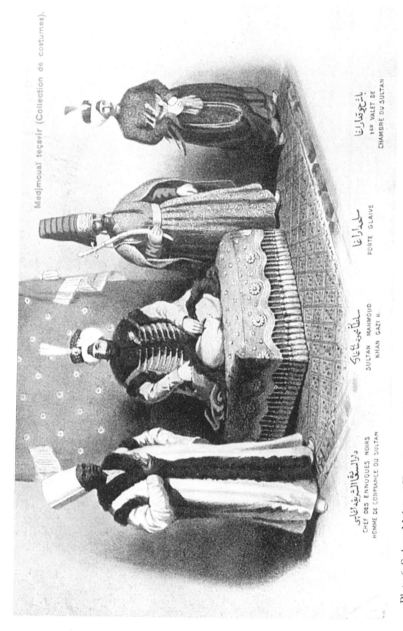

Medjmoual teçavir (Collection de costumes).

دراخ الثريفة الباشى

CHEF DES ENNUQUES NOIRS
HOMME DE CONFIANCE DU SULTAN

سلطان محمود خان غازى

SULTAN MAHMOUD
KHAN GAZI II.

سلادار اغا

PORTE GLAIVE

باغجنلاراغا

1ER VALET DE
CHAMBRE DU SULTAN

Plate 6 Sultan Mahmut II and some of his personal attendants
Postcard from the *Mecmua-ı Tecavir*, early nineteenth century. Personal collection of the author.

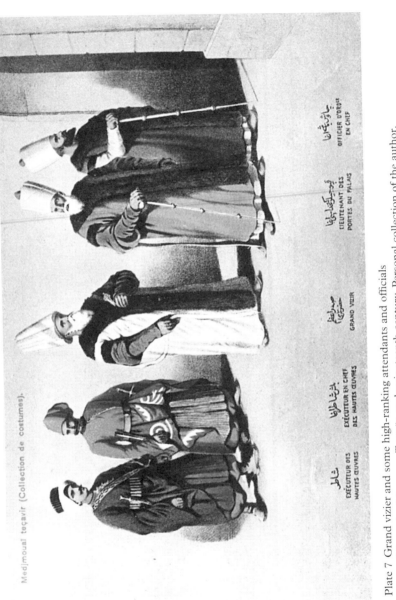

Plate 7 Grand vizier and some high-ranking attendants and officials
Postcard from the *Mecmua-ı Tecavir*, early nineteenth century. Personal collection of the author.

Plate 8 Police, military, and other officials
Postcard from *Mecmua-ı Tecavir*, early nineteenth century. Personal collection of the author.

groups began to emerge. First, thanks to mounting international trade and the general increase in the circulation of commodities, new Muslim and non-Muslim merchant groups developed. And second, the life-time tax farmers (*malikanecis*) who were created in the 1690s became a potent new source of political power, one bound to state wealth and functioning within the state apparatus.

Already during the Tulip Period, 1718–1730, the new wealth was evident and the court used competitive displays of consumption in order to keep the new rival groups at bay. Hence, Sultan Ahmet III and his son-in-law, Grand Vizier Ibrahim Pasha sponsored competitions of palace building and festivities, as well as other consumption displays such as tulip breeding. Their primary targets perhaps mainly were the lifetime tax farmers since international trade at this time was just beginning to become prominent.

Beginning in the Tulip Period and for the remainder of the eighteenth century, a host of clothing laws appeared, for example, in the 1720s, 1750s and 1790s. These laws preached for a status quo that was all too fugitive – for morality, social discipline, and order – and ranted against women's and men's clothing that was variously too tight, too immodest, too rich, too extravagant, or the wrong color. In the 1760s, laws condemned merchants and artisans for wearing ermine fur, reserved for the sultan and his viziers. In 1792, women's overcoats were said to be so thin as to be translucent and so were prohibited while, just a few years before, non-Muslims allegedly were wearing yellow shoes, a color permitted only to Muslims. Vibrant social change and mobility was occurring, to the consternation of the state and the social groups whose privileged place was being threatened. And so, they demanded that the state *do* something about it. To maintain its own legitimacy and the loyalties of the challenged groups – who often were from the older merchant groups and the state servant ranks – the state enacted this barrage of laws.

Social change and mobility became so extreme and so beyond the state's ability to control that, in 1829, Sultan Mahmut II overnight gave in and abolished the old social markers based on wearing apparel. Instead, a new set of regulations demanded that all officials wear the fez, that is, exactly the same headgear. With this action, all state servants looked the same: the different turbans and robes of honor were gone. The religious classes specifically were exempted from the legislation. Ottoman women, for their part, simply were ignored. Moreover, the Sultan intended that the non-official classes put on the fez as well, to create an undifferentiated Ottoman subjecthood without distinction. The 1829 law reversed the previous practice of using clothing legislation to create or maintain difference. Instead, it sought to impose visual uniformity among all male state servants and subjects.

Plate 9 Court functionaries at a ceremony in the Topkapi palace during the
reign of Sultan Abdülhamit II
Carney E. S. Gavin *et al.*, "Imperial self-portrait; the Ottoman Empire as
revealed in the Sultan Abdul Hamid's photograph albums," special issue
of *Journal of Turkish Studies* (1998), 98. Reprinted with permission of the
publisher.

Long-standing rules that had sought to distinguish cobblers from sil-
versmiths and merchants from artisans and Muslims from non-Muslims
disappeared overnight. In wearing the fez, government officials and the
rest of male society (outside of the religious classes) thereafter were to
look the same before the monarch and to one another. There were to
be no clothing indicators of occupation, rank, or religion. The 1829 law
thus anticipated the more famous Tanzimat decrees of 1839 and 1856
that sought to establish equality among all Ottoman subjects, regardless
of religious or other group identity.

Many welcomed the final disappearance of the old markers that had
strained and finally collapsed in the face of mounting social change
(plates 9 and 17). The fez, frock coat, and pants became the new
"uniform" of the official classes. Now free of legal restraints, many wealthy
merchants, who primarily were non-Muslims, immediately adopted the

Plate 10 Example of workers' headgear and clothing, later nineteenth century: kebab seller and others, probably Istanbul
Sébah and Joaillier photograph. Personal collection of the author.

new attire in order to escape the discrimination that difference sometimes had brought. But other Ottoman subjects rejected the effort to create uniform clothing and instead created new social markers. At the lower end of the social scale, for example, Ottoman workers – Muslims and non-Muslims alike – often rejected the fez. This was not a reactionary measure opposing equality of Muslim and non-Muslim. Rather, the workers were insisting on their identity as workers, on retaining class difference and a solidarity against a state that was attacking guild privilege, had destroyed their Janissary protectors, and was dismantling economic programs that long had afforded privilege and protection to workers. Many but not all Muslim and non-Muslim workers insisted on headgear that marked them as a distinct group. See plates 5, 10, and 11 that show some workers with the fez and others retaining distinctive headgear. Further up the social ladder, many wealthy Muslims and non-Muslims displayed their new wealth, power, and social prominence by dressing extravagantly in the latest fashions. In the process, they made a mockery of the 1829 legislation attempting to impose uniformity, modesty, and simplicity.

The mounting sartorial heterogeneity of the nineteenth century thus mirrored rising social fluidity and the ongoing dissolution of the old boundaries among various occupational and religious groups and ranks in

Plate 11 Example of workers' headgear and clothing, later nineteenth century: textile workers, Urfa, c. 1900
Raymond H. Kevorkian and Paul B. Paboudjian, eds., *Les Arméniens dans l'empire ottoman à la veille du genocide* (Paris, 1992). With permission.

Ottoman society. These extraordinary and accelerating changes in dress also occurred among Ottoman women, as seen below, reflecting the transformations that marked eighteenth- and nineteenth-century Ottoman society.

Ottoman private spaces

In the Ottoman world, the home often was the testing ground for social innovation. Women first tried out fashions in private, at home, and from there took them out into the public spaces. While this process likely was not uniquely Ottoman, it was not a universal principle either. In nineteenth-century Japan, for example, western clothing was worn in public spaces but inside the home older forms of clothing prevailed. In the eighteenth and early nineteenth centuries, Ottoman women in their residences had worn baggy pants (*shalvar*) and a flowing, three-skirted, household dress. As the nineteenth century wore on, however, urban elite women began to wear new fashions at home, shifting to puffy skirts, corsets for a thin-waisted look, and a chignon hairstyle. Following these experiments at home, they wore the new styles in the public spaces, taking care to conceal them with a long skirted veil that covered practically every part of the body. Over time, this long skirted veil became transformed into something resembling European women's coats and the veil became more and more transparent (plate 12). Still later, c. 1910, the flapper look appeared.

Not only fashions but also other social innovations were first tested in the home. For example, the prevailing Ottoman practice of separate socializing for males and for females was experimented with and then broken at home. Among elite nineteenth-century families, initially in Istanbul and the port cities and then elsewhere, couples began visiting close friends together, as couples, and the practices of women visiting women and men visiting men diminished.

Specialists argue over the meaning of the western clothing that Ottoman women and men wore. Some analysts state that the adoption of western attire and other cultural forms reflected westernization, or the desire to be part of the West. This view seems difficult to maintain. If this is true, how then are we to understand the widespread Ottoman use of Indian textiles in the early nineteenth century – were the Ottomans trying to become Indian? Others see the adoption of western fashions in a more complex way, *not* as an effort to integrate into western society but rather part of a larger "civilizing process" during the nineteenth century. By donning lace dresses or cutaway coats in the latest Parisian fashion, individuals were seeking to mark their social differentiation and modernity – that they were part of the new, not the old, and were superior to those in their own society who did not wear such attire (plate 13).

Structure of the home

We need to remember the extraordinary variety of the Ottoman world that stretched from Belgrade to Istanbul to Aintab to Damascus and Beirut. My goal here is not to make categorically true statements about all homes but rather to leave an impression of Ottoman domestic life, both urban and rural, during the 1700–1922 period. With that in mind, let us begin.

The spatial layout of urban homes before the nineteenth century was more conducive to separate gender spaces than rural homes. In many urban homes, there was a *selamlik* section, the predominantly male space, at the front while the *haremlik*, the female space, was located elsewhere. This *haremlik* may have been primarily an urban, upper-class phenomenon. Urban homes often held the *selamlik* room, which the oldest male had

Plate 12 Female outdoor attire, c. 1890, likely Istanbul
Edwin A. Grosvenor, *Constantinople* (Boston, 1895).

Plate 13 Female indoor attire: Muhlise, the daughter of photographer Ali
Sami, Istanbul, 1907
From the collection of Engin Çizgen, with thanks.

the prerogative to use, in the center with independent rooms off of it but without corridors linking these to each other. Males socialized in the one space, and females in the other. Before the nineteenth century, in virtually all urban elite and non-elite homes, furnishings consisted of pillows on raised platforms placed against the walls. People sat on pillows on carpeted or matted floors. When eating, they gathered around large trays, raised perhaps a foot above the floor, and ate with their hands from communal dishes. Wealthy people ate meat, previously cut into small pieces. Rooms tended to be multi-purpose; the entertaining areas of the male and female sections converted to bedrooms in the evening. Furnishings often were modest. For example, the home of a wealthy urban family in Syria in the 1780s contained carpets, mats, cushions, some small cotton cloths, copper and wood platters, stewing pans, a mortar and portable coffee mill, a little porcelain, and some tinned plates.

In the early nineteenth century, important furnishing changes were taking place. At the port city of Izmir, homes of wealthy merchants were filling up with goods from Paris and London, including knives, forks, tables, chairs, and English fireplaces along with English coal. By the end of the century, chairs, tables, beds, and bedsteads had become relatively common in elite homes in Istanbul and the port cities and were spreading to inland cities and towns. As the new furniture moved in, the functions of Ottoman domestic spaces changed. Multi-purpose rooms of the past became single purpose. Separate bedrooms, living rooms, and dining rooms emerged, each filled with specialized furniture that could not be moved about or stored in order to use the room for another purpose.

Turning now to homes in rural areas, we find that many peasant dwellings divided simply into three rooms, one for sleeping, and the others for cooking/storage and for sitting. These were very small spaces with no real spatial division by gender. Here is a nineteenth-century description of village homes in the Black Sea coastal areas around Trabzon:

The cottage is fairly clean, especially if its inhabitants are Mahometan [Muslim], and is much more spacious than the dwelling of the town artizan. Regularly it has three rooms, one for sleeping, one for sitting in, and one for cooking... Glass is unknown; the roof, made of wooden shingles in the coast region, of earth if in the interior, is far from water-tight, and the walls let in wind and rain everywhere...
The peasant's food is mostly vegetable, and in great measure the produce of his own ground. Maize bread in the littoral districts, and brown bread, in which rye and barley are largely mixed for the inland provinces, form nine-tenths of a coarse but not unwholesome diet. This is varied

occasionally with milk, curds, cheese, and eggs; the more so if the household happens to possess a cow and barn-door fowls. Dried meat or fish are rare but highly esteemed luxuries. Water is the only drink...[1]

To demonstrate the variety of rural housing in the various areas of the empire, consider another description, this one from the Bulgarian regions during the nineteenth century:

The houses of the better class of peasant farmers are solidly constructed of stone, and sufficiently comfortable. The cottages of the poorer class, however, are of the most primitive style of architecture. A number of poles mark out the extent to be given to the edifice, the spaces between them being filled up with wattles of osier, plastered thickly within and without with clay and cow dung mixed with straw... The interior of an average cottage is divided into three rooms – the common living-room, the family bedroom, and the storeroom. The floor is of earth, beaten hard, and is covered with coarse matting and thick homemade rugs. The furniture consists chiefly of cushions covered with thick woven tissues which also serve the family as beds... Like all the peasants of Turkey [the Ottoman empire], the Bulgarians are most economical and even frugal in their habits. They are content with very little, and live generally on rye bread and maize porridge, or beans seasoned with vinegar and pepper, supplemented by the produce of the dairy.[2]

The homes of nomads were even simpler than those of sedentary peasants. In the late eighteenth century, the bedouin of Syria lived in tents, within which were weapons, a pipe, a portable coffee mill, a cooking pot, leather bucket, coffee roaster, mat, clothes, black wool mantle and a few pieces of glass or silver.

In the 1870s, by comparison, some three-quarter million pastoral nomads of the Erzurum–Diyarbekir region lived in the following manner:

During the winter they live in small huts constructed of loose stone, but of a far more miserable character, if possible, than those ... situated in low-lying valleys. Their flocks and horses are penned and tethered in similar but larger buildings communicating with the dwelling chamber, as in other villages already noticed. In spring and summer they migrate to the hills in their or adjacent districts, where they live in spacious goathair or woollen tents. Their food is the same as that of the agricultural class... with them, also, meat is rarely used, unless travellers of consequence alight at their homes... Their furniture is rather better than that of the other classes, inasmuch as their females

[1] British consul Palgrave at Trabzon; cited in Şevket Pamuk, *The Ottoman Empire and European capitalism, 1820–1913* (Cambridge, 1987), 188.
[2] Lucy M. J. Garnett, *Balkan home life* (New York, 1917), 180; but written when Bulgaria was inside the Ottoman Empire.

manufacture good carpets, with which every family is provided, in addition to fine felts.[3]

New public spaces

The economic, social, and political transformations reflected by the changes in Ottoman apparel and private spaces, that were more pronounced in urban centers than rural areas, also can be seen in the emergence of new public spaces in the nineteenth century. Control of public space should be understood as an extension of the struggle for political clout and social pre-eminence. Unfortunately, virtually all of the evidence presented here applies only to the capital city. Istanbul and the port cities felt the kinds of developments traced below earlier and more acutely than elsewhere in the empire, for in these places the economic changes were the most pronounced.

Sites of public display, where persons came out to promenade and show their finery, were important places of socialization in pre-modern cities with their narrow, winding, and often very muddy streets. In Istanbul, the most important sites for centuries were two stream valleys named the Sweet Waters of Europe, situated up the Golden Horn, and the Sweet Waters of Asia, on the other side of the Bosphorus. There, the wealthy and powerful of the imperial capital long had congregated, picnicked, and paraded their wealth and power. In the early nineteenth century, "the poorer classes who are unable to command a carriage, or a caique [small boat], will cheerfully toil on foot from the city, under a scorching sun, in order to secure their portion of the festival" (see plates 14 and 15).[4] The major religions during the nineteenth century maintained a certain sharing of the spaces: on Fridays, crowds of Muslims dominated while on Sundays, Christians took over the places.

Over the course of the nineteenth century, however, the public gradually abandoned these sites in favor of new places of public display. Unlike at the two Sweet Waters locations, rich non-Muslims dominated these new public spaces, setting the tone with their fashion finery. Both of these new public spaces were cemeteries and adjacent open areas – named the Grand and Petit Champs du Morts – and were located in the Pera district, that is, in the predominantly European and Ottoman Christian sections of the city. To these places and not to the Sweet Waters increasingly went the fashion leaders, the fancy people, the trend setters, and those who wanted to know the latest fashions. Thus, non-Muslims replaced the

---

[3] British consul Wilkinson at Erzurum, cited in Pamuk, *The Ottoman Empire*, 186.
[4] Julia Pardoe, *Beauties of the Bosphorus* (London, 1839 and 1840), 8.

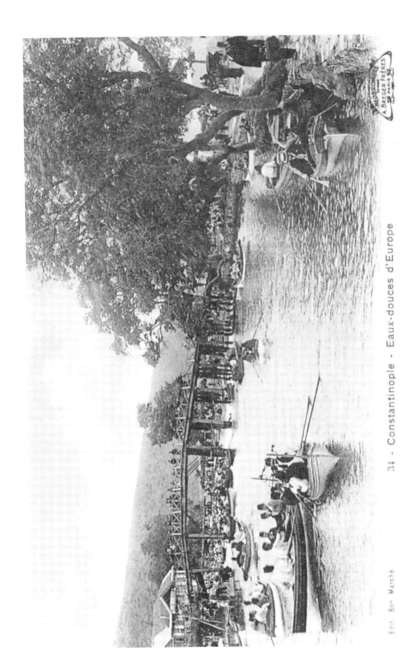

Edit Bon Marché   31 - Constantinople - Eaux-douces d'Europe

Plate 14 Sweet Waters of Europe, c. 1900
Personal collection of author.

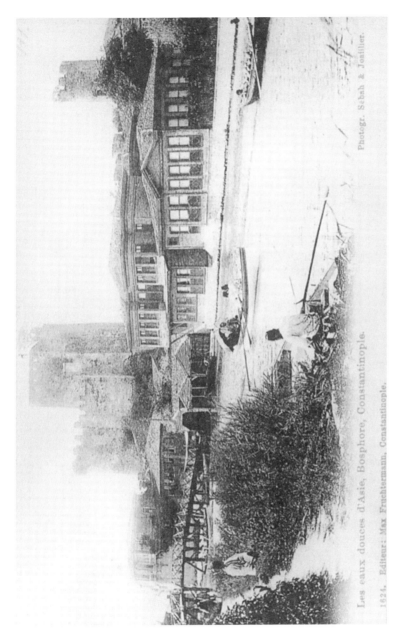

Les eaux douces d'Asie, Bosphore, Constantinople.

1624. Editeur: Max Fruchtermann, Constantinople.

Photogr. Sebah & Joaillier.

Plate 15 Sweet Waters of Asia, c. 1900
Personal collection of author.

Muslims as fashion leaders. Social status was contested in the clothing competitions of the public spaces. While the fez and frock coat became the standard attire of the official classes, the non-Muslims led the way in wearing elegant, expensive, up-to-the-minute fashions from Paris.

Significantly, non-Muslims as a group were the fashion setters and the economic leaders but not the political leaders. A tension existed between their mounting economic wealth, their social/sartorial leadership roles and their politically subordinate position, a contradiction which the 1829 clothing legislation and the 1839 and 1856 reform decrees sought to resolve.

The coffee house and the bathhouse

In the Ottoman world, the coffee house served as the pre-eminent public male space. Coffee houses initially appeared in Istanbul with coffee in 1555, entering via Aleppo and Damascus from Arabia, the source of the first coffee, mocha. Soon after, c. 1609, tobacco arrived. Thereafter, the combination of coffee and tobacco became hallmarks of Ottoman and Middle East culture, inseparable from hospitality and socialization. The two over time became the first truly mass consumption commodities in the Ottoman world. From its introduction until the second half of the twentieth century, the coffee house functioned as the very center of male public life in the Ottoman and post-Ottoman world. (Thanks to television, it now seems to be dying in most areas of the Middle East.) Coffee houses were everywhere: in early nineteenth-century Istanbul, for example, they accounted for perhaps one in five commercial shops in the city.[5] Hence, the vast expansion of male gendered public spaces in the Ottoman world was intricately linked with a consumer revolution that began in the seventeenth century (and took on new forms with the accelerating changes in clothing fashion of the eighteenth and nineteenth centuries). In these coffee houses, men drank, smoked, and enjoyed story telling, music, cards, backgammon, and other forms of entertainment that sometimes were held outside, in front of the coffee house.

Bathhouses, for their part, provided public gendered spaces for female (and male) sociability. In earlier times, indoor plumbing, although known, was exceptional. Most people did not have an in-home water source and so depended on public bathing facilities. This hygienic need for bathhouses was compounded by the powerful emphasis that Islam and the Muslim world places on personal cleanliness. As a result, bathhouses

---

[5] Cengiz Kırlı, "The struggle over space: coffeehouses of Ottoman Istanbul, 1780–1840," Unpublished Ph.D. Dissertation (Binghamton University, 2000).

were a routine presence in Ottoman towns and cities. Larger ones afforded separate facilities for men and for women while the smaller bathhouses scheduled times for women only and for men only. Bathhouses provided women with crucial spaces for socialization outside the home. There they not only met friends but also negotiated marriage alliances and made business contacts.

Other forms and sites of sociability

Eating out places were very uncommon until the later nineteenth century. But men and women routinely traveled to market places, an important public site. There, women, dressed in their public garb, bought and sold from merchants on a regular basis. Similarly, the areas before places of worship – mosques, churches, and synagogues – afforded spaces for conversation, entertainment, and business negotiations.

In such spaces, the Ottoman public enjoyed story telling by professionals who recited tales, some of them Homeric in length and speaking of sultans and heroes and great deeds. Other reciters spoke of life, of love, and emotion, often in poetic form, and sometimes quite explicitly. Take these examples from a seventeenth-century folk poet, very popular in later years as well:

> ... tell them I'm dead
> Let them gather to pray for my soul
> Let them bury me by the side of the road
> Let young girls pause at my grave

or

> Save me, O lord
> My eyes have seen her ripe breasts
> How I long to gather her peaches
> To kiss the down on her cheeks[6]

Shadow puppet theater (*karagöz*), that today still is enjoyed from Greece to Indonesia, was perhaps the most popular entertainment in Ottoman times. Audiences gathered before a translucent screen. Behind the screen worked one or more puppetmasters who used short poles to hold the paper-thin, colored, shadow puppets against the screen, moving them about as the plot dictated. These shadow puppets were made of scraped animal skin, incised and multi-colored. To the sides of the screen were fixed stage props (*göstermelik*), made of the same materials. There were

---

[6] Seyfi Karabaş and Judith Yarnall, *Poems by Karacaoğlan: A Turkish bard* (Bloomington, 1996).

scores of fixed stories immediately familiar to the audiences watching them – about love, politics, folly, and sagacity – based on folk wisdom with the characters representing the common voice. In addition, the performers prepared impromptu plots reflecting current political conditions. For example, *karagöz* masters in Aleppo ridiculed the Janissaries who were returning from their failed campaign in the Ottoman–Russian War of 1768. The shadow puppet theaters were places of social commentary, safe places from which to criticize contemporary events, the state, and its elites.

In the nineteenth century, competing forms of entertainment began arriving from Western Europe. Many foreign troupes performed operas in Istanbul during the late 1830s while Western theater arrived in 1840, also performed by a traveling company. Within several decades, the performances were by Ottoman subjects, not foreigners, and even some smaller provincial towns had their theater companies. Movies arrived in Istanbul in 1897, two years after their invention in France by the brothers Lumière.

In the world of Ottoman sports, wrestling was very popular, particularly in the Balkan provinces while archery and falconry enjoyed a following among elites. By the late nineteenth century, a host of competing sports activities had arrived from abroad in Istanbul and the port cities such as Salonica. These included football (soccer), tennis, cycling, swimming, flying, gymnastics, croquet, and boxing. Similarly, a football and rugby club appeared in Izmir in 1890. Football caught on somewhat while other sports did not; for example, tennis in Istanbul remained within the palace grounds (as it did in contemporary imperial China).

Sufi brotherhoods and their lodges

The Sufi brotherhoods and lodges, which included men and women, played a central role in Ottoman social life and were another important place of socialization outside the home. In this case, the place exclusively was Muslim and contained within it both male and female spaces, for visitors as well as adherents. Some brotherhoods had emerged with the Turkish invasions of the Middle East and had assisted in the Ottoman rise to power during the fourteenth century. Many thus were located in areas where ethnic Turks had settled, such as Anatolia and parts of the Balkans. But they also were thoroughly commonplace across the Arab lands as well. Everywhere, these brotherhoods were crucially important both in the realm of religion and for their social functions. Although the mosque, its prayers, rituals, and instruction were central to the religious life of Ottoman Muslims, the brotherhoods' religious importance can hardly be overstated. The beliefs and practices of the brotherhoods provided many women and men with a set of vital, personal, and intimate religious experiences that alternately combined with or transcended those of the mosque. Also, the brotherhoods served as among the most important socialization spaces for Muslim men and women in Ottoman society, providing members with a host of relationships important in social, commercial, and sometimes political life. It is often said that, during the nineteenth century, most residents of the imperial capital and many major cities were either members or affiliates of a brotherhood.

Brotherhoods formed around loyalty to the teachings of a male or female individual, the founding sheikh, usually revered as a saint. These holy persons, by their example and teachings, had formed a distinctive path to religious truth and to the mystical experience. The teachings of each brotherhood varied but shared in a common effort to have an intimate encounter with God and find personal peace. Members gathered in a lodge (*tekke*), for communal prayer (*zikr*) and to perform a set of specific devotional practices. The Mevlevi brotherhoods whirled about in circles seeking to gain the mystic vision, others chanted. Financed by members' contributions, lodges in nineteenth-century Istanbul most often were ordinary buildings, usually the house of the sheikh who was its living leader. Many lodges, however, consisted of a complex of buildings that included a library, hospice, and tomb, a cell for the sheikh and the students, both men and women, as well as classrooms, a kitchen, public bath, and toilets. In addition, "grand lodges" (*asitane*) held residential buildings for families, single persons, and for visitors, male and female, in addition to the library, prayer hall, and kitchen. In late Ottoman times, Istanbul alone contained some twenty different brotherhoods that together possessed 300 lodges (compared with perhaps 500 in the seventeenth century). Among the most popular brotherhoods in nineteenth-century Istanbul were the Kadiri with fifty-seven lodges and Nakshibandi with fifty-six lodges. The Halveti, Celveti, Sa'di and Rufai also were important, followed by groups such as the Mevlevi with fewer than ten lodges. The brotherhoods often drew on distinct social groups. The Mevlevis, for example, were small in size but politically powerful because its members belonged to the upper classes and included many state leaders. The Bektashis, by contrast, drew from the artisanal and lower classes. They had been chaplains of the Janissaries and thus were suppressed in 1826.

Tombs of the saints

The brotherhoods, as seen, had close connections to holy men and women, saints who were highly revered in the Ottoman world. Visiting their tombs was widely practiced and supplicants often arrived in families or in groups of lodge members. Visitors prayed at the tombs for the saint's intercession, lighting candles and sleeping near or on the tomb, a few hours for most illnesses but up to forty days for graver diseases and mental problems. Women often prayed to conceive a child or for a successful pregnancy. To obtain the blessings of the saint, supplicants frequently tied ribbons to the bushes nearby or to the grillwork of the tomb structure; or they placed a water offering or a shirt or piece of clothing on the tomb.

Many Muslim shrines arose on sites of religious importance that dated back to the Christian era, places which in turn often had pre-Christian significance. At least ten tombs in the Balkan provinces were devoted to the Muslim saint Sari Saltuk – who possessed the attributes of St. George – and one of these, in Albania, is in a grotto where the saint reportedly had killed a dragon with seven heads. Sanctuaries of saints frequently served both Christians and Muslims, for example a Bektashi shrine on Mount Tomor in Albania was dedicated to the Holy Virgin. In central Anatolia, within a single shrine stood a Christian church at one end and a mosque at the other while in the city of Salonica, the Church of St. Dimitri had become a mosque but the saint's tomb remained open to Christians. Not unusually, Christians and Muslims in many areas celebrated the holy day of the same person on the same day in the same place, but using different names for the saint. At Deli Orman, in the Balkans, the Muslim Demir Baba and the Christian St. Elias were both remembered on August 1. Near Kossovo, there was a shrine of a different sort, preserving blood from the body of Sultan Murat I, who was killed on the battlefield in 1389, and later transported to Bursa for burial.

Holidays

Holidays were a special time, to dress up in the best clothes, go for a promenade and enjoy special entertainments. Almost all Ottoman holidays commemorated religious events and drew on a number of different religious traditions and calendars. In the late nineteenth century, official calendars noted the day according to the Julian system for Christians; the hijra for Muslims (based on an event in the life of the Prophet Muhammad); and the financial calendar. The notable exceptions to religious festivals were celebrations connected to the life of the dynasty, including weddings and circumcisions and, during the late nineteenth century at least, empire-wide observations of the sultan's birthday. To give another example of another non-religious holiday: in the early twentieth century, miners and officials in the coal mining districts of the Black Sea coast gathered to commemorate the accession anniversary of the sultan, a ceremony intended to foster loyalty and a sense of wider identity, and perhaps community among managers and workers (plate 16). Some holidays

Plate 16 Holiday ceremony, Black Sea region c. 1900
Personal collection of author.

in earlier times had celebrated great military victories. In the eighteenth
century, when these were few, an annual banquet prior to the departure
of the fleet celebrated its coming tour of the Mediterranean.

Certain religious holidays went beyond the particular religion: the
Muslim Ramadan in part was a holiday for all (see below). The bless-
ing of Muslim fishing vessels occurred on the feast day of the Epiphany,
a Christian festival. Among Ottoman Christians, St. John's Day in July
and the Assumption of the Virgin in August were important days: Greek
women, even the humblest of them, the fishermen's wives, are said to have
worn elegant dresses of silk or velvet and cloaks lined with expensive furs.
There were many Muslim holidays, including days that commemorated
the birth of the Prophet or his ascent into heaven.

Ramadan, however, easily loomed as the most important holiday, the
most significant time of public life in the Ottoman world.[7] This greatest
of all Muslim holidays is the ninth month of the hijra calendar. In this

[7] The material on Ramadan is drawn from: François Georgeon, "Le ramadan à Istanbul,"
in F. Georgeon and P. Dumont, *Vivre dans l'empire Ottoman. Sociabilités et relations inter-
communautaires (xviie-xxe siècles)* (Paris, 1997), 31–113.

month, the Koran was revealed, the "Night of Power" (*Leyl ul qadir*). Ramadan was doubly and triply important for during this month fell the anniversaries of the birth of Hüseyin, and of the deaths of Ali and of Khadija – three vitally important figures in Islamic history and religion. Moreover, Ramadan also celebrated the anniversary of the battle of Badr, the first important military victory of the Prophet Muhammad. To honor these events, especially the Night of Power, Muslims observed a month of fasting, Ramadan. From the first crack of sunrise until sunset they are enjoined not to eat, drink (not even water), smoke, or have sex. Cannon shots signaled sunset as well as the onset of the fast at sunrise. The fast month ended with the *Şeker Bayramı*, one of the two major holidays in the Islamic calendar.

During Ramadan, a time of intense socializing, the rhythm of daily life profoundly changed. Istanbul and the other cities in effect shut down during the daytime, both in the public and private sectors. But then, shops and coffee houses stayed open all night long, lighted by lamps. Only during Ramadan did night life flourish – the holiday changed night into day. In the weeks before, houses were cleaned, insects removed, pillows re-stuffed and preparations begun for the many special foods. The daily breaking of the fast, a celebratory meal named the *iftar*, brought forth foods and breads especially prepared for the occasion. A central social event in this intensely social month, the *iftar* meal each day provided the occasion for visiting and for hospitality. Grandees maintained open tables and strangers – the poor, beggars – would show up, be fed and given a gift, often cash, on departure. In the eighteenth century, the grand vizier routinely gave presents – gold, furs, textiles, and jewels – to state dignitaries at *iftar*. Sheikhs of various brotherhoods were especially honored, often with fur-lined coats. These protocol visits at home among officials, however, actually were legislated out of existence during the 1840s; thereafter, official visiting occurred only in the offices. Lower down in the social order, masters gave gifts to their servants and to persons doing services for them, for example, merchants, watchmen and firemen (*tulumbacıs*). In the mid-nineteenth century, the poor presented themselves at the palace of Sultan Abdülmecit, to receive gifts from the sultan's aides de camp. (This had been a more general custom until the Tanzimat reforms but thereafter was restricted to the *iftar* during Ramadan.) During at least the eighteenth and early nineteenth centuries, on the fifteenth day of Ramadan, the sultans visited the sacred mantle of the Prophet Muhammad within the Topkapi palace and distributed sweets (baklava) to the Janissaries. After 1826, sultans continued to honor the army, giving them special Ramadan breads. During the reign of Sultan Abdülhamit II, a different regiment dined at Yildiz palace each evening and received gifts.

Ramadan provided a month of distractions, not only by exchanging home visits but also through a host of special public amusements. It was the grand season for *karagöz* shadow puppet theater and performers memorized twenty-eight different stories in order to present a different one each night up to the eve of the *bayram*. Similarly, as theater developed in the later nineteenth century, Ramadan became the theater season, with special shows customary by the early twentieth century. And, there were special Ramadan cinema shows in Istanbul within a decade of the introduction of movies. In the eighteenth century, social events had turned on the *iftar* and included promenades, *karagöz*, and coffee houses while, in the nineteenth century, these had expanded to include new entertainment forms such as the theater and cinema. Ramadan, in a certain sense, was a month of carnival when social barriers fell or, as in carnival in Europe, the rules were suspended. Hence, for example, the state during the early nineteenth century generally forbade men and women from going about together in public but an imperial command allowed them to do so at the *Şeker Bayramı*.

And, this month also was a time of heightened religious sensibilities and religious activity. Across the empire, ulema continuously read the Koran in the mosques of towns and cities until the eve of the *Şeker Bayramı*. During Ramadan, many visited holy places and the tombs of the saints including, in Istanbul, the Eyüp shrine as well as the graves of their relatives where they passed the entire night in tents. After the *Şeker Bayramı* prayer, families gathered in silence at the tombs of parents and close relatives. Also, the ranking ulema offered special lessons, with readings of the Koran, before the sultan. Students preparing for a career in the religious ranks left their schools during Ramadan and toured the countryside preaching, receiving both money and gifts in kind from the villagers. In Istanbul, in a practice that may have begun during the Tulip Period of the early eighteenth century, the mosques and minarets were strung with lights, sometimes in the form of words or symbols (called *mahya*). Until public lighting was installed in 1860, the effect of such lights must have been amazing. Imagine the impact of these strings of lighted words and symbols on an otherwise-darkened city of nearly a million, normally lighted only by the lamps that persons were required to carry.

Ramadan also promoted inter-communal relations. Many non-Muslims were invited to break the fast at the imperial palace, a practice that set and mirrored the standard of behavior for the rest of society; many Muslims opened their homes to non-Muslim neighbors and friends for the breaking of the fast. Thus, the festival both heightened the sense of Muslim-ness while also promoting social relations between Muslims and non-Muslims.

The actual observance of the fast of course varied enormously, by place, time, and individual. Overall, the public complied and transgressions were in private without wider consequences. In eighteenth-century Istanbul, the neighborhood exerted social pressure but levied no punishments beyond public condemnation – usually by the *imam* or a person (*kabadayı*) who acted as its guarantor of public honor. During the nineteenth century, this began to change. Fasting in Istanbul became an issue of public order as the old system of regulating public behavior dissolved. The clothing changes of Sultan Mahmut II, which rendered visible distinctions less clear, made it easier for transgressing Muslims to slip into non-Muslim quarters of the city in order to eat or drink. Other forms of state regulation of public behavior changed as well. A government official (*mühtesib*) had supervised the market and kept local order. But the post was abolished in 1854 and its functions split between two sets of law and order authorities, the police and the gendarmes. These changes, together with the enactment of new legal codes, spelled confusion in the regulation of public behavior. Unsure of their position, the ulema more stridently demanded adherence to fasting and sought new rationales – at one point arguing that fasting made for good health. The civil authorities were similarly uncertain: in one quarter of the capital, the police used a bastinado on those who publicly ate or drank during Ramadan. But the typicality of such public punishments remains uncertain.

From the very highest levels, the state during the late nineteenth century sent confusing signals about the observance of Ramadan. Recall Sultan Abdülhamit II, who powerfully stressed his role as caliph, leader of the Muslim faithful. It seems at first surprising to read that officials in his Yildiz palace offices ate, drank, and smoked all through Ramadan. Such behavior derived from the state's effort during the nineteenth century to create a new discipline and keep people at work in their offices. Hence, regulations declared fasting as incompatible with modern civilization. Work life was to go on as usual and the normal business hours for government offices would be kept. But the state behaved differently towards late nineteenth-century schools. Ramadan remained a holiday in the Muslim religious schools, the *medreses*, as in the past. And, when the state opened hundreds of schools of several types and at various levels – primary, secondary, medical, and military and others – it maintained Ramadan as a school holiday.

Reading and literacy

Only a tiny minority could read in what long had been and largely remained an oral Ottoman culture: in 1752, the largest library in the city of

Plate 17 Graduating class of the National College, Harput, 1909–1910
Raymond H. Kevorkian and Paul B. Paboudjian, eds., *Les Arméniens dans
l'empire ottoman à la veille du genocide* (Paris, 1992). With permission.

Aleppo contained only 3,000 volumes. At the time, Aleppo held thirty-
one Muslim *medrese* schools, altogether educating perhaps hundreds of
students. Among females, extremely few could read, a far smaller proportion than among males. Literacy overall increased sharply during the
nineteenth century due to both private and public initiatives. On the one
hand, the number of privately funded schools among Ottoman Christians
and Jews rose dramatically, as did the presence of foreign-run mission-
ary schools that catered mainly to the Greek and Armenian communities. For example, fifty private Jewish schools annually trained 9,000 students in late nineteenth-century Salonica, that contained a large Jewish
population. On the other hand, a state-sponsored educational system
emerged, especially in the final third of the century. A network of officially financed schools evolved at all levels, ranging from the elementary, lower secondary, and upper secondary to the professional. Estimates
suggest general Muslim literacy rates equaling about 2–3 percent in the
early nineteenth century and perhaps 15 percent at its end. In what remained of the Ottoman Empire at the end of the nineteenth century,
nearly 5,000 state primary schools enrolled over 650,000 students. Less
than 10 percent of these were girls (plates 17–19). And, in the early
twentieth century, approximately 40,000 students attended the state-run

Plate 18 Students at the secondary school for girls at Emirgan, Istanbul, during the reign of Sultan Abdülhamit II
Carney E. S. Gavin *et al.*, "Imperial self-portrait: the Ottoman Empire as revealed in the Sultan Abdul Hamid's photograph albums," special issue of *Journal of Turkish Studies* (1998), 98. Reprinted with permission of the publisher.

secondary schools. While these are impressive increases, the numbers of students being trained paled before the educational needs of the population. Strapped Ottoman finances continued to retard the fuller emergence of the state-run school system.

Another measure of literacy is to count the number of books and newspapers being published. Before 1840, only eleven books annually were published in Istanbul while that number had increased to 285, produced by ninety-nine printing houses, in 1908. Other statistics yield a similar impression of rapidly mounting book production and literacy. Between 1729 and 1829, c. 180 titles appeared in print while during the mere sixteen years between 1876 and 1892, the number increased to 6,357. And, remarkably, 10,601 titles appeared between 1893 and 1907. There were similarly impressive increases in the number of newspapers and

Plate 19 Students at the Imperial Medical School, c. 1890
From the Sultan Abdülhamir II's albums. Personal collection of the author.

journals being published: 1875 – 87; 1895 – 226; 1903 – 365, and 1911 – 548. Two of the leading newspapers in Istanbul daily printed 15,000 and 12,000 copies each during Sultan Abdülhamit II's reign, when censorship prevailed. Circulation soared after the Young Turk Revolution and the emergence of a free press, respectively to 60,000 and 40,000 daily issues.[8]

Suggested bibliography

Entries marked with a * designate recommended readings for new students of the subject.

*And, Metin. *Karagöz*, 3rd edn (Istanbul, n.d.).

Andrews, Walter *et al.*, eds. and trans. *Ottoman lyric poetry: an anthology* (Austin, 1997).

Artan, Tülay. "Architecture as a theatre of life: profile of the eighteenth-century Bosphorus." Unpublished Ph.D. dissertation, Massachusetts Institute of Technology, 1989.

*Atıl, Esen. *Levni and the surname. The story of an eighteenth century Ottoman festival* (Istanbul, 1999).

Barnes, John Robert. *An introduction to religious foundations in the Ottoman Empire* (Leiden, 1986).

Behar, Cem. "Neighborhood nuptials: Islamic personal law and local customs – marriage records in a mahalle of traditional Istanbul (1864–1907)," *International Journal of Middle East Studies* 36, 4 (2004), 537–559.

Bierman, Irene, *et al.* *The Ottoman city and its parts* (New Rochelle, 1991).

Birge, John Kingsley. *The Bektashi order of dervishes* (London, 1965).

*Brown, Sarah Graham. *Images of women: The portrayal of women in photography of the Middle East, 1860–1950* (London, 1988).

*Çelik, Zeyneb. *The remaking of Istanbul* (Seattle and London, 1989).

*Doumani, Beshara, ed. *Family history in the Middle East. Household, property and gender* (Albany, 2003).

Duben, Alan and Cem Behar. *Istanbul households: Marriage, family and fertility 1880–1940* (Cambridge, 1991).

*Esenbel, Selcuk. "The anguish of civilized behavior: the use of western cultural forms in the everyday lives of the Meijii Japanese and the Ottoman Turks during the nineteenth century," *Japan Review*, 5 (1995), 145–185.

Feldman, Walter. *Music of the Ottoman court* (Berlin, 1996).

Garnett, Lucy M. J. *Mysticism and magic in Turkey* (London, 1912).

The women of Turkey and their folk-lore, 2 vols. (London, 1890).

Gibb, E. J. W. *Ottoman poetry*, 6 vols. (London, 1900–1909).

Jirousek, Charlotte A.. "The transition to mass fashion dress in the later Ottoman Empire," in Donald Quataert, ed., *Consumption studies and the history of the Ottoman Empire, 1550–1922: An introduction* (Albany, 2000), 201–241.

Karabaş, Seyfi and Judith Yarnall. *Poems by Karacaoğlan: A Turkish bard* (Bloomington, 1996).

---

[8] Robert Mantran, *Histoire de l'Empire ottoman* (Paris, 1989), 556–557.

*Keddie, Nikki, ed. *Women and gender in Middle Eastern history* (New Haven, 1991).

Lifchez, Raymond. *The dervish lodge: Architecture, art and Sufism in Ottoman Turkey* (Berkeley, 1992).

*Marcus, Abraham. *The Middle East on the eve of modernity: Aleppo in the eighteenth century* (New York, 1989).

*Mardin, Şerif. "Super westernization in urban life in the Ottoman Empire in the last quarter of the nineteenth century," in Peter Benedict, Erol Tümertekin and Fatma Mansur, eds., *Turkey. Geographic and social perspectives* (Leiden, 1974), 403–446.

Quataert, Donald, ed., *Consumption studies and the history of the Ottoman Empire, 1550–1922: An introduction* (Albany, 2000).

*Quataert, Donald. "Clothing laws, state and society in the Ottoman Empire, 1720–1829," *International Journal of Middle East Studies*, 29, 3 (August 1997), 403–425.

Social disintegration and popular resistance in the Ottoman Empire, 1881–1908 (New York, 1983).

Scarce, Jennifer. *Women's costume of the Near and Middle East* (London, 1987).

Somel, Selçuk Akşin. *The modernization of public education in the Ottoman Empire, 1839–1908* (Leiden, 2001).

Sonbol, Amira El Azhary, *Women, the family, and divorce laws in Islamic history* (Syracuse, 1996).

*Tunçay, Mete and Erik Zürcher, eds. *Socialism and nationalism in the Ottoman Empire, 1876–1923* (London, 1994).

*Wortley Montagu, Lady Mary. *The Turkish Embassy letters* (reprint, London, 1994).

Zilfi, Madeline. "Elite circulation in the Ottoman Empire: great mollas of the eighteenth century," *Journal of the Economic and Social History of the Orient*, 26, 3 (1983), 318–364.

Politics of piety: The Ottoman ulama in the post-classical age (Minneapolis, 1986).

Women in the Ottoman Empire. Middle Eastern women in the early modern era (Leiden, 1997).

9   Inter-communal co-operation and conflict

Introduction

Nationalism – a highly sensitive and difficult subject at the root of shifting understandings of identity – forms an important focus of attention in the present chapter. In its essence, nationalism speaks of one dominant nationality; for example, the Turkish republic is said to rest on a Turkish identity. Yet the Ottoman Empire for much of its history brought together multiple and different ethnic and religious groups. At times their interaction was co-operative and harmonious; but under the pressures of "modern nationalism" those ethnic and religious relations deteriorated into hostilities and worse, massacres, that remain a difficult subject in memory and national accounting. This issue is particularly acute in the interactions among, for example, modern-day Turks, Armenians, Greeks, and Kurds, as well as Palestinians and Israelis.

Inter-communal relations: an overview

The subject of historical intergroup relations in the Ottoman Empire looms large because of the many conflicts that currently plague the lands it once occupied. Recall, for example, the Palestinian–Israeli struggle, the Kurdish issue, the Armenian question, as well as the horrific events that have befallen Bosnia and Kossovo. All rage in lands once Ottoman. What then, is the connection between these struggles of today and the inter-communal experiences of the Ottoman past?

Let me begin with the assertion that there was nothing inevitable about these conflicts – all were historically conditioned, that is, produced by quite particular circumstances that evolved in a certain but not unavoidable manner. Other outcomes historically were possible but did not happen because of the way in which events unfolded. Nor, it is important to repeat, are these struggles ancient ones reflecting millennia-old hatreds. Rather, each can be explained with reference to the nineteenth and twentieth centuries, through the unfolding of specific events rather than inherent animosities of an alleged racial or ethnic nature. But because these contemporary struggles loom so large and because we assume that present-day hostilities have ancient and general rather than recent and specific causes, our understanding of the Ottoman inter-communal record has been profoundly obscured.

Despite all stereotypes and preconceptions to the contrary, inter-Ottoman group relations during most of Ottoman history were rather good relative to the standards of the age. For many centuries, persons who were of minority status enjoyed fuller rights and more legal protections in the Ottoman lands than, for example, minorities in the realm of the French king or of the Habsburg emperor. It is also true that Ottoman inter-communal relations worsened in the eighteenth and nineteenth centuries. In large part, this chapter argues, the deterioration derives directly from the explosive mixture of Western capital, Great Power interference in internal Ottoman affairs, and the transitional nature of an Ottoman polity struggling to establish broader political rights. Such an assessment does *not* aim to idealize the Ottoman record of inter-communal relations, which was hardly unblemished. Neither does it seek to explain away the major injustices and atrocities inflicted on Ottoman subjects by the state or other subjects.

The goal is to replace the stereotypes that too long have prevailed regarding relations among the religious and ethnic Ottoman communities. One's religion – as Muslim, Christian, or Jew – was an important means of differentiation in the Ottoman world. Indeed, ethnic terms confusingly often described what actually were religious differences. In the Balkan and Anatolian lands, Ottoman Christians informally spoke of "Turks" when in fact they meant Muslims. "Turk" was a kind of shorthand for referring to Muslims of every sort, whether Kurds, Turks, or Albanians (but not Arabs). Today's Bosnian Muslims are called Turks by the Serbian Christians even though they actually share a common Slavic ethnicity with these Christians. In the Arab world, Muslim Arabs used "Turk" when sometimes they meant Albanian or Circassian Muslim, one who had come from outside the region.

Stereotypes present distorted and inaccurate pictures of Ottoman subjects living in sharply divided, mutually impenetrable, religious communities called *millet*s that date back to the fifteenth century. In this incorrect view, each community lived apart, in isolation from one another, adjacent but separate. And supposedly implacable hatreds prevailed: Muslims hated Christians who hated Jews who hated Christians who hated Muslims. Recent scholarship shows this view to be fundamentally wrong on almost every score. To begin with, the term *millet* as a designator for Ottoman non-Muslims is not ancient but dates from the reign of Sultan

Mahmut II, in the early nineteenth century. Before then, *millet* in fact meant Muslims within the empire and Christians *outside* it.

Let us continue this exploration of inter-communal relations and look at two different versions of the past, taken from Ottoman Bulgaria during the 1700–1922 era. In the first version, we hear the voices of Father Paissiy (1722–1773) and S. Vrachanski (1739–1813) calling their Ottoman overlords "ferocious and savage infidels," "Ishmaelites," "sons of infidels," "wild beasts," and "loathsome barbarians." Somewhat later, another Bulgarian Christian writer Khristo Botev (1848–1876) wrote of the Ottoman administration in a similar vein:

> And the tyrant rages
> and ravages our native home:
> impales, hangs, flogs, curses
> and fines the people thus enslaved.

In the first quotation are the words of Bulgarian émigré intelligentsia who were seeking to promote a separate Bulgarian nation state and break from Ottoman rule.[1] To justify this separation, they invented a new past in which the Ottomans had abruptly ended the Bulgarian cultural renaissance of the medieval era, destroying its ties to the West and preventing Bulgaria from participating in and contributing to western civilization.

And yet, hear two other Bulgarian Christian voices speaking distinctly differently about Bulgarian Muslims, the first during the period just before formal independence in 1908 and the other a few years later:

Turks and Bulgarians lived together and were good neighbors. On holidays they exchanged pleasantries. We sent the Turks *kozunak* and red eggs at Easter, and they sent us baklava at Bayram. And on these occasions we visited each other.[2]

In Khaskovo, our neighbors were Turks. They were good neighbors. They got on well together. They even had a little gate between their gardens. Both my parents knew Turkish well. My father was away fighting [during the Balkan Wars]. My mother was alone with four children. And the neighbors said: "You're not going anywhere. You'll stay with us . . . " So Mama stayed with the Turks . . . What I'm trying to tell you is that we lived well with these people.[3]

Thus, as the various quotations demonstrate, some Bulgarian Christian writers emphasize the differences between "Bulgarians" and "Turks"

---

[1] The quotations provided from the oral interviews conducted in Bulgaria by Barbara Reeves-Ellington.

[2] Interview with Simeon Radev, 1879–1967, describing his childhood before 1900, provided by Barbara Reeves-Ellington.

[3] Interview with Iveta Gospodarova, personal narrative, Sofia, January 19, 1995, provided by Barbara Reeves-Ellington.

while others stress the everyday, friendly relations existing between two sets of neighbors.

Concepts of the "other", that characterize the first set of quotations, abound in history. The ancient Greeks divided the world into that of civilized Greeks and of barbarian others. Barbarians could be brave and courageous but they did not possess civilization. For Jews, there are the *goyim* – the non-Jew, the other – whose lack of certain characteristics keeps them outside the chosen, Jewish, community. For Muslims, the notion of the *dhimmi* is another way of talking about difference. In this case, Muslims regard Christians and Jews as "the People of the Book" (*dhimmi*), who received God's revelation before Muhammad and therefore obtained only an incomplete message. Thus, *dhimmi* have religion, civilization, and God's words. But since they received only part of that message, they are inherently different from and inferior to Muslims.

In the Ottoman world, people were acutely aware of differences, for example, those between Muslims and non-Muslims. Muslims, as such, shared their religious beliefs with the dynasty and most members of the Ottoman state apparatus. The state itself, among its many attributes, called itself an Islamic one and many sultans included the term "*gazi*," warrior for the Islamic faith, among their titles. Later on, as seen, they revived the title of caliph, one with deep roots in the early Islamic past. Further, for many centuries military service primarily was carried out as a Muslim duty, although there always were some non-Muslims in the military service, such as Christian Greeks serving as sailors in the navy during the 1840s. Yet, in a real sense, the military obligation had become a Muslim one. Even when an 1856 law required Ottoman Christian military service, the purchase of exemption quickly became institutionalized as a special tax. A 1909 law ended this loophole but in response hundreds of thousands of Ottoman Christians fled the empire rather than serve. Thus, subjects understood that Muslims needed to fight but non-Muslims did not.

A variety of mechanisms maintained difference and distinction. Clothing laws, as seen earlier, distinguished among the various religious communities, delineating the religious allegiance of passersby. They reassured maintenance of the differences not simply as instruments of discipline but also as useful markers of community boundaries, immediately identifying outsiders and insiders. Apparel gave a sense of group identity to members of a specific community.

Until the nineteenth century, the legal system was predicated on religious distinctions. Each religious community maintained its own courts, judges, and legal principles for the use of coreligionists. But Ottoman realities made the Muslim courts more powerful. Since Muslims theologically were superior, so too, in principle, was their court system. Muslim courts thus held sway in cases between Muslims and non-Muslims. The latter, moreover, simply did not possess the necessary authority (*velayet*) and so, with a few exceptions, could not testify against Muslims. The state used the religious authorities and courts to announce decrees and taxes and, more generally, as instruments of imperial control. The ranking government official of an area, for example, the governor, received an imperial order and summoned the various religious authorities. They in turn informed their communities which negotiated within themselves over enforcement of the order or distribution of the taxes being imposed.

Because of their inherently greater authority, Muslim courts often provided rights to Christians and Jews that were unavailable in their own courts. And so non-Muslims routinely sought out Muslim courts when they were under no obligation to do so. Once they appeared before the Islamic court, its decisions took precedence over the decisions of other religions' courts. Thus, non-Muslims often appealed to Muslim courts to gain access to the provisions of Islamic inheritance laws that absolutely guaranteed certain shares of estates to relatives – daughters, fathers, uncles, sisters. Persons who feared disinheritance or a smaller share in the will of a Christian or Jew placed themselves under Islamic law. Christian widows frequently registered in the Islamic courts because these provided a greater share to the wife of the deceased than did ecclesiastical law. Or, take the case of *dhimmi* girls being forced into arranged marriages by fellow Christians or Jews. Since Islamic law required the female's consent to the marriage contract, the young woman in question could go to the Muslim court that took her side, thus preventing the unwanted arranged marriage.

With the Tanzimat reforms, the old system of differentiation and distinction and of Muslim legal superiority formally disappeared. Equality of status meant equality of obligation and military service for all. The clothing laws disappeared almost entirely and, while the religious courts remained, many of their functions vanished. New courts appeared: so-called mixed courts at first heard commercial, criminal, and then civil cases involving persons of different religious communities. Then, beginning in 1869, secular courts (*nizamiye*) presided over civil and criminal cases involving Muslim and non-Muslim. Whether or not these changes automatically and always improved the rights and status of individuals – Christian, Jew, or Muslim – currently is being debated by scholars. Some writers, for example, argue that women's legal rights overall declined with the replacement of Islamic by secular law, but others disagree.

So, how equal were Ottoman subjects and how well were non-Muslims treated? Quite arbitrarily, I offer the testimony of the Jewish community of Ottoman Salonica, as recorded in the "Annual Report of the Jews of Turkey" of the *Bulletin de l'Alliance Israélite Universelle* in 1893. French Jews had founded the Alliance Israélite Universelle in 1860 to work for Jewish emancipation and combat discrimination all over the world. The organization placed great stress on schools and education as a liberating device, establishing its first Ottoman school in 1867 and within a few decades, some fifty more. It published a journal, the *Bulletin*, in Paris, to which Jewish communities from all over the world sent letters reporting on local conditions. Here then is the statement which the Jewish community of Salonica sent to the *Bulletin* in 1893:

There are but few countries, even among those which are considered the most enlightened and the most civilized, where Jews enjoy a more complete equality than in Turkey [the Ottoman Empire]. H. M. the sultan and the government of the Porte display towards Jews a spirit of largest toleration and liberalism.[4]

To place these words in context, we need to consider several points. First, the authors of the statement were quite aware that the treatment of Jews in many parts of Europe was atrociously bad and, by comparison, Ottoman Jews truly were better off. Second, the statement possibly can be read at face value since it was not prepared for circulation within the empire (but, nonetheless, the authors could surmise their views would become known to the Ottoman state). And third, Ottoman Jewish–Muslim relations were better than Muslim–Christian (or Jewish–Christian) relations. Even after all these reservations are taken into account and although this statement explicitly is about only Ottoman Jews, it likely also represents the sentiments of large numbers of Ottoman Christian subjects as well during the eighteenth and nineteenth centuries.

Residential patterns and inter-communal relations

Residential patterns – whether people of the different communities lived separately or apart – provide an important key to understanding inter-communal relations. The example of mid-nineteenth-century Salonica at first glance seems to suggest a pattern of segregation by religious community. The city map of Salonica at the time indicates separate Jewish, Muslim, and Greek Orthodox quarters and further depicts these respective quarters generally clustered together. Thus, thirty-eight of the forty-three Muslim quarters are concentrated in the northern part of the city,

---

[4] Paul Dumont, "Jewish communities in Turkey during the last decades of the nineteenth century in the light of the archives of the Alliance Israélite Universelle," in Benjamin Braude and Bernard Lewis, eds., *Christians and Jews in the Ottoman Empire* (London, 1982), I, 221.

while eight of the twelve Greek quarters are in the central and southeast corner and all sixteen Jewish quarters in the south-central district. And yet, quarters of the three communities also are scattered about, sometimes in the middle of quarters of a different religious community. Thus, one Greek Orthodox quarter appears right in the middle of a group of Jewish quarters while another is embedded among the Muslim quarters. Also, it is unclear if quarters designated as Jewish, Greek Orthodox, or Muslim held any persons of another religion. That is, we do not know if large numbers of Christians or Muslims resided in a "Jewish" quarter in Salonica but we do know this was the case elsewhere in the empire.

Overall, residential exclusivity by community was not the rule in the 1700–1922 era. In the European provinces, Muslims in the city of Resen did not live in separate quarters of the city (although they did in Ohrid). In many regions, households of different religious communities clustered together according to wealth. This pattern held for Istanbul during the nineteenth century, where the wealthy lived near the palace. But elsewhere in the capital, different economic strata lived together in many residential neighborhoods. In nineteenth-century Ankara, an unimportant provincial town and thus very different from the imperial capital, certain quarters had been cohabited by both Muslims and non-Muslims for several centuries. Mid-eighteenth-century Aleppo provides a well-documented, strikingly clear example of residential patterns according to wealth and not religion. Here we know both the patterns by quarter and even who lived in the particular houses of the quarter. In this carefully studied case, no quarter was inhabited by only a single religious community. And, names could be deceiving: hence, the so-called Jewish quarter of Aleppo held only part of its Jewish population while many Muslims called the neighborhood home as well. The Kurdish quarter at the time in fact was empty of Kurds; none remained from the original Kurdish settlement there in the medieval Mamluk era. Indeed, in the early twentieth century, 93 percent of the residents of this so-called Kurdish quarter were Christian (Kurds almost exclusively were Muslim). Thus, while Muslims, Christians, and Jews in Aleppo often lived with their own kind, they also often inhabited mixed neighborhoods. In Aleppo, Jewish homes nestled up to a mosque while Muslim homes were adjacent to a synagogue. Instead of separation by religion, quarters in Aleppo tended to be strikingly homogeneous in social and economic status. Thus, the inhabitants of this important Arab city often preferred to live with others of similar wealth rather than the same religion. Elsewhere, as in Istanbul and Ankara, rich and poor and middling often resided together in the same neighborhoods. In sum, when Ottoman families chose their home sites, they used a host of criteria and not simply religion. Depending on time and place and whim, the economic status of neighbors, the convenience of the neighborhood as well as religion affected their selection. Overall, there was a high degree of inter-communal residential mixing.

Other evidence of inter-communal sharing

The argument for intimate daily contact among members of the various religious and ethnic communities is further supported by the very languages spoken in the Ottoman Empire, as well as the liturgical music employed. Even the most cursory glance at the official Ottoman language demonstrates an incredibly rich intermixing rather than separation of communities. The Ottoman language largely is Turkish in syntax and grammar, but written in the Arabic script. It contains massive infusions of Arabic vocabulary (perhaps 40 percent of the total), an equal amount of Turkish and a lesser measure of Persian. Many other languages are represented as well. Among nautical terms, for example, there are perhaps 1,000 Greek and Italian loan words that entered into Ottoman usage, together with many words from Spanish, English, French, German, Portuguese, Bulgarian, Old Serbian, and Russian, among others. When new foods came into the Ottoman diet, the names given by their lenders often entered with them. Thus, tomatoes and potatoes in Ottoman were called by words derived from those spoken by the Nahuatl peoples of southern Mexico and the Taino in the Caribbean. In addition, there are numerous German, French, English, and other loan words for objects ranging from bread to carriages to the machinery of the industrial age, including steam itself. The name of the Ottoman coin *kuruş*, derives from the German *groschen*. Nor is Ottoman the only language of the empire to reflect such richness. In Cilicia, in southeast Anatolia, Armenians spoke Turkish but wrote it in the Armenian script. Similarly, Greek Christians in western and northwestern Anatolia, mainly around Kayseri, spoke Turkish but wrote it in the Greek alphabet (a language called Karamanlıca). The Greek spoken at Kayseri contained so much Turkish that knowledge of both languages was needed to understand it. Many Greeks in Istanbul spoke only Turkish in the late eighteenth and early nineteenth centuries. Similarly, consider that, in Aleppo during the mid-eighteenth century, the Christian, Jewish, and Muslim religious liturgies all were based on the same Arabic melodic system (*makam*). Such linguistic and musical interpenetrations demonstrate communities in constant and intimate contact rather than groups sealed off from one another.

Inter-communal relations in the workplace

Relations in the workplace, in common with residential patterns and linguistic and musical borrowings, demonstrate intimate daily contact among the various religious and ethnic communities. Here too, gross and untenable generalizations have prevailed, often under the name "ethnic division of labor." In some of the scholarship on Ottoman history, this widely used term essentially meant that particular ethnic or religious groups in general inherently were especially well suited to carry out certain tasks. And so, they were said to dominate that activity throughout the empire. Thus, Turks (taken to mean Muslims) allegedly did certain jobs but not others, while Christians of the various denominations respectively performed other tasks. In agriculture, Turks supposedly were cereal growers while Armenians and Greeks grew fruits and vegetables. In the industrial sector, Armenians were said to be the silkweavers and Greeks the tailors; Turks for their part allegedly excelled in the applied arts, such as carpet making and woodworking. Further, according to this division of labor, Greeks and Armenians were gifted in commerce but often dishonest, particularly the former. Turks on the other hand were unimaginative and dull but honest and, to boot, made good administrators. Such crass generalizations, rightfully, are seen as inappropriate in other areas of historical writing. For example, it is considered both inaccurate and unacceptable to state that Jews are especially skilled in business or Irish-Americans in bricklaying. And yet such stereotypes still reside in Middle East history.

As in many stereotypes, there is a nugget of reality. While there was no empire-wide division of labor, certain groups in particular localities did monopolize a particular industry. In some areas, most cereal farmers were ethnic Turks and most silkweavers Armenians – but the statements do not hold true for the empire as a whole. Elsewhere, the Greek Christians were cereal growers and Muslims silkweavers. Some observer might have noticed that Armenians in a particular Istanbul neighborhood dominated shoemaking and then assumed this pattern to be true both of the whole city and of every city of the empire as well, which it was not. Indeed, in another town or city a different group dominated the same activity. In fact, in a big city such as the Istanbul capital, Armenians controlled shoemaking in one quarter while in another quarter of the city, at the very same moment, Greek shoemakers thrived. Muslims, Christians, and Jews all were active in the industrial sector of Damascus, and were well represented in the city's famed textile industry. There, many Christians and Sunni as well as Shii Muslims wove silk and silk-cotton cloths. Sometimes one group dominated a particular craft within the general textile industry. Damascus's dyers, for example, almost all were Christians, while those placing the warp thread on the looms, a very skilled activity, predominantly were Muslim. This is not to imply that Muslims were uniquely or more gifted than Christians, but only that they were not the dull farmers depicted by the ethnic division of labor stereotype. In the Balkan provinces, similarly diverse and non-generalizable patterns of work prevailed. In nineteenth-century Bosnia, proportionately more Muslims owned industrial firms than Catholics while Orthodox Christians were the least well represented among industrial owners. Not far away, in Montenegro, Muslims and Albanian Catholics rather than Orthodox Christian, Greek-speaking, Montenegrins dominated trade and commerce. Armenian and Greek Christians formed the majority in the silk industry of the Anatolian and Arab provinces but many Muslims and some Jews as well were employed. And, elsewhere, at Trabzon for example, both Muslims and Christians wove silk. Moreover, each of these particular patterns has a specific historical explanation. Take the vast carpetmaking sector of Anatolia, for example. Most workers had been Muslims. In the mid-nineteenth century, however, European-dominated merchant houses in Izmir began competing with Muslim firms in Uşak in west Anatolia for control of the carpetmaking business. These Izmir houses formed rural carpetmaking networks and, needing labor, they relied on their Ottoman Christian business associates who utilized existing relationships among coreligionists to provide the workers. Hence, Christian workers formed the majority of those who entered the carpet industry after 1870 while Muslims continued to occupy the older sector of the industry. Such examples show clearly that no one group dominated a particular economic activity and that the ethnic division of labor was a myth.

Occupational patterns of ethnic and religious heterogeneity also show up in labor organizations, both guilds and, at the very end of the Ottoman era, unions. These organizations' members sometimes were drawn exclusively from one or another community. But mixed guilds were commonplace. Thus, the members of one guild might be both Christian and Muslim while another contained members of only one community. There was no general pattern. An early nineteenth-century study partially surveyed the guilds of Istanbul, revealing that about one-half of all the enumerated members belonged to mixed guilds, containing both Muslims and non-Muslims. By contrast, a listing of guilds in the city of Salonica revealed that only one-quarter of its guilds were mixed. The difference between the two cities likely derives from the fact that Salonica's population was more homogeneous and thus had less diversity to draw on. In the empire as a whole, perhaps one-quarter to a half of all guild members belonged to labor organizations that contained members of more than one religious community.

The role of communal identities in the workplace is seen clearly when labor mobilized to present its demands, protest, or strike. In such instances, religious community affiliation sometimes seemed irrelevant and at other times important. For example, coreligionists in a guild on occasion mobilized along religious lines, even when the body as a whole was religiously heterogeneous. Take, for example, a greengrocers' guild in Istanbul that contained both Christian and Muslim members. In 1860, some 100 members of this guild signed a petition to the government (regarding coal prices). All of the signatories on this occasion were Christians who, for whatever reasons, temporarily had banded together on the basis of their shared faith. In Aleppo, similarly, only Christian members of a mixed guild of textile merchants signed a petition in the 1840s while the tables were turned in the 1860s, when just the Muslim members petitioned. In both instances, which had no apparent religious content, the petitioners asserted that they were acting on behalf of the entire guild and not merely their coreligionists.

Unions as a form of labor organization arrived very late in the Ottoman period; some dated back to the 1880s but most evolved only after the July 1908 Young Turk Revolution. Rarely were the unions religiously homogeneous. For example, Muslim and Christian commercial employees originally organized themselves in 1908 as two separate unions but, within weeks, the two merged into a single organization. In most cases, membership of these unions was heterogeneous with many Christians and Muslims and, sometimes, Jews as well. The most important unions, and perhaps all of them, emerged in the context of foreign capital. Take, for example, the railroad unions with their Christian and Muslim members; or the Salonica-area tobacco workers' union with Jewish, Greek, Muslim, and Bulgarian members; or the various utility company unions in Izmir, Beirut, and elsewhere, with Muslim and Christian members. The inter-communal quality of unions is vividly illustrated by a June 1909 protest meeting (against state labor policies) held in Salonica where speakers harangued the crowds in Ottoman, Bulgarian, Greek, and Ladino (archaic Spanish written in Hebrew characters).[5] Salonica was noteworthy for the multi-ethnic, multi-religious character of its working class activities, some of which evolved into socialist movements.

The hiring practices of foreign corporations provide a useful tool for understanding the inter-communal tensions that became too familiar in the nineteenth-century Ottoman world. These corporations numbered in

---

[5] Yavuz Selim Karakışla, "The emergence of the Ottoman industrial working class, 1839–1923," in Donald Quataert and Erik Zürcher, eds., *Workers and the working class in the Ottoman Empire and the Turkish Republic, 1839–1950* (London, 1995), 19–34.

the dozens and included banks, railroads, port companies, and utilities as well as textile and food processing factories. Altogether, they employed large numbers of Ottoman subjects – more than 13,000 worked on the railroads while the Ottoman Public Debt Administration hired more than 5,000 employees. The issue here concerns the stratification of the workforce in these newly founded, often large, foreign corporations. As we have seen, there was no overall division of labor in the Ottoman workforce as a whole. But in foreign companies, over and over we find the same hiring and stratification patterns present. These corporations always hired foreigners for the very top jobs in the company, the executives who sat on the board of directors and those who most often were the department and bureau chiefs. Just below them were the Ottoman Christians who served as the middle managers and held most of the skilled jobs. Muslims rested at the bottom of these corporate hierarchies, filling the lowest-ranking, lowest-paid jobs. Moreover, in times of crisis, the corporations tended to hire disproportionate numbers of non-Muslims and foreigners, as if they distrusted Muslim employees and workers. In a roughly similar fashion, the labor unions tended to have a largely Christian leadership with a mixed, Muslim and Christian, rank and file. It should be stressed that there was nothing inherently necessary about this development. Capitalism need not generate ethnically or religiously stratified labor unions, although sometimes it has. In this particular Ottoman case, however, foreign capital interacted with the local (Ottoman) society to produce a workforce in which the coreligionists of the foreign investors were privileged. This hierarchy placed foreigners and non-Muslims in positions of superiority over Muslims and thus reversed the centuries old Ottoman pattern of Muslim political and legal predominance.

The effect of the foreign corporations' hiring policies on the workforce of those companies stands as a metaphor for the impact of west European penetration on Ottoman society as a whole. The increasing economic, political, social, and cultural power of the West had set in motion a transformation that was overturning the existing order in the Ottoman Empire. Indeed, during the final Ottoman century, three sets of social hierarchies competed for supremacy. The first, which had existed formally for centuries until the early nineteenth-century changes, placed Muslims in positions of political and legal dominance over non-Muslims. The second, the model of the foreign corporation, began to emerge in the eighteenth century, positioning foreigners at the top, non-Muslims in the second rank, and Muslims at the bottom. The third, the Ottomanist model, called for a state administrative cadre recruited from every religious and ethnic community, ruling over a society in which all members were equal before the eyes of the law and state.

We will never know whether the new society of equality before the law or the new order of foreigner/non-Muslim superiority that the foreign corporations seemed to predict would have replaced Muslim supremacy. The old Ottoman order was fading but the new one had not yet been born. In sum, Ottoman society in the nineteenth century was undergoing an evolution; but that transformation remained unfinished because of the destruction of the empire in 1922.

The Armenian massacres of 1915–1916[6]

Ottoman inter-communal relations, I have argued, were comparatively peaceful for most of the history of the empire. Differences among subjects always existed but only sometimes, as seen, did these lead to conflicts and violence. But, as in all societies, communal bigotry, intolerance, and violence flared intermittently for different economic, social, and political reasons. Thus, after Greek Uniates left Greek Orthodoxy and established their own church in 1701, the "hostility of the Orthodox Christians towards these perceived renegades degenerated into threats, persecution and riots in which members of one Christian sect burned down the churches of another rite."[7] In another example, Orthodox Christians in Damascus, in 1840, found the mutilated bodies of a high-ranking cleric of the Spanish monastery and his servant near some Jewish homes. And so local Christians whipped up charges of the blood libel, saying that Jews needed Christian blood for their religious rituals, forcing the arrest and torture of some wealthy Jewish merchants. Similarly, when a Greek child drowned in a river near Izmir at Easter time, local Greeks blamed the Jews and began assaulting them.[8]

Both the scale and the frequency of violence among Ottoman communal groups increased during the nineteenth century (see Chapter 4). Unparalleled in ferocity and scope were the attacks against the Ottoman Armenian population. These began with massacres of Armenians in 1895–1896 which were repeated in 1908, 1909, and again in 1912. In this last set of assaults, recently arrived Muslim refugees from lost provinces in the Balkans played an important role. During the Balkan Wars, vast numbers of Muslims had been driven from the European provinces, to towns

---

[6] There is an enormous scholarship on this subject, much of it polemical but some of it increasingly constructive. See the Hovannisian and Suny works cited in bibliography for this chapter as well as studies by Michael Arlen, Michael M. Gunter, Heath Lowry, Robert Melson, and Justin McCarthy for different points of view.

[7] Youssef Courbade and Philippe Fargues, *Christians and Jews under Islam* (London and New York, 1997), 69.

[8] For example, Lucy M. J. Garnett, *The women of Turkey and their folk lore* (London, 1890), 6–7.

such as Tekirdağ/Rodosto and Malgara on the north shore of the Marmara Sea and in Adapazarı in west Anatolia. In these places, the refugees vented their frustration and anger on hapless and innocent Ottoman Armenians. By far the worst, however, were the massacres of 1915–16. An estimated 600,000 Armenian Ottoman subjects died during and after forced deportation from their east Anatolian homes, as they moved towards the Arab provinces. These events are the centerpiece of debates around the Armenian genocide. Every year, for example, the halls of the US Congress reverberate as the Greek, Armenian, and Turkish lobbies try to win support for their respective positions for and against an official American commemoration of these World War I tragedies.

The story begins as war erupted in 1914 between Russia and the Ottomans along the east Anatolian frontier. With the Russian invaders came Russian Armenian soldiers as well as some Ottoman Armenians who had defected to the enemy. In 1915, Ottoman Young Turk ruling circles issued orders for the deportation of the entire Armenian population of east Anatolia out of the battle zone, southward to the Syrian deserts. These orders exist and can be examined and read; they are authentic materials and not forgeries or part of a hoax and are full of directives commanding the protection and care of the deportees and their properties. Order after order speaks of the need to guard the deportees and their property and assure their safety. Those deported often walked since there were few trains. As they walked, they suffered and some died of malnutrition or an accompanying disease. Others died at the hands of bandits or other Ottoman civilians who preyed on the weak. But, the solicitous state documents notwithstanding, there is abundant evidence that low and high Ottoman officers, soldiers and bureaucrats – the very persons who had the sworn responsibility to defend and protect the lives of all Ottoman subjects regardless of religion or ethnicity – murdered vast numbers of Armenian civilians, men, women, and children alike. Moreover, the patterns of the killings were chillingly similar in the various areas, powerfully suggesting the presence of a coordinated program.

How can we reconcile the orders commanding care and diligence with the murderous and apparently coordinated slaughter by state military and civil officials? Consider this assessment of the events, one that seems to be gaining acceptance among scholars on both sides of the controversy.[9] There was a circle, acting like a state within the state, within the ruling Committee of Union and Progress group. Coming to power in early 1913,

---

[9] Derived from Erik J. Zürcher, *Turkey: A modern history*, 3rd edn (London, 2004), 114–17. This line of argument also is present in some of the writings noted in Suny *et al.*, above.

members of this circle secretly sought to use deportation as a guise for exterminating the Armenians. As World War I developed, they increasingly feared the potential ability of Armenian revolutionary organizations to overthrow the Ottoman state and/or the consequences of mass Armenian defections in east Anatolia to the Russians. Under the leadership of Talat Pasha, a major Union and Progress figure, the group employed the Special Organization (*Teşkilat-ı Mahsusa*) to carry out the massacres, outside the formal government apparatus and lines of communication. This parallel Special Organization organized and coordinated the killings, often using government officials and troops who were its members. Those who were not members or objected to the orders were overruled or replaced. The Special Organization sent directives to the many locations where the killings occurred, using its own networks rather than state channels of communication. Since the records of both the Special Organization and the Committee of Union and Progress were either lost or destroyed, this argument cannot be established without doubt. On the evidence presented, it seems plausible that high-ranking officials of the Ottoman state, utilizing the Special Organization, directed a concerted, centrally orchestrated program that murdered massive numbers of Ottoman Armenians.

Asking the question whether this crisis was the first twentieth-century genocide runs the risks of being submerged in semantic arguments and thus avoiding the real issues. After all, most Armenians died because of their presumed identity, not because of their own actions or beliefs. On the one hand, these atrocities in 1915 were not Nazi-style events that sought to concentrate and eliminate every single member of a group as such. There were numbers of Armenians outside of the battle zones who were not targeted for deportation or murder. In some of these non-conflict areas, Armenians were treated brutally but it does not appear that either the government or the Special Organization sought to deport or murder the majority of Ottoman Armenians living in western Anatolia and the Southern Balkans. In places such as Istanbul and Izmir, large Armenian communities in 1915–16 remained intact, going about their lives in the midst of war. On other hand, this situation does not gainsay the slaughter of hundreds of thousands of their compatriots in the war-torn eastern provinces. Debates now seem to be centering on the context to this slaughter in the east. The new perspective asks a different question: would such atrocities have occurred in the absence of World War I?

Nationalism and the end of the Ottoman Empire

The fate of the Ottoman Armenians likely is linked intimately to the role that nationalism played in the destruction of the Ottoman Empire.

Was the empire destroyed from within by separatist or nationalist forces or from without, by the imperial powers? This is a highly controversial question. In my own view, external rather than internal factors played the key role. The overwhelming majority of Ottoman subjects were not seeking separation or withdrawal. Rather, they would have remained within an Ottoman state framework had that political entity continued to exist into the 1920s and 1930s.

To be sure, important changes in personal and group identities were occurring. During the nineteenth century, ethnic identities were becoming more important while the designators "Muslim" and "Christian" became more complicated. Earlier, in the eighteenth century, the Greek Orthodox clergy had eradicated many formerly separate clerical institutions in the Balkans and brought them under its own hegemony. Hence, in 1766, it suppressed the Serbian patriarchate of Peç and, in 1767 the Bulgarian archbishopric of Ohrid. Similarly, the patriarchate of Antioch gradually became the dominion of Greek prelates. Thus, by the end of the eighteenth century, Greek Orthodoxy reigned. That is, at the end of the eighteenth century, the term Greek Orthodox Christian covered many Christian groups of quite different ethnicities.

During the nineteenth century, ethnic distinctions became more important among Ottoman Christians in the Balkans, a process accelerated by the emergence of the separate church organizations. Indeed, the separatist movements of the nineteenth century often fought against Greek ecclesiastical and cultural imperialism as much as Ottoman rule. In 1833, after the formation of the Greek state, an autocephalous Greek Church emerged there, while in the same decade a separate Serbian Church similarly followed upon formation of a Serb state. Later on, a Bulgarian exarchate emerged in 1870 and then an autocephalous Rumanian Church in 1885. Thus, each separate Church sought to create or reinforce a sense of separate ethnic, for example, Serb or Rumanian, identity: the "Orthodox Church" went from embracing almost all Orthodox subjects to, largely, only the ethnically Greek ones. At the same time, nationalists in the various communities worked to purify the various languages of "alien" elements. Hence, for example, Greek nationalists worked to eradicate the Turkish spoken by many Ottoman Greeks. In sum, there can be little doubt that new notions of separateness were at work in the Ottoman Balkan world.

And yet, in common with developments elsewhere in the globe, nationalist movements in the Ottoman Empire were minority movements, orchestrated and promoted by a few. In (probably) every case of successor state formation in the Ottoman Empire, state preceded nation and not the other way around. The formation of independent states derived not from groundswell movements but rather from the actions of certain groups in the societies who sought economic and/or political privilege that they believed they could not obtain under Ottoman domination. That is, a relative handful of individuals established a government apparatus, drew boundaries on a map and prepared the national flag and anthem. With these in place, the creation of a national community actually began to be based on a shared feeling of being Bulgarian, Serbian, Greek, etc. In the Balkan lands, Russia, Austria-Hungary, Britain, and/or France supported these aspirations since they believed (usually correctly) that the new states were likely to fall under their own respective influence. Throbbing in the breast of every Christian in the Balkans was not the idea of breaking away from the Ottomans. The foundation of independent Balkan states in the nineteenth century is no proof of mass discontent with Ottoman rule on the part of the Balkan Christian subject populations. Their creation, however, is testimony to the determination and organizational skills of the separatists and the assistance of the Great Powers. On this basis, they created the new states and within them began constructing the new nationalities, often using the foil of the "savage infidel."

We also need to understand the unimportance, until after World War I, of Arab, Turkish, and Kurdish nationalisms on the territories that remained under Ottoman sovereignty. Here, too, the basic point deserves reiteration: most Ottoman Muslims of whatever ethnicity remained fundamentally content with Ottoman rule and did not actively seek separation.

Several issues are important here. First, the nineteenth-century state-supported ideologies of Ottomanism and pan-Islamism were failing to protect the empire: territories continued to fall away. Nonetheless, Ottoman state elites, including the Young Turks who came to power after 1908, by and large remained loyal to Ottomanism and did not opt for Turkish nationalism, although it is often alleged that they did. It is true that some leaders, after 1908, personally pursued a new cultural identity as Turks and came to believe in Turkish superiority to others. And yet, they and their political party continued to argue for and promote the imperial policies of Ottomanism and pan-Islamism. And it is also true that, despite the personal secularist tendencies of many Young Turks, the Islamist component of Ottoman identity became more important after 1908 because of the accelerating dismemberment of the (largely Christian) European provinces of the empire. Within months of the 1908 revolution that had promised an end of territorial dissolution, many lands nominally still Ottoman became formally separate or independent: Bulgaria, Crete, and Bosnia-Herzegovina. Such fragmentation meant that, in 1914, the majority of remaining subjects were Muslims, mainly ethnic Turks, as well as Arabs and Kurds, although considerable

Christian Armenian and Greek populations remained. It nonetheless is clear that a secularist, Ottomanist world view prevailed among the Young Turks, who remained determined to mold a new identity among subjects. One measure of their effort to create this common Ottoman identity is the Election Law, passed after the 1908 Revolution, that sought to eliminate representation by religious community and replace communal politics with party politics. Overall, the post-1908 policies of the Ottoman regimes reflected strong centralization policies, a pressing for close control and an imposition of uniform, standardized, imperial standards rather than Turkish nationalism.

How, then, can we explain the accusations of Armenian and Arab nationalists of our own day, that the Young Turk Ottoman regimes were harshly Turkish nationalist? They point, for example, to the famous Young Turk leader Cemal Pasha who executed a group of local notables in Damascus during World War I. And, most significantly, they recall the Armenian massacres of 1915–1916. Rather than viewing these as the actions of fierce Turkish nationalists aimed at Turkish racial dominance over others, it may be more accurate to see them as policies enacted by centralizing state officials ruthlessly determined to stamp out threats to its stability. In the first case, the hangings reflected the Istanbul government's relentless determination to impose and maintain control over Damascene notables who were trying to replace central authority with a decentralized regime that they themselves would lead. Regarding accusations that the regime was pro-Turkish, consider that the post 1908 Young Turk regimes aggressively recruited more Arabs into the state apparatus than at any other time, except the reign of Sultan Abdülhamit II, who was exceptional in this regard. In the second case, the Armenian massacres, the state may have killed not from racialist or nationalist reasons but rather because it feared the Armenians as actual or would-be rebels seeking to break with Ottoman control and ally with enemies of the government. The state warred against its own subjects; but it was not a nationalist civil war among competing groups of equals or near equals.

Neither Turkish nor Arab nor Armenian nor Kurdish nationalism pushed a dying Ottoman state over the nationalist cliff after 1914. Indeed, there were scarce few of these sentiments during the final decade of the Ottoman Empire. Some Armenians did call for a separate nation state but the overwhelming majority continued to opt for the Ottoman system. Very few Kurds spoke of autonomy. Similarly, most Arabs acted as if they expected to remain within the Ottoman polity, although it is true that a few leaders sought a separate cultural identity and promoted regionalism with greater autonomy within the Ottoman imperial system. In sum, the vast majority of Ottoman subjects in 1914 – of whatever religion and ethnicity – were not seeking to break away but instead retained their identities as Ottoman subjects.

A key to understanding the accusations of Turkish xenophobia and nationalism lies in the Middle Eastern events following World War I. The Great Powers forcibly dismantled the empire. Britain and France divided the Arab provinces between them, setting up "mandatory regimes" under their own supervision within the League of Nations framework and ruling these regions in various guises until the mid 1950s. They had intended to hand over a large chunk of Anatolia to their protégés in Athens and to leave a rump Ottoman state. Instead, Ottoman resistance forces gathered and, unable to restore the empire, settled on founding a smaller state in its Anatolian fragment, one that later became the Turkish nation state. In both the Arab and the Anatolian areas, nationalist movements after the Ottoman demise worked to create nations in the states that had emerged from the imperial debris: notably Turkey, Syria, Lebanon, Iraq, Jordan, and the special case of Palestine. Leaders respectively were working to create and propagate Turkish and Arab nationalist identities. Each found it useful to invent, find, or magnify – for quite different reasons – the Turkish nationalist elements that were present in the late Ottoman period. For the Turkish group of state and nation builders, who viewed these elements positively, finding Turkish nationalism in the Ottoman era served to legitimate the new Turkish state and gave it historical roots. For Arab state and nation builders, Turkish villainies both reinforced and helped justify their own separate state identity. And, perhaps, such villainy made more palatable the Great Power occupation that had ensued without their consent after World War I. Ironically, this anti-Turkish interpretation also helped Britain and France to justify their destruction of the empire itself. Thus, insisting on the presence of significant Turkish nationalism before 1918 promoted many post-World War I agendas, including that of Britain, France, the Turkish Republic, and the Arab politicians and intellectuals struggling to gain independence from the Great Powers.

Suggested bibliography

Entries marked with a * designate recommended readings for new students of the subject.

Adanir, Fikret. "The Macedonian question: the socio-economic reality and problems of its historiographic interpretations," *International Journal of Turkish Studies*, Winter 1985–6, 43–64.

Ahmida, Ali Abdullatif. *The making of modern Libya: State formation, colonization and resistance, 1830–1993* (Albany, 1994).

Akarlı, Engin. *The long peace: Ottoman Lebanon, 1861–1920* (Berkeley, 1993).

Anastassiadou, Meropi. *Salonique, 1830–1912. Une ville ottomane à l'âge des réformes* (Leiden, 1997).

*Andric, Ivo. *The bridge on the Drina* (Chicago, translated edition of 1945 Serbo-Croat original, 1977).

Braude, Benjamin and Bernard Lewis, eds. *Christians and Jews in the Ottoman Empire*, 2 vols. (London, 1982).

Cleveland, William. *The making of an Arab nationalist: Ottomanism and Arabism in the life and thought of Sati al-Husri* (Cleveland, 1971).

*Cole, Juan. *Colonialism and revolution in the Middle East: Social and cultural origins of Egypt's Urabi movement* (Princeton, 1993).

Davison, Roderic. "Nationalism as an Ottoman problem and the Ottoman response," in William W. Haddad and William Ochsenwald, eds., *Nationalism in a non-national state: The dissolution of the Ottoman Empire* (Columbus, 1977), 25–56.

Edib, Halide. *Memoirs* (London, 1926).

Hasluck, F. W. *Christianity and Islam under the Sultans*, 2 vols. (London, 1925).

Hovannisian, Richard G., ed. *The Armenian people from ancient to modern times, II: Foreign dominion to statehood: The fifteenth century to the twentieth century* (New York, 1997).

Kahane, Henry, Renée Kahane, and Andreas Tietze. *The lingua franca in the Levant: Turkish nautical terms of Italian and Greek origin* (Urbana, 1958).

Karpat, Kemal. *The politicization of Islam: reconstructing identity, state, and community in the late Ottoman state* (New York, 2001).

*Kayalı, Hasan. *Arabs and Young Turks: Ottomanism, Arabism and nationalism in the Ottoman Empire, 1908–1918* (Berkeley, 1997).

Kevorkian, Raymond H. and Paul B. Paboudjian, eds. *Les Arméniens dans l'empire ottoman à la veille du genocide* (Paris, 1992).

Levy, Avigdor, ed. *Jews Turks, Ottomans: a shared history, fifteenth through the twentieth century* (Syracuse, 2001).

*Lockman, Zachary. *Workers and working classes in the Middle East* (Albany, 1994).

*Marcus, Abraham. *The Middle East on the eve of modernity: Aleppo in the eighteenth century* (New York, 1989).

*Quataert, Donald, ed. *Workers, peasants and economic change in the Ottoman Empire 1730–1914* (Istanbul, 1993).

Rodrigue, Aron. *French Jews, Turkish Jews: the Alliance Israélite Universelle and the politics of Jewish schooling in Turkey, 1860–1925* (Bloomington, 1990).

*Suny, Ronald Grigor, Engin Deniz Akarlı, Selim Deringil, and Vahakn N. Dadrian, "Exchange" *Armenian Forum: A journal of contemporary affairs*, Summer 1998, 17–136.

Tibi, Bassam. *Arab nationalism: A critical inquiry* (New York, translation of 1971 German original, 1981).

*Tunçay, Mete and Erik Zürcher, eds. *Socialism and nationalism in the Ottoman Empire, 1876–1923* (London, 1994).

*Vatter, Sherry. "Militant textile weavers in Damascus: waged artisans and the Ottoman labor movement, 1850–1914," in Donald Quataert and Erik J. Zürcher, eds., *Workers and the working class in the Ottoman Empire and the Turkish Republic, 1839–1950* (London, 1995), 35–57.

Zürcher, Erik. *The Unionist factor: the role of the Committee of Union and Progress in the Turkish nationalist movement of 1905–1926* (Leiden, 1984).

Turkey: A modern history, 3rd edn (London, 2004).

10 Legacies of the Ottoman Empire

The nationalist sentiments that have pervaded most nineteenth- and twentieth-century history writing seriously have obstructed our assessment and appreciation of the Ottoman legacy. The biases come from many sides. West and central Europeans rightly feared Ottoman imperial expansion until the late seventeenth century. Remarkably, these old fears have persisted into the present day and arguably have been transformed into cultural prejudices, for example, now being directed against the full membership of an Ottoman successor state, Turkey, into the European Union. Moreover, nationalist histories have dismissed the place of the multi-ethnic, multi-religious political formation in historical evolution. Furthermore, as a model of economic change in an emerging European-dominated world economy, the Ottomans have had to bow to the manufacturing, exporting, highly productive Japanese success story. In the more than thirty countries that now exist in territories once occupied by the Ottoman Empire, the Ottoman past until recently has been largely ignored and/or considered in extremely negative terms. With some exceptions, this remains the situation today in the former Balkan provinces. Regarding a number of Arab states, by contrast, scholarly works on the Ottoman period recently have proliferated. In Israel, a comparatively strong Ottoman studies tradition dates back decades, often linked to Zionism and its justification. And finally, academic and public awareness of the Ottoman legacy in Turkey is growing and an active public debate over its meaning is taking place. Given the presence of the Ottoman Empire in many of these successor states for five to six centuries – an extraordinarily long period of time – the overall lack of public awareness and debate at first seems remarkable.

Let us begin with the paucity of the Ottoman linguistic legacy. At one time, there was a considerable penetration of Ottoman Turkish into the various languages; for example, Turkish words accounted for one-sixth of all Rumanian vocabulary during the pre-independence nineteenth century. Today, however, just a few words survive although, generally, somewhat more Turkish elements persist in other Balkan languages, including Greek, Serbo-Croatian, and Bulgarian. In the former Anatolian and Arab provinces, relatively little of the Ottoman language survives and it is vanishing quickly. Part of the explanation lies in the size and character of the Ottoman literary elite that was both small and mainly Muslim. Hence, when the successor states launched their literacy drives after gaining independence, they were working mainly with an illiterate populace and thus had few existing literary conventions to overcome. In the Balkan provinces, moreover, the Ottoman administrative elites fled with the success of the breakaway movements, leaving few living links to the Ottoman literary heritage. These features, however, only partially explain the absence of an Ottoman linguistic heritage. We also must consider that all of the post-Ottoman regimes launched linguistic purges, that were sustained efforts to eliminate Ottoman usages from the emerging national languages of the successor states. Hence Turkish governmental programs eliminated the Arabic and Persian words (more than 50 percent of the total) that had crept into Ottoman while the Syrian and Bulgarian states – otherwise so different – respectively erased Turkish words from Arabic and Bulgarian.

The linguistic purges derived from negative views that policy-makers in almost all of the successor states held of the Ottoman past, a function of their determination to fully expunge Ottoman elements from the national identities they were creating. That is, the hostility owes less to actual Ottoman policies in the past and more to the post-Ottoman history of these countries, specifically, their state building processes. In all of the successor states – from Serbia to Bulgaria to Turkey to Syria and Iraq – vilification of the Ottoman past accompanied state formation. For each people, the Ottomans served as the "other" – what they were not – and as the suppressor of long-cherished "national" values that had been submerged during the long Ottoman centuries. Thus, the Balkan, Arab, and Anatolian successor states for decades rejected the Ottoman legacy in their respective quests for identity in the post-Ottoman era. Here, it is important to consider that the imperial system being rejected died quite recently, just over seventy-five years ago. Hence, the process we are observing is very much in a state of flux.

In the former imperial lands, some nationalists continue to wax eloquent about the cultural destruction wrought by the Ottomans. This is ironic, for the heterogeneous variety of cultures, customs, and languages that presently exist in the successor states in fact is powerful testimony to the light hand of the Ottoman state on society. That is, the very fact that peoples who were speaking Bulgarian or Greek and professing Christianity at the moment of the Ottoman conquest still retained those languages and religion many centuries later following the departure of the Ottomans, speaks to Ottoman tolerance of linguistic and religious difference. Nonetheless, many writers, politicians, and intellectuals in areas of the Balkans, such as Bulgaria, Greece, and Serbia, resonate with a terrific hostility to the Ottomans, the "Turks." For many Bulgarians, the "Turkish" yoke until today stands out as the darkest, most deplorable period in Bulgarian history. In most textbooks of Bulgarian history (as well as those in Greece), the Ottoman period, which is six centuries long, scarcely warrants a chapter of coverage, and then only in the bleakest terms. This seems amazing, the equivalent of writing the history of the United States without mentioning the British occupation of eastern North America.

For decades, historical writing in the Arab states similarly remained silent about or hostile to the Ottomans. In their efforts to create a sense of Arab community, nationalists decried the dead hand of the Ottomans. During the Ottoman period, 1516–1917, they said, Arab national rights had been extinguished. In their search for a foundation for the emerging new states, they ignored the Ottomans and went back to the Abbasid caliphate (750–1258) to find Arab history, or, sometimes, to find more secular roots, to the pharaohs or the kings of Babylon. There are some signs of positive change in places like Syria, Lebanon, and Egypt (and in pre-occupation Iraq as well). Scholars of and from these countries sometimes now are analyzing rather than vilifying the Ottoman period of the Arab lands and beginning to incorporate the Ottoman years into their own pasts. Many have moved away from overly simplistic dark characterizations of the Ottoman era and acknowledge its place in the Arab present. As a part of this discussion, there is a growing scholarly consensus that most Arab subjects neither consented to nor participated in the death of the Ottoman empire.

In Anatolia, Turkish nationalists building their new state aimed to foster a common sense of Turkish identity by connecting to the land of pre-Ottoman Anatolia. They created the Hittites as their national ancestors and sought to skip over the Ottoman period as irrelevant to modern Turkish identity, not unlike the use of the pharoahs and Babylonians in modern Egypt and Iraq. In Iran similarly, the last Pahlevi Shah had reached back to the ancient Achaemenids at Persepolis for legitimation. More, they argued that the Ottoman state was corrupt, decadent and weak and thus deserved replacement by the Turkish nation state. But counter-trends were present from the first years of the Republic, building over decades. Already in 1940, some mainstream Turkish academic works discussed the authentic significance of the Ottoman past for the Turkish present. In 1953, the Republic held a vast celebration commemorating the 500th anniversary of the Ottoman conquest of Constantinople and acclaiming Sultan Mehmet II as a national hero. In some provincial areas, locals began wearing Ottoman costumes in historical commemorations during the 1960s, making clear that the imperial past had no claim on present loyalties. Since the 1980s, rejection of the Ottoman past generally has given way to its use, although there is considerable debate over the nature and meaning of that past. By the 1990s, a best-selling Turkish author, Orhan Pamuk (and others), routinely used the Ottoman years as a backdrop for his books, demonstrating how popular Ottoman themes have become. There is today quite considerable popular and scholarly interest in the Ottoman era: Ottoman architectural monuments glisten again after restoration and Ottoman artifacts are widely sought items of display in the homes of the Turkish middle classes. They buy Ottoman books they cannot read, displaying them as well as Ottoman copper utensils, coins, stamps, clothing, and furniture. A huge market exists for these Ottoman antiques while television shows abound using Ottoman themes and settings. So too, in the world of cartoons there now are Ottoman sultans and heroes, often replacing the pre-Ottoman Turkic warriors of past decades.

And yet profound disagreement in Turkey exists over the meaning of these Ottoman events, antiques, and personages. Some nationalists portray the Ottoman state as a Turkish one, seeking to make this multinational empire into what it never was – a nation state. Some avowed secularists are beginning to look to the vastness of the empire as a model for Turkish military expansion, very much contrary to the decades-long direction of Turkish foreign policy. Others point to the Ottoman era as a model for the implementation and respect of Islamic values, part of an Islamist movement that has become politically powerful. These hold Sultan Abdülhamit II in high regard because of his pan-Islamic programs and stress his position as the caliph of Islam. On the one hand, this view distorts the past since it downplays Ottoman state efforts to hold onto the loyalty of all subjects, regardless of religion and ethnicity. And, on the other, the endorsement of Sultan Abdülhamit is complicated and risky because he presided over the massacre of Armenians in 1895.

If we consider west European hostility towards contemporary Turkey, we can see yet another legacy of the Ottoman past. Mistrust, dislike, and fear of modern-day Turks abounds in countries like Germany, notably symbolized by the European Union's initial rejection of Turkey's application for admission in 1998. Certainly the economic reasons for the rejection were important: namely, the consequences of a massive influx of Turks into Europe and of Turkish industrial competition. And there are other issues promoting rejection, generally, modern Turkey's poor human rights record and, specifically in the case of Greece, its disputes with Turkey over Aegean oil and Cyprus. But history also plays a role, if often unacknowledged, in stimulating west European fears of Turkey. Old memories of Ottoman military successes against the European states are at work. Here, western Europeans falsely treat Turkey as the only Ottoman successor state, rather than one among many. In part this posture derives from several factors: the origins of the Ottoman Empire in Anatolia and the Turkish migrations into that area; and from the fact that, in the end, Anatolia remained the most populous area left in the empire, with ethnic Turks as the largest single group.

Ottoman administrative borders that had existed were ignored more or less in the state-making decisions that occurred after World War I in the Anatolian and Arab provinces. In the Balkans, however, present-day political frontiers follow old Ottoman provincial administrative boundaries. But few administrative practices or structures transferred from the Ottoman to the post-Ottoman states in the Balkans. The main reason seems to be because, following independence, almost all of the Muslim administrative classes fled or were expelled. By contrast, former Ottoman elites directed affairs or exerted considerable influence in many Arab states, for example, Iraq, Jordan, Egypt, and Syria. The case of Iraq is an arresting example; there, a small group of former Ottoman military officers and administrators thoroughly dominated state and society until the revolution of 1958. Elsewhere, for example in Syria and Egypt, distinguished families from the eighteenth century and before continue to be prominent. In Turkey, former Ottoman generals served as presidents of the Republic until 1950 while comparatively large numbers of Ottoman civil and military personnel staffed the Turkish bureaucracy. Overall, Turkey inherited more Ottoman personnel than any other successor state.

Sometimes present-day patterns falsely are attributed to an Ottoman legacy. For example, some scholars argue that the general Turkish and Arab prevalence of large bureaucracies and of the dominion of public over private economic direction owes something to an Ottoman legacy. Since, however, these patterns persist elsewhere in the world, they likely are due to other factors. Others, for example, point to Ottoman influences to explain the allegedly patient and cautious style of Arab politics that balances one force against another in an effort to neutralize them all, leaving the enemy time and scope for self-destruction. While Ottoman diplomacy surely possessed these features, so did that of Machiavelli's Florence and Ming China. On the other hand, there may be some connection between the Ottoman and modern Turkish administrative traditions of a very strong central state.

The Ottoman legacy in landholding is held to be a key to understanding the present in many areas. Landholding in twentieth-century Iraq evolved in a peculiar way – thanks to the interaction of capitalism, colonialism, and Ottoman land legislation. There, tribal chiefs manipulated the Land Law of 1858, became great estate holders, and held sway until the 1958 revolution finally broke their power. In most other Arab and Anatolian areas, the relatively free peasantry and absence of a landed nobility is said to be a key carryover from Ottoman times. In some cases, the statement seems to be valid: small plots do predominate in modern Turkey. And yet, perhaps the point has been overemphasized. Many families now holding political and economic power in the Anatolian and Arab areas have done so for several centuries. For example, in northeastern Turkey during the 1960s, the local elites almost always were descended from families which had been prominent in the empire. In the Balkan lands, by contrast, economic patterns from the Ottoman era were obliterated: the independence regimes often embarked on land distribution programs that reversed the landholding patterns of the Ottoman era. And then, the Communist regimes completed the destruction of the former Ottoman economic and political elites.

The Ottoman legacy, however, clearly stands out when we look at a number of population distribution patterns. Migrations imposed by the Ottoman imperial system compelled the movement of peoples within the empire, with effects down to the present. Turks on the island of Cyprus are descended from Anatolian settlers arriving during the sixteenth century while the Circassians in Jordan came in the nineteenth century. Serbs and Croats left their earlier homelands and fled northward to escape invaders or migrated later when they sided with the Habsburgs. Everywhere these demographic legacies remain, although the post-cold war migrations are diluting their importance.

Ottoman policy failures resonate down into our own time. First, Ottoman inability to keep Great Britain out of the Persian Gulf during the later nineteenth century led to the formation of a British client state in Kuwait, from what had been part of the Ottoman province of Basra in the Iraqi lands. Saddam Hussein's invasion and the Gulf War of the early 1990s to reclaim Kuwait thus is traceable, in part, to this Ottoman political failure. Similarly, the Ottomans tried but failed to prevent Jewish immigration into Palestine, giving Zionism a demographic toehold there, an event that still resonates today. Also, as is well known, the chronic Turkish–Greek hostilities directly stem from the breakaway of the Greek subject peoples, while Armenians and Turks still bitterly clash over the events of 1915.

In modern Turkey, Syria, pre-occupation Iraq, Lebanon and other Arab states, popular attitudes and official policies sometimes are tinged with a Turkish sense of imperial superiority and an Arab sense of being colonized. In Turkey, for example, the word "arap" has quite negative connotations. The past repeatedly comes to haunt the present. In the Balkans, intervention by the Turkish state during the Bosnian crisis sometimes was criticized and opposed as a latter-day version of Ottoman imperialism. Here, again, we see the common but nonetheless incorrect tendency to see Turkey as the only successor state of the Ottomans.

In sum, the Ottoman legacy, both in the lands the empire once occupied and beyond, is mixed. For some, it remains an object variously of opposition, derision, scorn, and even hatred while others along this spectrum view the Ottoman past as irrelevant for their own present. Admirers of the Ottoman legacy, however, are divided. They disagree over whether the Ottoman entity they seek to emulate is a secular, nationalist, or Islamist state and society. In these pages, I have argued that the Ottoman legacy is of a political and social system offering non-national, multi-religious and multi-ethnic forms of organization for a world increasingly divided by nationality, religious belief and ethnicity.

Suggested bibliography

Entries marked with a * designate recommended readings for new students of the subject.

*Abou-El-Haj, Rifaat. "The social uses of the past: recent Arab historiography of Ottoman rule," *International Journal of Middle East Studies*, May 1982, 185–201.

Anscombe, Frederick F. *The creation of Kuwait, Saudi Arabia and Qatar* (New York, 1997).

*Brown, Leon Carl, ed. *Imperial legacy: The Ottoman imprint on the Balkans and the Middle East* (New York, 1996).

*Kayalı, Hasan. *Arabs and Young Turks: Ottomanism, Arabism and nationalism in the Ottoman Empire, 1908–1918* (Berkeley, 1997).

Kiel, Machiel. *Art and society of Bulgaria in the Turkish period* (Aassen/Maastricht, 1985).

Meeker, Michael. *A nation of empire. The Ottoman legacy of Turkish modernity* (Berkeley, 2002).

*Schacht, Joseph and C. E. Bosworth, eds. *The legacy of Islam*, 2nd edn (Oxford, 1979).

Sells, Michael A. *The bridge betrayed: Religion and genocide in Bosnia* (Berkeley, 1996).

Todorova, Maria. *Imagining the Balkans* (Oxford, 1997).

Several suggestions on the history of the post-Ottoman Middle East and Balkans

*Beinin, Joel. *Workers and peasants in the modern Middle East* (Cambridge, 2001).
*Cleveland, William. *A history of the modern Middle East* (Boulder, CO, 1999).
*Esposito, John. *The Islamic threat: myth or reality*, 3rd edn (Oxford, 1999).
*Goldberg, Ellis, ed. *The social history of labor in the Middle East* (Boulder, CO, 1996).
*Hourani, Albert, Philip S. Khoury and Mary C. Wilson, eds. *The modern Middle East* (Berkeley, 1993).
*Khater, Akram Fouad. *Sources in the history of the modern Middle East* (Boston, 2004).
Neuburger, Mary. *The Orient within. Muslim minorities and the negotiation of nationhood in modern Bulgaria* (Ithaca, 2004).
*Smith, Charles D. *Palestine and the Arab–Israeli conflict*, 5th edn (Boston and New York, 2004).

Index

NEW APPROACHES TO EUROPEAN HISTORY